Moeller Law Office
424 W. Broadway
Farmington, NM 87401

SOLOMON TIME

*An Unlikely Quest in
the South Pacific*

WILL RANDALL

SCRIBNER

NEW YORK   LONDON   TORONTO   SYDNEY   SINGAPORE

☯

SCRIBNER
1230 Avenue of the Americas
New York, NY 10020

First Scribner Edition 2003
Originally published in Britain in 2002 by Abacus,
an imprint of Time Warner Books UK

SCRIBNER and design are trademarks of
Macmillan Library Reference USA, Inc., used under license
by Simon & Schuster, the publisher of this work.

For information about special discounts for bulk purchases,
please contact Simon & Schuster Special Sales:
1-800-456-6798 or business@simonandschuster.com

Designed by Colin Joh
Text set in Fairfield Light

Manufactured in the United States of America

1   3   5   7   9   10   8   6   4   2

Library of Congress Cataloging-in-Publication Data
Randall, Will.
Solomon time : an unlikely quest in the South Pacific / Will Randall.
—1st Scribner ed.
p.   cm.
Originally published: Great Britain : Abacus, 2002.
1. Randall, Will, 1966—Journeys—Solomon Islands.
2. Solomon Islands—Description and travel. I. Title.
DU850 .R36 2002
919.59304—dc21   2002036698

ISBN 0-7432-4396-X

Extract from *A Pattern of Islands* by Arthur Grimble reproduced
by kind permission of John Murray (Publishers) Ltd.

This is a book for anyone who thinks it might be time for a change.

Acknowledgments

Without the generosity of spirit and general goodwill of countless friends and acquaintances I would never have found myself in a position to write these few lines. I am very grateful to all of them.

There are a number of people, however, who held my hand and patted my head, who geed me up and reined me in, and who made sure that I lasted the course. It would be remiss of me not to mention them by name and to take this opportunity to thank them most sincerely.

In the Solomons, Dave Cooke, Mariana Cooke, and Dicky Anning showed me the ropes and kept me afloat on the Roviana Lagoon. I was lucky to have met them and to have benefited from their experience and their broad sense of humor. Grant Griffiths was my forthright adviser on all things feathered, and Marilyn and Richard Somerville provided me with lavish Honiaran hospitality.

In Australia, Paul Greguric, Terry Mansfield, and my fellow residents at the Crystal Palace Hotel, Sydney, kept me well oiled while I bashed out the first draft in Room 4. My good friends John, Alexa, Daniel, Jack, and Greta Duke offered me the inspiration for this book as well as their wonderful home, great tucker, and a solid kitchen table at which to write. Ray Francis, too, was an excellent and enthusiastic host.

In France, my neighbors Michael and Jenny Boys-Greene and Jean Perrier provided me with superb *gastronomie* and an abundance of *bonhomie*.

Back at home in England, Christopher and Jennifer

Palmer were the catalyst for this tale, and it is only thanks to their kindness and quiet assistance that I found myself in the South Pacific at all. Peter Palmer and I will always enjoy swapping Solomon stories. He is very good company. We will all remember N.S.-E. with affection. It is with very much gratitude, too, that I want to thank my great friends Robin, Sue, and Patrick Grant-Sturgis, whose generosity, hospitality, and kindness over many years are beyond my powers of description.

If it had not been for Crispin Sadler, I should never have met Kate Hordern, and if it had not been for Kate Hordern, I would still be sitting at my computer. Her support, encouragement, and positive good nature have been inspirational. I am deeply appreciative of all her efforts on my behalf. I am grateful, also, to Richenda Todd, who provided me with cool insight, and to Richard Beswick for his confidence. In the United States, Leslie Breed has been tirelessly efficient; both she and Colin Harrison, an endless fund of good advice and ideas, have had great faith in *Solomon Time*.

It is with love and affection that I want to thank my mother for all her support—not least in managing to stay awake to read me all those stories when I was a child—and my brothers, Michael and Patrick, for their friendship and for putting up so cheerfully with all their older brother's peccadilloes. This book is for them, and for my father, who would have enjoyed the adventure.

However, my biggest vote of thanks must go, of course, to all my Solomon Islands friends for their gentle welcome and for very happy times in the Happy Isles. *Tanggio tu mus*.

WR
France
Summer 2002

Contents

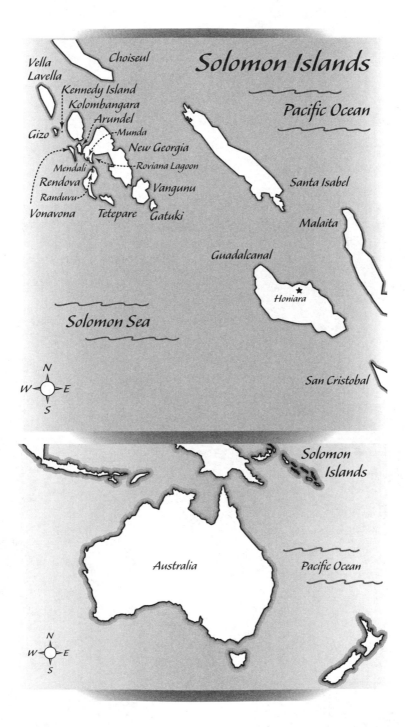

SOLOMON
TIME

Prologue

Opening one eye, I snapped it closed hurriedly against the white glare of the sand. I tried again. A small hermit crab was making its way up the beach with deliberate determination. Stopping, it turned its two black-tipped antennae to glare at me disdainfully.

I managed to raise myself onto one elbow, leaning, to my surprise, on my inflated, yellow life jacket. With my free hand I brushed the grit from my eyes, cheeks, and forehead, out of my ears and nose, the fine grains stinging against my skin. Gently lap-lapping, the water around my ankles was calm blue, the light breeze of an early morning just frosting its surface. The sun, casting shadows through the coconut leaves high above me, was already preparing for its daily offensive and, as a vanguard, a squadron of brightly colored parrots zoomed from its furnace center. They flew in small swoops directly overhead. Aiming with pinpoint accuracy, their leader released his payload. A direct hit, it landed with a wet splash on my salt-stiffened T-shirt. The bird flew off, waggling his wings. The rest followed, screeching their congratulations as they banked away toward the cover of the trees.

I discovered that my tongue had been mysteriously glued

to the roof of my mouth. Squeezing my finger between cracked lips, I dislodged it, but when I did so thirst thundered through me. Every joint crackled as I heaved myself to a sitting position and unsuccessfully tried to run my fingers through my hair. It had set saltily solid. Parted just above the right ear, it stood out at an angle, a lopsided crest.

Staggering to my bare feet, and shading my eyes with both hands, I peered up and down the shoreline. White beach. More white beach. I looked up at the deep green, impenetrable jungle. It stared back implacably.

Trudging to the next point, I squinted further on round the island.

No leaf huts, no children throwing themselves into the water with great screeches of delight—fortunately, because now my head was beginning to throb like a big bass drum—no wisps of smoke from the kitchens signaling kettles and tea, no fishermen in wooden canoes waving their paddles in greeting. In fact, none of the familiar sights and sounds of the small village that I was, by now, so used to waking to. Nothing, just the quiet stillness, the untouched haphazardness of a desert island.

Along the length of the water's edge, shells, leaves, twigs had all been discarded by the risen tide as it slunk back out to rejoin its parent ocean. White-capped noddies, those beady, bargain-hunting birds, picked the tangled mass over, scavenging for any useful junk or tasty leftovers. Nowhere, though, among all this flotsam was there the cheering sight of a beached canoe or even a wet footprint in the sand. No, absolutely nothing, just miles of sand, acres of jungle, and several billion gallons of bloody sea.

My thirst, now fearsome, had me by the throat. Poking a coconut out from the fringes of the bush, I tried light-headedly, halfheartedly really, to break it apart on a washed-up giant clamshell. In frustration, I hurled it into the sea, where it bobbed and winked in a self-satisfied fashion. I turned in disgust and headed for the shade of some small sago palms.

No need to worry, said a small, slightly high-pitched voice in my head, someone is bound to turn up soon enough, you'll see.

Hang on a minute, interjected another, considerably deeper and gloomier voice, doesn't that leave just a few unanswered questions? You know, just for example . . . Where am I? How did I get here? And why is someone bound to turn up?

Try as I might, I could not piece together the events leading up to my mysterious presence here. I did, however, succeed in deducing, from various elementary clues, two near certainties. First, from the nature of the scenery, I was pretty sure that I was on one of the Solomon Islands. Which one of course was still open to debate—with myself. Second, the tranquillity of the morning led me to conclude that I was now this particular island's only occupant.

CHAPTER 1

Spirit of Adventure

"Class, I think it's important that I let you know at this stage that, as of the beginning of next year, you will be having a new French teacher," I said, staring down at my fingertips, which rested among the dusty slag heaps of paperwork on my desk.

"Yes, I shall be leaving at the end of this summer term." Hoping for at least some muted sign of disappointment, I was greeted by a blank wall of fourteen- and fifteen-year-old faces.

"Yes, I shall be leaving teaching and shall be going to live in a little village in the Solomon Islands." This revelation, too, was met with impressive indifference.

Oh, come on! It was quite interesting surely. A stirring in the front row. Good, the class swot. Robert was fresh-faced, keen, all hands up and smug glances to his left and right whenever he handed in another tome of homework. We all loathed him, but he would probably ask a bright question, the answer to which would kill off the last five minutes of the class.

"Yes, Robert, what is it?" I stood and pointed to him enthusiastically. Everyone else sat and cast their eyes heavenward.

"Sir, I just thought I would remind you that you haven't set us any homework yet, sir." He simpered.

"Robert!" we chorused. I searched around haplessly for the textbook, trying to work out which exercises had already been completed, while the others prayed that I wouldn't be able to remember.

"So where are these Sodomon Islands, then?"

"Thank you, er, Sonia, err, Sarah. Yes, well, the Solomon Islands, Solomon Islands, Sarah, are in the Southwest Pacific, about a thousand miles off the northeast coast of Australia."

This much I had ascertained. Checking the map of the world on my classroom wall, I had eventually found the microscopic dots. It had not been an auspicious introduction. Seconds later the rickety wooden chair on which I had been standing for a closer view had collapsed. Falling, I had sliced my chin on the corner of the empty filing cabinet. The next thing I knew I was lying on my back, bleeding onto my favorite tie and blinking up at a piece of graffiti inscribed on the underside of one of the desks: "Randle is a wanker!"

"So what kind of stuff can you do there?"

"Excellent question, Ricky, excellent question. Err, yes . . ." I picked at the scab doubtfully.

With a boxer's relief, I heard the bell ring.

"I tell you what, why don't we have a prize for the person who can come back and tell us the most about the Solomon Islands next time, eh?"

"But what has that got to do with French, sir?"

"Robert, why don't you just shut up and fuck off?" (Actually I said, "Robert, let's get going, shall we, or we will be late for our next lesson, won't we?" but the sentiment was much the same.)

Once again, I had little more knowledge of the matter in hand than did my dear pupils. I had signed on the metaphoric dotted line and agreed to go to live in the furthest reaches of the back end of outer nowhere but knew next to nothing about it. So, in the hour-long lunchtime break I made a brief appearance in the school library but hastily backed off when I came upon half the class in the geography section. I grimaced as I caught a snippet of their conversation:

"I bet it'll just be some crappy old Mars bar."

"Yeah, like all the other 'prizes' he owes us."

Classes finished at three-twenty, so after school that day I ambled down the High Street of the small market town, past the door of the travel agents, waving briefly at the harried-looking manager. He was half out of his seat the moment he saw me. I hurried on: he wanted paying for the ticket. The one thing I did already know about the Solomon Islands was that it was not one of your cheap holiday destinations. I strode enthusiastically into the public library.

"Ah, yes!" I said to the steely librarian who stood behind the counter, her half-moon glasses swinging from a chain around her neck.

"I shall be going off to the Solomon Islands pretty soon and would like to do a bit of research." I laughed a sort of we're-all-in-this-together kind of laugh. We obviously were not.

"Are you a member?"

"Err . . . no, I don't think so."

She snapped on her spectacles. After a few formalities and a good deal of snorting, I was directed, by the point of a carefully sharpened pencil, to the travel section. After a brief distraction by a slim but illustrated publication entitled *Bournemouth: A History of Sun, Sea and Sex,* I ascertained that there were no books with any mention of the Solomon Islands in the title. In fact there was nothing that I could find with any mention of them, inside or out. I moved to the reference section. I pulled down a dusty red *Sl–Tr* volume of the encyclopedia. As I riffled past "Slov'yansk," "Snoilsky (Carl Johan Gustaf [Count])," "snoring," and "Social Darwinism" (all of which, had I had the time, would no doubt have been fascinating), the page fell open upon the following entry:

Solomon Islands, island nation in the southwestern Pacific Ocean, extend southeastward from Papua New Guinea and Bougainville—Yes, knew that—*Formerly British Solomon Islands Protectorate (independence 1978), democratic government, Head of State: Queen Elizabeth II. Discovered by Spanish explorer, Don Álvaro de Mendaña y Neyra, in 1587*—Ah, sí, sí, Don Alvaro!—*Center of widespread missionary activity from mid-nineteenth century but slow acceptance due to strong tribal beliefs and headhunting*—Hmm—*Center for slave trade. Fierce rebellion Malaita Island (1927), subdued by British with great brutality*—Wonderful. Should make me really popular—*Scene of intense fighting WWII between American and Japanese (Battle of Savo, August 1942). Recent political unrest and fighting between rival militia groups over land rights*—Not exactly a history of tropical harmony, then?—*Capital: Honiara*—Well, that sounded nice enough. "Horniarra"; I tried it with my best Spanish accent, a quick stamp of my feet, and a very quiet click of my fingers—*Total population: 360,000*—About the same as . . . err . . . Northamptonshire? Maybe?—*Total area: 1.35 million sq. km.; 992 islands, approx. 350 inhabited. Total land area: 27,556 sq. km.*—Not quite the same as Northamptonshire, then— *Tropical climate, hot and humid. Flora and fauna: virgin rain forests, six varieties of rats and two of crocodiles*—Virgin rain forests, six varieties of rats . . . and two of crocodiles. Marvelous—*Malaria is a problem*—Of course—*The population is largely Christian of various denominations although animist beliefs*—Animist . . . hmm?—*still exist and cannibalism is thought to be practiced in remote areas*—As in they still eat people. Great—*No more than 3,000 visitors a year.*

Well, that was hardly a heel-rocking surprise. I wondered how many of them made it back intact.

"The capital is called 'Oniara, sir."

"Good, anybody else? Yes, you there, um . . ."

"John, sir. There's loads of rats and crocodiles, sir."

"You don't have to tell me anything I don't know already, thank you," I said irritably as I gazed out through the diamond panes across the small courtyard at the back of the school. An elderly caretaker creakily snipped the edges of a square of grass.

"And sharks, sir."

"Sharks? Who said anything about sharks?" I turned as if, as only very occasionally happened, someone had fired a paper pellet at my backside.

"My mum says it sounds horrible, sir."

"And my mum says it hasn't got anything to do with French, sir."

"Oh, will you just shut up, Robert!" I sat down behind my desk with a jolt. The figures in front of me swam away and into the way swam smiling sharks, tearful crocodiles—and six varieties of synchronized rats.

I suddenly felt very hot and humid. Was I really doing the right thing giving all this up: the holidays, the house, what was left of the car? Teaching was fun, and there weren't too many drawbacks, apart from marking papers. Even Robert was nice enough really, just a bit misunderstood—by everybody.

For ten years now my life had been steered by the comfort of bells, the regular ringing shaping my days, putting their events in order. In the main, the course had been smooth and I had carved myself a cozy niche in the life of the school, in the soft valleys of the West Country. As I gazed above the faces that must surely one day become distorted from all the leaning on fists and jaw-cracking yawning, I realized that my classroom had become very much my own; clothes, books, the jumble of pictures and mementos all gave my work a setting, a backdrop. From the leaded windows I was used to watching the seasons come and go, scattering the quadrangle with petals or leaves. I was used, too, to watching the youngsters arrive as bright-faced innocents, only to slope off a few years later with a "Seeya," never to be seen again apart from, perhaps, the occasional appearance in the court report of the local newspaper.

My home, the other side of the stone bridge, high above the valley where the sharp incline of the road met the top of the hill, provided me my landscape. Green always but for the occasional smearing of wet snow, the countryside stretched from my bedroom window away to the sea. My wages were fair, boys like Robert a rarity, and the pub was on the way home.

I opened the classroom window. The room could be insufferably stuffy on warm days, but then again so could most of my colleagues all the year round. On balance, I was happy with my world. Swapping all this for a few bouts of malaria before featuring as the main course at the Sunday barbecue was the action of a madman.

I would get out of it. That was it—I would just say no. I had reconsidered and, in light of my professional aspirations, whatever they were, I was terribly sorry but it was just not possible. I couldn't imagine that anyone—apart from a few rapacious reptiles—was going to be that upset. So that was that. Easy.

Sadly, as so often seemed to happen, any plans that I had for my own future had already been wrestled from my grasp. I had again been relegated to the role of timid onlooker at this runaway disaster. It soon became clear that I had discussed the venture with far too many people. It had become a fait accompli.

"So, you are off to new pastures, Will? Or should I say jungles, ha, ha!"

"Well, I, actually, I was thinking that perhaps . . ."

"Damn good idea. Do something a bit different. Breath of fresh air, eh?"

No, breath of hot air. Hot, disease-ridden air.

"Wish I'd done something like that myself, you know, when I was a bit younger. Too late now, of course." The elderly headmaster shook his head as he looked down rheumily at his frayed tweed turnups.

"Still," he said more cheerfully as he looked up again, "we'll accept your resignation, of course."

"Oh, yes, well, thank you very much," I faltered, "but I don't want to leave anybody in the lurch, you know, perhaps it would be better if I stayed. I hear the hockey team needs a coach next season and err . . ."

"Nonsense. Nobody is indispensable. Least of all you, eh? Ha, ha!"

In hindsight I am not sure how flattered I should have been by this last remark, but I suppose it must have been a joke.

"I always thought you had a bit of the old spirit of adventure about you."

As my employer turned on his heel and walked quietly down the parquet corridor, I reflected on how quickly events were overtaking me, how helpless I was to change their course, and how extraordinarily baggy was the seat of his trousers. Anyway, I realized, as I wandered off in the opposite direction for the two-forty German class, that my fate was sealed because my lips had not been.

The end of term came in a flurry of kind things being said and some, at least, meant. On the final afternoon, I sat in a large tent and listened patiently to interminable speeches of self-congratulation about the good old school and there always being an England. I decided, though, to forgo the tepid cup of tea and the "He's doing fine, fine, bit more effort, nice lad, do have a lovely holiday" conversations that were twittering away on the lawn as everybody took this last chance to be appallingly nice to each other and the sparrows hopped around the curling sandwiches.

Skulking away, I found myself alone, glum and grumpy, in my classroom. After a desultory attempt to tidy up my belongings, I gave up. Having convinced myself that the new incumbent of my job and therefore room would find the mounds of yellowing files and folders invaluable, I was doodling absent-mindedly on the blackboard and wondering whether the pub was open when a knock came at the door. It burst open, and in bounced Tom and David. The two sixth-form school leavers wore smart suits and the wide grins of those who realize that liberation is at hand. They were glowing at the prospect of leaving, full of belief that the worst was over, that life, from now on, was going to be fun; that you would not, through your own inherent ineptitude, find yourself banished to the other side of the world to meet your fate.

"We just came to say bye sir, so bye sir." They ran back out, only to burst back in.

"Sorry, forgot we've got a present for you, for you to take to your island." They laughed.

Reaching into a schoolbag, David pulled out a package, which he thrust under my nose. The pink bow was a work of art.

"My girlfriend wrapped it," he answered my look of surprise.

"Hope it's useful," said Tom. "Go on, open it then, sir."

I did and inside, neatly folded in its own neat container, was an inflatable life jacket. A rip cord dangled from a small gas canister, waiting for the dire emergency that would require it to be tugged. I was touched. I was actually quite moved.

"Thanks, thanks very much," I stumbled, "but it must have cost you a fortune."

"Not really. Nicked it off of a plane when we went to America last year. Couldn't think what to do with it. Cheers then, sir."

And with that they disappeared through the door to their futures, leaving me alone to face mine.

They say that selling your house, packing up, and moving is to be considered on a par, in terms of stress, with getting divorced, married, or bereaved. I cannot understand why anybody should wish to leave his home, let alone the country, for all the palaver it causes. In fact, looking back now, I see it was a much more momentous time than I had realized. Over the years I had amassed not much more or less than most, but my possessions were not just material belongings that could simply be thrown away without a second thought, cast aside in order to adopt a new identity. Actually most of them were, but some things did seem to have a particular hold . . .

But eventually it was all done and lightly dusted. Everybody wanted to say good-bye. Either they were truly sorry to see me leave or they wanted to make absolutely sure that I really was going. Friends, on hearing of my intentions, seemed to divide themselves into two distinct groups: those who said that they thought I was *so* lucky, who *really* wished they were doing what I was, and who were clearly not telling the truth, and the rest, who informed me with startling sincerity that they thought I was barking mad. I was unsure which group I sympathized with more.

The only person who did not seem to pass any judgment was my ninety-three-year-old great-aunt, who had lived through all the major events of the twentieth century and therefore had a better sense of the ridiculous than most. One afternoon I visited her in her book-lined cupboard in the hinterland of West London to say my farewell and, of course, have a cup of tea.

"I'm sure you'll have a lovely time, dear, but you'll need something to read, so I've made you up a little parcel."

From under her lace-covered armchair she produced a package of brown paper and white string and made me promise not to open it before I arrived. "It'll be more fun like that," she assured me.

As it was, I only just had time to cram it into the top of my rucksack and do up all the complicated zips, clips, and drawstrings before I had to leave. Time was plodding on, and I was being forced to follow. The car was sold, covering the cost of a couple of last-minute parking fines, and furniture and belongings were spread evenly between ungrateful friends and relations. Finally, the date on my ticket, now paid for, caught up with me. Grasped firmly by the arm, I was frog-marched off to the South Pacific.

~⊇~

CHAPTER 2

Welcome to Solomon Islands

Impenetrable, the cloud that sat overhead was almost dense enough to stifle the drone of the bumper-to-bumper planes taking off from Heathrow. Sour gray and wet, the sky reminded me of that late November afternoon; the day that the odd-shaped ball with my name written on it had been booted out of my feeble grasp.

Slithering and squelching my way to the touchline of the bog-wet rugby pitch, I had been preparing myself, as their reluctant coach, to witness the glorious Fourth Fifteen being pounded viciously into the red slime for the umpteenth time that season. At a distance I had recognized my next-door neighbors standing on the far side of the field, and I went to join them. Buried in scarves, clapping their warm gloves together, they intermittently ran on the spot as they waited for the Big Match in which their youngest son was to star later in the dank, freezing afternoon. In the meanwhile, they had come to offer the unwilling junior coach moral support.

"So, what do you reckon of your chances this week?" asked Charles, comradely.

I made a face. "My" team was huddled together underneath the far posts, more for warmth than for camaraderie, I imagined, as the white wisps of their breath disappeared on the light ice wind.

"Oh, come on, Will, where's your team spirit?" Juliet, Charles's saintly wife, laughed. Sadly the last drop of team spirit had been consumed well before half term. It was now a question of damage limitation.

"Will, have you met the Commander? Commander Somebody Something-Something, Will Randall."

"Sorry, no I don't . . . What?" Distracted, I was at that moment wondering what they had been feeding the opposition team that was now lumbering into view.

Turning, I met the sharp, blue gaze of stone-hard eyes set in an ancient face. Blood vessels brought to the surface by the scouring of the elements ran widely across both cheeks; a few gray whiskers bristled from the end of a determined nose. Wrapped in a battered, stiff mackintosh that looked tough enough to withstand musket shot let alone the rain and girded by a thick belt of the same material, a short, uncompromising man looked up at me. On his head resided a deerstalker of incalculable age. From my height advantage, I checked for signs of life.

"Will Randall, Commander Something Somebody-Whatnot."

Despite Charles's solicitous formality, I had still failed to catch his name. Never mind. It was hellish cold, and the quicker this whole fiasco was over and we all went home, the better.

"How do you do?" I said with absentminded politeness, holding out my hand.

"Dying a little bit more every day," he replied, not releasing my hand from a nutcracker grip. My vision blurred.

"Oh, yes how nice, good, great . . ."

A colleague, who had bounded spotless out of a washing powder advertisement and onto the field of play, brought the two captains together. The first whistle blew, and my cohorts churned slowly through the mire. I closed my eyes as the first strangled "Oh, God!" was expelled from a pair of lungs somewhere at the bottom of a pile of bodies.

The "Commander" had been as good as his word. Within six months of our meeting he had died. The seasons drifted one into the next regardless, and it was on the side of a cricket pitch in the middle of one strangely warm May that Charles told me of his demise.

"Of, course he was getting on. Eighty-four this year. Extraordinary man. We ever tell you about him? Amazing chap, the Commander."

"No, I don't think so." A smattering of applause came from the deck chairs that lined the white rope boundary. I clapped along with everyone else and wondered what could have happened out on the field to cause such approval.

"Of course he had a very distinguished war career."

"Oh, yes . . . What was he in?"

"The Navy."

"Oh, yes, of course."

"But the amazing thing was that after it was all over he went off and bought a plantation in the South Pacific."

"What, like the musical?"

"Well, yes, as a matter of fact. It's funny you should say

that but the musical was actually set in these particular islands. The Solomon Islands. Anyway, he was there and he ran it for about thirty years: coconuts and cocoa. He sold it off to the government, but it's pretty much disused now. He came back to England in the early eighties to retire."

"Oh, right . . . retire, oh really? Interesting." I could see a particularly garrulous mother approaching.

"Actually, I'm the executor of his will—he was friendly with my parents, served with my father during the war. Here's a thing for you, Will. He left a bit of money for the welfare of the islanders who used to work for him because they're still living out there, you see. I have just received a letter from them very sad to hear of his death. They were very close to him and he to them, of course."

"Of course." I could still see the mother waiting until the end of the over before she bore down on us.

"Yes, do you know over all these years he has kept in touch with them? Never missed a birthday or a Christmas card. He was a tough old chap, but he would get very cut up if he heard that one of his old workers had died. He never married, so they were pretty much family to him. In many ways he probably regretted ever leaving. Well, anyway, so he has left this money, not much—to prevent poverty and promote education—that sort of thing. We're looking for someone to go out and organize something. I was chatting to my father, he's an executor too, and we thought you might be interested."

"Me?"

"Just the thing for you—bit of a change."

"What, *me*? No, no, not me." I laughed. Ridiculous. "Not me."

"Why not? Good chance to get away from all these awful kids."

"Over."

There was some languid shuffling about on the field.

"No, no way. Huh, blimey, no. Hello, Mrs. Edmunds. Anyway, look, I've got loads of marking to do. Got to get it done by tomorrow. Sorry. Bye then." I checked my watch rather obviously and made a less than polite retreat.

King Solomon's Island? Who'd want to go there for God's sake? I'd never even heard of the place.

Of course, I should have realized that I was not going to have any hand in steering the juggernaut of fate as it tore off downhill, roaring toward an unimaginable destination. On the way it pulled in briefly for supper at Charles and Juliet's:

"Of, course, I've done a bit of traveling. School holidays and that sort of thing, you know . . ."

Admittedly, a pre-Christmas trip to the supermarket in Dunkirk or even a two-week school exchange to the petrochemical fields outside Le Havre with seventy twelve-year-olds and attendant disasters did not really set me alongside Thesiger, Theroux, Burton, or Bryson. It was, on the other hand, worth stretching things a bit if it went any way to impressing the lovely Czechoslovakian trainee doctor next to whom I was sitting.

"So, why do you not go to help in Solomon Islands? It is a wery important job, isn't it not?"

Not that one again. It was the last thing I wanted to talk about, although she did have the most charming double-yous.

"Well, err, I, yes, I'm sure it is." I took another deep swig of wine. "Perhaps we could go together?" I added with skewed inspiration and an eye-wateringly embarrassing wink.

"Naturally, this is not possible because I must study." Naturally.

"But you must go. 'Wariety is the spice of life,'" she added vehemently as she made an incision in the skin of her potato and inserted a microscopic piece of butter, before performing a skillful dissection of her trout.

"Yeah, well, I just might," I burbled grumpily into my glass.

"Did you say you would go, Will? That's great. Darling,

Will's said he'll go. Darling . . . ?" Juliet, sitting on my right, turned away from me to attract Charles's attention.

"Well, hang on, wait, when I said—"

Too late.

A few days later the phone rattled loudly on my bedside table, slicing through a Sunday morning dream.

"Look, Will . . . did I wake you up? Sorry. Look, can't talk now. Just spoken to the other trustees and they are fine about you going." Charles was at his most genial—and his most businesslike. I had to put a stop to this.

"Now listen, I'm afraid the other night, you know, perhaps I'd had a couple too—"

"I shouldn't worry too much about that, it's all pretty much forgotten about. Anyway, she's going back home next week." He laughed.

Sitting up, I dredged through the murk.

"Pop into the office next week, perhaps Wednesday afternoon, and we'll discuss dates. Take a bit of planning. Off out to lunch now . . . all right, see you Wednesday. Bye now."

"Charles . . . I . . . look."

But come that Wednesday, I was in a very different frame of mind. A terrifying amount can happen in a short space of time, and on this occasion, perhaps by coincidence, perhaps not, it had.

"Raring to go?" Charles looked up in surprise from his appointments diary. Leaning forward in his leather chair, he had slipped on his glasses to better understand my bizarre change of heart. "But, I thought . . ."

"What a wonderful challenge. Yes, I'm very excited by the opportunity. Very good of you to consider me. Yes, absolutely raring to go."

"Well, I see. You do know a bit about the Solomons then? What to expect?"

"Yes, Solomon Islands. That's right, South Pacific," I

waved a hand at a vague point on an imaginary map of the world that hung in the air between us.

"Oh, well that's great. You've done some research, then? You know what's involved, I suppose?"

"Sure, sure. Help out a bit, be useful?" I hazarded.

"Well, yes. More specifically, we hope that you will be able to use the money I mentioned to create some sort of local project that will provide a bit of income for the villagers to use on community improvements."

"Yep, sounds fine, fine. When do you want me to go?"

"Well, that was rather what I was going to ask you, Will. I mean, you will have to give some notice, I suppose?"

"Yes, I suppose. A term, I think." It was the end of the spring term in a week's time. I was sure I could get a letter written up by then.

We shook hands on the deal. I left Charles looking slightly dazed.

What Charles did not know was that during the few days between our telephone conversation and my arrival in his office much had happened that gave me good cause to have a significant change of heart—at least so I thought at the time.

Perhaps it was coincidence or perhaps it was a natural juncture, but a variety of concerns, uncertainties, and regrets had simultaneously bubbled to the surface. It had suddenly become clear that some action needed to be taken to relieve the irritation or I ran the risk of scratching myself to bits.

On Monday morning, in a last attempt to be on time for school assembly, I had narrowly avoided killing Jim, the postman.

"Morning, Jim. Okay?" I greeted him lightly.

"Morning, Will. You in a bit of a rush again?" He smiled as he unsnapped my mail from an elastic band and handed it to me from the ditch.

Thanking him, I pressed on, the wheels spinning slightly

in the muddy lane. I waved into my rearview mirror and thought I saw Jim raise his hand in return. Driving through the damp town, I ripped open the three stiff envelopes with my teeth as I fought to do up the top button of my shirt and tie my tie. Not one, not two, but three invitations to friends' weddings that summer. Normally I would have been delighted to go, to wish them well for the future and lift a glass of champagne to send them on their happy way. However, as my own romantic prospects, in the shape of la belle Sophie, had disappeared in the exhaust roar of a plane bound for Toulouse, I could feel only a triple measure of irritation.

She had, she said, *"finalement piquée une crise de nerfs."* This, from what I could gather from the way she had treated a few of the more fragile objects in the house, meant that she had thrown an enormous and terminal Gallic fit. Undoubtedly, she had had endless lists of good reasons for being so angry with me. Sadly, however, I never found out what they were because when she talked that fast and shouted that loudly I could not really understand what she was saying.

It had been an affair that, like many, had started with something of a bang but had slowly disintegrated into a relationship that had been life-changing only to the extent that I now had to wait to use the bathroom every morning. Indubitably, however, and as I was the first to admit, I had not paid her enough attention. I had been too wrapped up in the minutiae of school life. She was fed up with my late-night rehearsals of the school play and surely bored to sobs with my endless stories about the Mystery of the Stolen Football Boots or the new dish in the school canteen. (Although it had to be admitted that Barry had been a caterer possessed of a rare talent.)

Sophie had been an undergraduate studying English at university and still found many of the customs and eccentricities of my fellow countrymen and -women intriguing, refreshing, and amusing. I just took them for granted. When the school day ended or the weekend finally began, I felt inclined only to recline, preferably in bed. I did not want to go on a trip to "see" something, which really meant, more often than not, "buy" something. I had no desire to go and visit people, surrounded by them as I was for every second of my working life. I mistook lethargic domesticity for a healthy relationship, laziness for love, lack of communication for mutual contentment.

Sophie had tried to coax me into a world outside the classroom. She created social occasions at which I was produced and where I would play along by laughing at the right moments. If I felt it was unavoidable, I could also provide an anecdote, which would suit the company and environment and might even elicit a little mirth in return. As time went on, though, I became idle in my efforts to please, and Sophie, despairing of my inertia, attempted first to cajole, then to coerce me into action. Finally, she started to tell me what to do. This had quite the opposite effect from the one that she had been hoping for. I buried my head in the pillows. When I reemerged she had gone.

No, no, I did understand why she had left, and consoled myself that, for both our sakes, it was much better that things had come to a head sooner rather than later. I convinced myself, after Sophie had slammed the last door behind her, that I had learned a lot from this experience, that I had matured as a result and that, next time, things would be quite different. Unfortunately, the opportunity to test this theory had not been forthcoming for quite some while now.

When my natural buoyancy occasionally deflated in the early hours of a lonely morning, I was reminded of a tearful, profoundly drunk girl I had once met at a wedding party. Late on, she had mumbled into my shoulder her theory that if you weren't married by the time you were thirty-two, you might as well grab the first person who walked past—in her case, that person appeared to be me. Otherwise, she concluded, you might as well give up and go abroad. I was eighteen months past my departure date.

On Tuesday morning, Jim had delivered a fourth wedding invitation. Still clutching it, I went into the headmaster's study. The atmosphere of academic competence and neat self-discipline always slightly unnerved me, just as it had done on the unhappy occasions that I had found myself in similar circumstances as a teenager. Now as then, I checked the cleanliness of my shoes.

"Ah, Will. Sorry to get you in like this. I'm sure you are very busy. It's just that . . . It's a rather delicate matter." My toes curled in my less than spotless footwear, and I riffled through a mental drawer marked "Guilty." I found it refreshingly empty. "It's just that the groundsman found these on the side of your rugby pitch on Saturday. Quite rightly, he brought them to me."

Pulling open an oak drawer of his colossal desk, he carefully removed a plate. Lying on it were the chewed and mangled remains of five or six quarters of halftime oranges. Resisting the surging urge to laugh, I rearranged my face into an expression of tragic mortification more in line with his own.

"Litter." The word that he had been searching for suddenly hit him with all its truly awful resonances, resonances that spelled the certain and imminent collapse of Western Civilization.

"What can I say, Headmaster? What an appalling oversight. Don't worry, I shall have a full investigation at the next practice."

"If you would and get back to me. Standards, Will, standards. That will be all. Thank you."

No, no, thank you, Headmaster.

Fortunately, I was outside, the door closed between the two of us, before I had the chance to suggest how he might best dispose of the offending articles.

Christ, the sodding things were biobloodydegradable, I thought as I pounded back down the corridor, glaring at the portraits of countless other pompous idiots, whoever they were. I was livid.

"Good morning, sir," said a fluting, syrupy voice behind me. I glanced over my shoulder. Oh, no.

"Morning, Robert," I growled as I charged on. "Have you seen the groundsman?"

"No sir, but *siiir!*" He skipped along to keep up. "My mother wonders when we will get our exercise books back."

"You can tell your dear mother"—dreary, neurotic old hag that she was—"you can tell her that you can have them back when I've finished counting in the oranges."

The door of the staff room slammed most satisfactorily.

"Sir?"

I can see now that my departure was not perhaps as spontaneous an event as I had initially considered. In fact, my life then as now had been directed by confusing, confluent currents of coincidence, outside influence, inherent sloth, and a hitherto undiscovered ability on my part to react remarkably badly to being told what to do. Anyway, it was high time I left school.

My final briefing had taken place in the comfortable sitting room of Charles and Juliet's house, a few hundred yards down the lane. Fortunately, Charles was a man of great method, which made up for all my inefficiencies, and now he filled me in, painstakingly, on important background. Although I was still smarting from the oranges incident, I tried to take as much onboard as possible and nodded and agreed at what I hoped were the correct moments.

It was true that this Commander did seem to have been an interesting character. Not content with having escaped from the Germans during the war by dropping through the floorboards of a cattle truck and onto the railway tracks, he had skied a season in Switzerland before making his way home to rejoin his ship. When the fighting was over he had chartered a yacht. This he had sailed to the South Pacific, where he had bought himself the plantation.

"Not many like him, I suppose," I commented with a spectacular lack of imagination.

"Now, you can get a pretty good idea of what the island looks like from this." Charles spread out a map on the floor, and we both leaned over it on all fours. To my surprise, instead of the veins and arteries that I was used to seeing on my very nice *Reader's Digest Deluxe Motorist's Atlas of Britain,* this chart was decorated only with concentric sea level lines.

"So, here it is: Randuvu. About the size of the Isle of Wight. About forty by twenty, something like that."

"What, yards?" I blurted in alarm.

"No, Will, miles."

Oh, God, the embarrassment!

"And here's the volcano in the middle—extinct, of course."

"Oh, yes, that's good . . ."

I peered more closely and tried to picture beaches and hotels, bars and restaurants. Charles pointed to a cross drawn on the map.

"Here you are. Mendali, the village, on the northwestern tip, about ten miles across the water, an hour or so by boat with outboard from Munda, the little town where the shop is."

The shop? The one shop?

"Oh, and the rest house."

Well, that was something.

"Anything else then . . . you know . . . on Randuvu?" I raised my eyebrows helpfully as if to jog his memory.

"Yes, a couple of other villages, much the same. Not much there—few huts, gardens."

Fancifully, I imagined roses and daisies, gnomes and sundials—parties.

"The villagers just grow vegetables and go fishing. Subsistence farming. Very poor, really. Trouble is that they have a lot more expenses than they used to. Petrol for a start, for the engine. They want to maintain the church and eventually save for a water standpipe in the village. One day it might be worth trying to get electricity laid on for street lighting."

I mentally unpacked my electric shaver.

"Of course, the fund won't last forever. So the best thing would be to get a moneymaking project up and running and then pay for the improvements with the profits."

"Okay, fine, thanks, good," I muttered weakly

"So, what sorts of things do you think you might try and do?" asked Juliet as she poured another cup of tea.

"Well, I think probably better to get the lie of the land, probably get some ideas then, don't you think?" I replied rather doubtfully.

My two neighbors nodded their agreement. Yes, probably get some ideas out there.

"There" suddenly seemed to have come significantly closer as I pushed my way through the squash of chaotic, animated holidaymakers in Terminal One. They were dressed in incongruous, patterned clothes, the occasional shop tag apparent, and festooned in essential gear. At last I took my place at the end of the check-in queue. Cool sunglasses, cameras, and headphone leads tangled themselves around necks as tickets and passports were rummaged for in arm-deep bags. Tea and Marmite wrapped in plastic bags were pulled out ostentatiously and announced to be necessities without which life in the wilds of a European seaside resort would be unimaginable. Stiff upper lips were kept and a little-exercised bonhomie reserved for such occasions was employed as we waited with national ease, content in the knowledge that Patience was a virtue.

"Only five hundred days to the millennium!" a television

screen flashed excitedly as I headed for Departures. "Where will you be?"

More apposite a question than it probably imagined. My "contract" was open-ended. I had no idea how long I might be gone for. How long was a piece of string? Perhaps I could chop a length off with my new penknife if things didn't go well. I handed my passport to the official at the desk, had it returned, and stepped through the doors.

I arrived in Australia, and at five o'clock the following morning, after a character-building night in Brisbane airport, I was the last to board the once-weekly plane to the Solomon Islands. A few freshly shaved businessmen, comfortably occupying the huge seats in which they were sitting, stared blankly at boring sections of the newspaper, yawning cavernously. The seats behind them, I noticed as I wandered lonely down the aisle, were all but empty.

Once arrived in "Oniara," my instructions were to take a domestic flight directly on to the small town of Munda, New Georgia, Western Province. There I would find a canoe hired from someone called Gerry to take me to the village of Mendali on the island of Randuvu. The villagers would be waiting for me. No worries, as they say, without much conviction. I was beginning to feel distinctly nervous.

The sun glanced off the starboard wing as we swung and dipped northeast from Australia. As we leveled off, I saw below me the glimmer of the sun as it edged up over the wide-open horizons of the Pacific.

At the end of a two-and-a-half-hour, uneventful, quite normal flight, we touched down and I got out.

Shuffling along in the queue, scooting my bag along the floor with my toe, I attempted to fill in the landing card. Deciding against asking a brisk-looking lady in front of me if I could make use of her shoulder, I made do with the flat of my hand. A quick mental check that I had not inadvertently packed any pornography, firearms, or explosives confirmed that I was pretty much in the clear. I ticked the last "no" box, kicked my backpack once more, and found myself standing in front of a counter behind which stood a tall, uniformed customs officer.

"Welcome to Solomon Islands." He beamed as he thumped a stamp into my passport.

CHAPTER 3

Coming in to Land

Yes, thank you," I mumbled. No mistake then. I really was in
the Solomon Islands. In my mind's eye I pictured the map of
the world on the classroom wall. Bloody hell. "I mean, err, yes,
thank you. Can you tell me how to get to the domestic terminal,
please?"

He smiled again. "Through the doors. There is a minibus
to take you."

"Thank you, yes, well, good-bye and thank you." As I
backed through the doors into the outside, I resisted the desire
to lift my hat to him. Totally absurd, I know. I wasn't even wearing one.

Arms folded around their briefcases, the businessmen
ahead of me disappeared, evaporating in a cloud of dusty green-
and-white taxis. Sure enough, a few yards distant stood a mud
brown bus, its side door slid open. On it someone had written in

bold lettering the slogan "Klin mi plis"—whatever that meant.

So rattled was I by my arrival and the need to make my connection that I had hardly had time to take in these new surroundings. It was only as another beaming man stepped forward to help me put my bags into the battered vehicle that the searing heat caught me. Hot and humid—just as it had been described in the book. As I swung my bag from my shoulder to hand to him, every pore sprang a leak and dark patches of sweat appeared on my chest.

"All inside, please."

To my mild alarm, I appeared to be the only person leaving the capital by air. I climbed in. Inside the rear of the minibus there were a number of freestanding webbing-and-tubular-metal folding stools arranged in no particular way at all. I picked one up, positioned it carefully on the corrugated floor, and sat on it. Off we set. We'd just slalomed round a particularly sharp corner on the dirt road and were whizzing along in front of an outlying workshop or some such when, with a clattering of camping seats, we suddenly stopped.

"Domestic terminal, now."

He climbed out, and once we'd both confirmed that the inside handle was temporarily elsewhere, pulled back the sliding door. I climbed out, dragging my luggage by its straps. He beamed, I beamed. He drove away. Solomon Islanders, I was discovering, smiled for the best part of the day. It was infectious.

Wooden and elderly, the building stood at an original angle and, as I approached, I could see that it was almost shaking with activity. Struggling my bag onto my back, I stumbled in through the double doors and found myself behind a crowd of eager black faces facing the far end of the room. Inching forward, I could see, as I grew closer, uniformed attendants busy behind a wide counter. They were enthusiastically employed throwing a great assortment of objects onto large penny-in-the-slot weighing machines, which, it seemed, had coins jammed permanently in their workings. Trays of eggs, vegetables, engine parts, even whole frozen fish carefully wrapped in Chinese, or possibly Japanese, newspaper were all weighed. Men, women, and children climbed on, clutching sacks of flour and rice as well as all their own bags and belongings. Once they were in position, relatives and friends would pile on more items until they could hold no more. Children, being the lightest, suffered most, the smallest all but disappearing under a welter of packages. Everybody was, it appeared, proposing to take the maximum allowed weight of goods, bought in the capital and unavailable elsewhere, back home. I wondered idly what would happen if they tipped the scales too far. What would they dispense with? A spare part here, a tuna there?

My turn eventually came, and I climbed uncertainly aboard. My total weight, my rucksack on my back, was recorded on a small pink sheet. If I were underweight, would I be given something extra to carry? All seemed to be well, however, and I made my way as directed to the door marked DEPARTURE LOUNGE FOR PLANE, followed by a crowd of fellow travelers.

I turned the handle, but it appeared to be locked. "Err, sorry, but this door won't open."

"That is because it is locked," replied the clerk.

"Oh, yes, I see," I said in some confusion and stepped smartly back onto the foot of a small child behind me who, quite understandably, burst into tears. With small robotic steps to avoid any further havoc that might be caused by my backpack, I turned around to apologize, but as I did so, suddenly the door was open. Turning giddily through the other half of the circle, I was propelled through the door as we poured out onto the tarmac.

On the edge of the runway, by a glass-fronted office, there was a small lean-to roof, shelter from the steaming heat of the sun. Swinging my bag to the ground, I looked around for something to sit on. In one corner was a wheelchair of rusting chrome and faded khaki. Attached was a notice that read, "Not for you to sit and relax but for sick people and nurses." At different times I supposed.

I squinted through the heat haze to the faded hills on the other side of the runway. At their foot was a helicopter. Its blackened, buckled tail section and warped rotor blades suggested that it had not landed according to plan. I cleared my throat and glanced at my watch. Ten forty-seven. Perfect. The plane was due to take off at eleven.

At just past three we were still waiting. Dizzy, my legs involuntarily twitching, I was beginning to regret the lack of any minor ailment or professional nursing qualification. I asked the man standing next to me if he knew why there was a delay. Was the plane broken down? A technical problem perhaps? No, no everything fine, he assured me. In that case, why, well, you know, why was it taking off four hours late?

"Oh," he said, "Solomon Time."

Everyone laughed.

"Oh, Solomon Time!" I joined in, somewhat perplexed.

Solomon Time, Solomon Time—how it was to dominate future events I then had no idea. It is liquid, a fluid that cannot be contained, that has no master, that sloshes backward and forward and even from side to side. It has no symmetry or order. Solomon Time plays by nobody's rules, yet it loosely dictates that something may happen a little late or perhaps a little early or days late or even days early; it may have happened already or it may never happen at all. Schedules and timetables become irrelevancies, arrangements, meetings, deadlines inconsequential.

Solomon Time trickles through every stream in every forest and pumps through the veins of every man or woman born of Solomon. Clocks stop ticking; wristwatches become mere ornaments. Time is governed by the sun and the moon, by light and dark. Months slip by indistinguishable one from the next, December as hot as May, November as wet as June. Daily routine, apart from the two bookends of morning and evening prayer, is as higgledy-piggledy as a child's toy box. Mealtimes become movable feasts. Work, rest, and play are as confused as three scoops of ice cream melted in the tropical sun.

Days, weeks, years slip by as they do in every other corner of the world, but the islanders pay scant attention to the upturned hourglass. Intent on living, they have no time for Time. Solomon Time can be magical; it can blur, twist, distort; it can transport you into an almost ethereal state of blissful calm and serenity—but then, of course, sometimes it can just be bloody irritating.

Sitting on the concrete, I leaned my back against the faded weatherboarding. On cue, a plane taxied up, and out jumped a white man with black-and-gold sunglasses that matched his epaulets and gave him the appearance of an irate insect.

"Munda, Munda."

Never, ever had I seen such a small plane; it was like a model. I struggled to my feet, partly in readiness, partly out of astonishment. If the hundred or so people waiting were going to fit in, I was to be witness to one of the greatest miracles since the fish and the loaves—in reverse as it were. There was no time to consider this problem further, however, as our pilot, an Australian of the type who fails to recognize a smile let alone return one, was in a hurry.

"All aboard. We're running a bit late," he ordered as he opened a square door in the tail of the plane and seven of us scurried over to throw our baggage into the small hold. Under his marshaling, impenetrable gaze, we piled in. Not one of the more popular destinations then, Munda, I thought as, bent double, I made my way down the two yards of aisle.

I found myself sitting just behind the pilot's right shoulder, the other six passengers in pairs behind me. I peered at the dashboard, if that is the correct aviation term. There were not nearly enough instruments. Our captain flicked a couple of light switches, and with a good deal of spluttering and black smoke the propeller engines fired. I happened to notice that some of the few dials that were in front of the driver's seat did not seem to be working. Others flicked momentarily and then came lazily back to rest.

Anyway, I was sure it would all be fine as I fingered the emergency instructions. They were printed on worn card and accompanied by diagrams. All the men in the pictures were white, wore suits, and smoked pipes. All the women were dressed in hats, their gloved hands fiddling nervously with their handbags. We taxied past the glass front of the terminal, and as I looked out of the window, which seemed, to my surprise, to open—for ventilation I supposed—I caught a glimpse of the plane resplendent in its livery: the colors of the national flag, green and royal blue, divided by a yellow stripe, the sand between the sea and the forest. Over one of the wings the pale circle of my face was reflected back at me as I peered out.

Perhaps the Commander had sat in this very plane, this very seat, and looked out of the very same window? Both man and machine seemed to be of the same sort of pre-jet vintage. Now I was seconds away from seeing the very same sights as he had at a height of God only knew how many thousand feet. The chances were that I was going to be rather closer to Him than I had ever been before.

Then all of a sudden we were off. Effortlessly the pilot eased back his steering wheel, twisting as he did so a knob on the side of his gray headphones. I could just hear the tinny pop music over the hair dryer roar of the engines as we sailed upward, leaving our shadow to make its own way along the ground.

Checking that the two halves of my seat belt were tightly

clicked together, I glanced back over my shoulder, just to see how the other passengers were coping with the takeoff. All six faces were already cast in various configurations of deep slumber.

One moment the view through the windscreen was of a large hedge and the odd hangar, and the next it was of the clearest blue sky, so blue that it was almost tangible; you could almost taste it, drink it. After a steep climb, we leveled off. As my ears became used to the noise and my eyes registered that I could see out through the cracks round the door, I began to enjoy the experience.

"The Solomon Islands, or 'The Happy Isles' as they are known, is a remarkably beautiful country consisting of six main islands." So explained the glossy in-flight magazine that proudly advertised itself as the only such publication in the country. There on a map they were: Guadalcanal, Makira, Malaita, Santa Isabel, Choiseul, and, after a worrying search, New Georgia. In that moment, it had crossed my mind briefly that this might all be some incredibly elaborate hoax and that I would discover that my destination did not really exist at all.

The view from the window looked reassuringly as I had thought it should. Tiny islands clustered round the larger ones like little splashes of land on the huge deep azure of the Pacific. Rising up from the ocean floor, the outer atolls protected the inner islands, encircling them with long, pale, protective arms of interlinking coral reefs. Inside the reefs lay the lagoons, the secret waterways where the Solomons shelter and hide away their riches. Only from the air could you peer into this hidden world, and it was the realization of every childhood dream: desert islands, coconut palms overhanging waters of every shade of green and turquoise, secluded bays, little rivers and great cliffs that fell like the walls of ancient fortresses sheer into the sea, mountains that slid gracefully down to small, bleached sand beaches or into the dark tangles of mangrove swamps.

Occasionally, only very occasionally, did I see signs of habitation. Squares and rectangles of leaf houses on stilts crowded to the water's edge; the long, thin shapes of canoes were drawn up on the shore. Sometimes, hidden from view, villages in the bush, deep into the jungles and hills far from the sea, living their own private existences, betrayed their presence: streaks of smoke rising up from the cooking fires.

Straining round, I looked down over the edge of the strangely quivering wing strut. Here was a vast distance of open water, an infinity of ocean, its surface blurred like paint dried in the wind.

Quite suddenly, the calm of the surface exploded into a wild, foaming turbulence. It was as if someone had turned a tap to unleash a gigantic and inordinately powerful jet of air from the seabed perhaps some ten or twenty miles across, as much as, at this distance, I could judge. Huge waves thundered away from the epicenter, throwing up great tails of spray.

"Err . . . Did you see . . . ?" I yelled at the back of the pilot's head.

"Underwater volcano," he bellowed in answer.

"Right, underwater volcano. Right."

The kind of thing that within a few weeks I would no doubt find entirely commonplace. I looked down again. From the effervescence, dark objects were projected high above the surface before crashing back into the spume: rocks and boulders thrown from the depths. I half-expected some dreadful sea creature to rise up and strike out with a dripping, gnarled claw to swat our buzzing airplane. Anyway, luckily, none did, which was a relief.

The vast, open expanses of water made the great landmasses of our planet seem inconsequential, distances across continents derisory. Like a constellation in the night sky, the Solomon Islands glimmered in the Pacific and, as I watched our shadow faithfully tracing our course, I could feel myself beguiled by the prospect of discovery. Of course, I was also beginning to get rather nervous. We were nearly there, very nearly there.

"Munda coming right up, mate."

Oh, dear. I peeked over his shoulder again as the nose of the plane dipped, dipped a bit more and then quite a bit more. As far as I could see, we were dropping into the dirty brown airstrip almost vertically. The little plane started to scream like a war movie soundtrack, and I waited for the pilot to disappear through the roof, twisting away on the end of his parachute. Feeling casually under my seat, I half-turned to see the reaction of the others. A sleeping mouth had sagged open, and a nose was now squidged uncomfortably against a window, vibrating to the tune of the engine. Otherwise all was undisturbed. I turned back and stared down.

I was on the point of voicing my concerns to the pilot when he nonchalantly pulled back on his handlebars and we glided gracefully parallel with the ground. With the smallest of bumps we made contact and, after a couple of gentle bounces, slowed to a halt.

Stepping out onto the tarmac, I thanked the captain wholeheartedly, complimenting him roundly on his flying skills. He still did not smile. Lazily, the other passengers tottered out. Little did they realize.

Collecting my bags, I took stock and a few deep breaths. It appeared that the plane had landed in the middle of a small town. To my left was a tiny post office with rusty bars, behind them the brown panels of its closed shop front. To my right stood a modern-looking bank, its business, too, finished for the day. There were, I was pleased to see, a couple of general stores, and through the open doors of the larger I could see rows of tins and packets, glass-fronted cupboards with clothes, tools, pots and pans all neatly piled up on them. Directly opposite me was the airport terminal—a low, rickety building a little like a village hall. It appeared to have been the target of a recent bomb attack. Shredded, faded curtains flapped in the breeze that blew through the doorless entrance. A man in a smart blue uniform was leaning out through a smashed window, cheerfully chatting on a radio that was powered by a car battery. In between the various constructions grew scrubby grass, picked out with orange and white wildflowers and crisscrossed by single-track dirt paths that etched lines from one door to another. The whole was pleasant and tidy in the late afternoon.

As the sun began to tip toward the sea, I wandered down the hill in search of the rest house where I was to meet my canoe. A leathery old man in bare feet and a pair of shorts was slowly climbing the shallow incline from the water's edge, heading in the direction of the "town center." On his back, tied around him with string, was a shiny fishing net; this and a long stick, which turned out to be a spear, in one hand gave him the appearance of Neptune up from the depths to do his weekly shopping. I stopped him at a safe distance and asked for directions.

"Hem long der." He pointed toward the sea. "Hem no long way tumas."

"I'm sorry? Perhaps you could try that one more time."

He repeated.

"Perhaps just once more?"

The man laughed.

"Iu no save tok-tok Pijin? You don't know any Pijin then?" he translated.

Pigeon?

"No, I'm afraid not. I don't know anybody. You see, I'm new here. I was just looking for Gerry."

"It's over there, not very far. Through the red gate. You just go straight. Gerry, him inside there."

I followed the instructions and, walking down a tidy coral path bordered by clumps of bright purple flowers that heaped over coconut stumps, I crossed the veranda of three numbered rooms. Their creamy blue fronts, with frames and sills picked out in yellow, shone prettily in the slanting light. Through the mosquito mesh of one of the glassless windows, I could see a ceiling fan turning wonkily.

Poking my head through an open doorway at the end, I found myself in a small office where a middle-aged white man with black hair and Irish eyes sat barefoot at a desk looking rather perplexed by a calculator that lay in front of him. He looked up when I came in. Standing and smiling, he stuck out his hand.

"You must be Will."

I nodded.

"Well, you can't go over to Randuvu now because it'll be too dark for the driver to come back. You'll have to stop here tonight. You better come and drink some beer. I'm Gerry, by the way," he said with a gentle lilt.

I followed him down some narrow ship's steps into a large wooden room open on one side to the sea. A short bar at one end was guarded by two enormous wooden carved figures—a warlike man and an equally ferocious woman, each pendulous according to its sex. His back against the warrior lady's sturdy thigh, another white man of a similar age to Gerry with tight blond curls and friendly blue eyes sat on a barstool.

"Hi, I'm Geoff. How are you? Good trip?"

"Oh . . . Yeah, fine, great, really good, loved it. No worries."

Throwing in this last piece of Australiana gave me a well-traveled edge, I thought, as my voice echoed round the barn of a room.

"I run the dive shop here. Are you a diver?" he continued in a cheerful but businesslike way.

"No, no, not really." I do not like overfilling the bath. I felt confused, tired. This was not what I had expected. It all seemed so, well, normal.

"You'll find it a bit different on Randuvu, boy." Geoff grinned, his voice rich with the soft undulations of the east coast of England. He was surely telepathic. Marlene, his wife, who had just joined us, smiled in agreement.

"But nice," she added as she read, correctly, an expression of concern cross my face. I followed their gaze out over the lagoon. Walking to the threshold of the airy room, I leaned against one of the rough doorposts. Dreamlike, the volcano reared up out of the water, three or four of its crenellated peaks piercing the motionless cloud that hung over the island. Randuvu looked neither sinister nor inviting, neither welcoming nor ominous. It simply did not look real.

I returned to my new acquaintances. They had lived here for ten years, providing "tourism" for the trickle of foreigners that wandered through. Gerry had married a Solomon Islands girl, and none of them had any intention of leaving.

"Very laid-back here you'll find. Quiet. Could never go back to the rat race. Not a great deal of competition, here. That's the real attraction."

Or custom for that matter, I thought as I looked around the empty hotel.

That evening we talked of home, of points in common, of differences. Swapping barroom stories and laughing at old jokes, I felt far removed from the South Pacific, almost at ease in this convivial company. Forgetting momentarily where I was, I filled my three companions in on the latest news and weather from home. Politics, celebrity gossip, and cricket almost eclipsed the brightness of the fireflies that blazed their trails over the jetty. The one about the Englishman, the Irishman, and the Scotsman on a weekend away in Amsterdam with an inflatable lady produced enough laughter to drown the drone of the huge moths that whirred round the conch shell lamps that hung on the pillars of the great leaf house. I ordered fish and chips for supper.

Later that night, as I made my way, somewhat unsteadily, to bed in one of the sparse but clean rooms in the rest house, Gerry asked me an exceedingly interesting question. "So what exactly will you be doing over on the island?"

"Well. . . . Perhaps just play it by ear to start off with and perhaps see how it goes . . ."

"So you don't really know?"

"No."

"Oh, well. Good night. See you tomorrow; probably try to set off sometime in the morning."

Solomon Time.

≈

CHAPTER 4

Mr. Will, I Presume?

The following morning at ten-forty sharp I left through the same red gate and climbed into a narrow, speedy fiberglass boat with an outboard engine and a cheery driver named Reuben. I waved farewell to Gerry, Geoff, and Marlene, thanking them for everything, including a bit of a headache.

So off we set—ten miles of water took about forty minutes to cover in the shallow-draft "canoe." It was the longest journey I've ever made. As the milky wake lengthened from our stern and small schools of sparkling flying fish zoomed ahead, my past disappeared behind me. Rounding the first island, we emerged into a wide channel of water. Without warning, the shallow reef dropped sheer away and, as if soaring over a cliff's edge, we floated out over a bottomless blue. Dark forms twisted and turned indistinct against the coral wall. Ahead of us, the peaks of a mountain rose up to a summit at the northern end of

Randuvu, and what had for so long been the far distant future became suddenly and undeniably the present.

As we rode the swell rolling in from the open sea, I glimpsed the outline of a figure sitting stiffly on the seat behind me. I just had time to catch sight of a furry green hat and the dirty white creases of a musket-proof raincoat before the light flickered again and the old man disappeared. Just checking that I was not attempting to bail out at this late stage.

Spray puffed up from the bow, and I tasted the salt. No, I was here, most definitely here. How I had allowed it all to happen, on the other hand, was another question entirely.

Twenty minutes later Reuben, who had sat silently cross-legged at the tiller, raised his arm and pointed. "Mendali," he shouted above the noise of the engine. I peered over the bow and bit by bit, on a point off to my right, I could make out the forms of houses, a clearing, a small jetty built from coral. Inside the reef, the water turned again to turquoise patched with the floating green shadows of clouds overhead.

The village grew imperceptibly larger and intelligible, a slide coming into focus, until, a few hundred yards off, I could make out its every detail. Every window and door was outlined, each tree distinct. I could see, even count, a few chickens pecking beneath the trees. Yet strangely, the scrawny birds apart, there was no sign of life, no one to be seen.

Reuben switched the engine into reverse, slowing us down alongside the small wharf, and threw a couple of turns of rope expertly around one of the wooden uprights that acted as fenders against the sharp coral. Climbing inelegantly out, I grabbed the bags as they were dumped down at my feet. I glanced around anxiously. Still nobody. Then, from the shadow of a low building, a tottering, naked boy of about two or three appeared. With one finger in the corner of his mouth, he approached cautiously, gazing up at me with round, brown eyes.

"Hello," I said. He just gazed.

Slowly figures began to appear. They came from behind trees and the backs of houses; some appeared at windows and at doorways. One little girl stood up from the middle of a bush, leaves still sticking out of her great fuzz of hair. This all as if everyone had been hiding, waiting to see what this strange man was like before they showed themselves. I smiled, mainly because I couldn't really think of anything else to do, and did not move. Behind me the engine puttered out of earshot. I waited, the blood pumping a reggae beat in my temples, my tongue huge in the back of my throat. After a few minutes a group of perhaps one hundred or one hundred and fifty extremely curious people had gathered in front of me. My smile was beginning to ache. Discreetly wiping the sweat from my forehead, I shifted from one foot to the other.

From the midst of this melee, the crowd parting on a muttered, indistinct instruction, there approached a man, slight in build but wiry. He wore shorts and a T-shirt. His curled hair was cut short, his face tattooed or rather, it seemed, carved, intricate patterns tracing either cheek. He thrust out his hand. Clearing his throat, he said in quiet and excellent English and without a hint of irony, "Mr. Will, I presume?"

He was staring fixedly at the ground just to the right of my shoes. I mistakenly thought that he had spotted something I had dropped as I disembarked. Shaking his hand, I too looked searchingly at the same spot, but as I did so I became aware that he was fixing his gaze there only because, through shyness or custom, he chose not to meet my eye. Unfortunately, when I bent down everybody else presumed that *I* had spotted something of the greatest significance on the ground. The assembled company shuffled forward en masse, leaning to peer at the same significant spot in search of a mythical something. Fortunately this impasse was dissolved when the man said softly, "My name is Luta. You are a friend of Commander, one of his friends in England, and we are happy that you come this long way. Now, of course the Commander is dead, thank God."

I managed to suppress laughter at this unfortunate turn of phrase and immediately felt ashamed when I looked at the genuine sentiment in the other man's face as he went on. "But you are welcome here in our village. Now everybody must shake hand with Mr. Will."

So, after the instruction was relayed in a language I did not understand, everybody did. Eager hands, firm ones, old ones and shy ones, even perfectly smooth baby hands that were tendered by their mothers, generally resulting in wails of terror.

"Small pickaninny no look any white man before," Luta explained matter-of-factly, unaware, of course, that the term was nearly archaic and considered offensive in the Western world. Some minutes later he made a suggestion: "So now you come and look around our village."

Turning, he started to walk back barefoot along the sharp coral of the jetty. I followed him, and everyone else followed me, and in a silent gaggle we wandered gently around the small settlement.

The houses were built on a narrow, sandy point perhaps one hundred yards wide and three hundred yards long. Running down one edge, they were all of much the same design. Raised on stilts perhaps four feet tall, the front two legs dipping their toes in the waters of the lagoon, the houses were made of leaf. That is to say that the walls and roofs were made of leaves cut and folded over long flat sticks and held in place with the bark skinned from the same sticks, interlacing the leaves. The whole formed panels some ten feet long. These had then been tied with more bark, each overlapping the one below, to the wooden frame of the house and to the roof. Most houses, it seemed, were divided into two or three different rooms, and each accommodated an extended family, which, judging from the number of children running around, meant that most were at pretty full stretch. Across the way from each dwelling stood a kitchen or cookhouse built from the same materials. On the dirt floor were open fires and piles of stones.

In the center of the village there was a clearing used for meetings and feasts and special days. On normal days, someone explained, the youngsters would use it to kick a football, if they had one. If not, they would just use one of the smaller children.

We wandered to the middle of the point. The church stood in an area of its own, which was laid to grass. Every Friday from then on I would see the women religiously trimming the neat churchyard. Bent double at the waist, one arm tucked behind their backs and swinging bush knives with the other, they would advance in line from the church to the graveyard until it was all cut. The cemetery was enclosed by a low bamboo fence. In one corner small, round mounds bore testament to those who had been born in the village but were destined to remain children for eternity. Some of the more recent graves showed signs of continued grieving—woven mats, a pile of pretty shells, a bunch of wilting flowers lay against the white of the coral that was strewn over each grave. The church itself was made of sawn planks and round trunks, roofed with sheet iron rusted brown and beige by the salt sea air. Inside, peeling light blue walls were decorated with carvings of boats and fish picked out in red and white.

Luta and I went in. Everybody else waited silently outside. Uncomfortable, I was beginning to feel like a visiting dignitary. Yet I was falling into the role. I adopted a measured, solemn walk, clasping my hands, fingers interlocked, across my stomach as we stepped through the open door.

"Commander build this church for us. Before we'd no place for worship, but in 1956 we bless this place and now we come here every day in the morning and in the evening. It is very nice for prayer."

Twice a day . . . Well, it would be good for me.

It was cool and quite dark inside. Sand, carefully swept, covered the floor, and down either side of the aisle stood pews of roughly hewn timber, smoothed shiny by the passage of time and innumerable bottoms. Following my host's lead, I achieved an awkward nod of the head as we approached the altar. It was simple, perhaps humble—a table decorated with a white cloth emblazoned with a hand-stitched red cross. On top stood two wooden candlesticks and beside these two tall, highly polished brass containers, which on closer inspection turned out to be hefty shell canisters. They served as vases for long, feathery leaves, yellow and bright red.

"Japanese forget to take these home." Luta grinned as he held them up for the light to glint off them. I guessed he was referring to the war, but I was not entirely sure what he meant, so I just smiled and nodded and shook my head. Only later did I come to understand better the brief but violent role that these islands had played in the course of world history.

We turned again to leave, and it was then that I noticed by the door, standing on a wooden plinth waist high, a giant upturned shell some two feet across. I looked into it. It was half full of water—the font.

We walked back outside into the aggressive heat. The others smiled, and we moved on.

"Next one, we show you house for rest but first 'smolhaus' belong you. Him number-one important one."

Led through a screen of flowering shrubs, I found myself standing in front of a child's tree house. Built precariously in the lower branches of a large tree that grew out over the sea, my lavatory had a green canvas door and a sloping tin roof. It could be approached only by a twisting, serpentine root that, even at a leisurely pace in the daylight, was going to require acrobatics. Ushered up for an inspection, I made my wobbly way to the threshold and held the sheet aside. Inside were splintery wooden floorboards, into which someone had cut a neat hole. I peered down.

I had only ever peed into a tropical fish tank once before and then only rather late on at a party. It had all been a bit of a mistake, particularly as I seemed to remember that I had not made myself very popular with the owner or, for that matter, the fish. This, though, was a positive invitation to do so. I was greatly relieved. Reversing back, I stepped out onto the root.

"So now Mr. Will make nice speech."

Speech!

Looking down at the assembled crowd, I saw that all eyes were upon me, waiting kindly and patiently. To my surprise I noticed several blue pairs among them and shocks of blond hair set against the black and copper skins. Later it was suggested to me that this was the genetic legacy of some passing Dutch sailors or perhaps just a hereditary anomaly—whatever the reason, they were a very striking and handsome people. Men and boys wore only shorts, while the women wore long skirts of designs best described as boisterous. Many of the younger women and girls had hitched the elasticated waistbands up over their breasts, thus creating fetching minidresses.

"Err, well yes, very nice . . ." I teetered. "I am very happy to be with you and bring you greetings from your friends in England."

I cringed at my effortless pomposity. My arms held out like those of a tightrope walker, I blundered on. "The Commander would have been very happy to see you all, but he cannot because he is, err . . . well . . . um . . . he's dead."

Suddenly a still passed over the company, and I realized that all eyes were now cast down.

Bugger.

"Anyway, this is a particularly fine building . . ."

Turning my head, I gestured with one thumb, fell sideways into a small shrub, and disappeared. To my relief, there was a ripple of good-natured laughter and, to polite applause, I was helped up.

Three wooden steps led up to a little picket gate that opened into my "house for rest." With a great deal of excitement, my bags were dragged in, and I was left to unpack and make myself at home. It was wonderful, possessing what could be described as a superb waterfront location. Indeed, so close was it to the sea that the high tide had left its mark on the front two stilts. A sitting room at the front looked out across the lagoon, over to the island of New Georgia and in the distance the cloud-crested, conical Kolombangara Mountain. Just outside the window to the right were a table and two benches shaded by a sloping roof.

Inside, a flimsy wickerwork chair stood at a low writing desk, above which had been nailed a short plank—a bookshelf. I reached for my rucksack and pulled out my brown paper parcel tied up with string. Three smartly bound hardbacks were to be the beginning of my library. I inspected each volume closely; a good deal of thought had been put into their choice. *In the South Seas* by Robert Louis Stevenson told the tales of his travels in the Pacific, which was also, I noticed with a frown, described on the flyleaf as "his final resting place." At least he had been correct to surmise on the first page that he "had come to the afterpiece of life and had only the nurse and the undertaker to expect."

Robinson Crusoe was going to be a good long read—well, long anyway, I thought nervously, as I flicked through pages of *thou*s, *thuse*s, and *Year of our Lord*s. Mind you, there were lots of illustrations.

The third book, which to my mild embarrassment turned out to be a "Junior Version," was entitled *A Pattern of Islands* and written by a man who went by the unlikely name of Arthur Grimble. Although he sounded more like a Victorian stand-up comedian, he had in fact spent the best part of a lifetime as a

district commissioner in the Gilbert and Ellice Islands, which
appeared to be stuck even farther out into the Pacific than the
Solomons. I sat down on the wobbly chair and flicked through
the three books to see if I could elicit their authors' initial reac-
tions to life in the islands.

Robinson Crusoe had, I was soon to discover, an ability to
make remarks of the astonishingly obvious and demonstrated
an impressive, self-satisfied insouciance while doing so. His
comment on his arrival on his uninhabited island possesses the
essence of his style: "I used to look upon my condition with the
utmost regret. I had nobody to converse with; no work to be
done but by the labour of my hands; and I used to say I lived just
like a man cast away upon some desert island."

Disconcertingly, both Robert Louis Stevenson and Arthur
Grimble expressed concerns about this island life. Grimble
reckoned it took a little while to acclimatize. Shortly after arriving, he had discovered that a giant cockroach had eaten the sole
of one of his feet while he slept. On waking he had been com-
forted by a more experienced friend: "Take it easy, son: it's only
the first ten years in the islands that's hell."

But even after that RLS believed that there was no escape.
"Few men who come to the islands leave them; they grow gray
where they alighted; the palm shades and the trade-wind fans
them till they die, perhaps cherishing to the last the fancy of a
visit home, which is rarely made, more rarely enjoyed and yet
more rarely repeated."

I closed the book firmly and put it away with the others on
the shelf. Right, fine, no need to worry about all that; anyway,
better have a bit more of a look around; that was all years ago.
Things were bound to be different now, bound to be.

I continued to investigate my new house. Through an
opening at the back of the room lay a bedroom with an old
enamel-topped table and a narrow bed built from wood. On the
bed lay a wafer mattress, the thinnest I had ever seen, let alone

planned to sleep on. I tested it with a bump. I was sure that I would get used to it—in time. I erected my mosquito net, a box arrangement advertised as being "for the expat." That was me. After tying its four corners to various rafters, using a system that did not look very much like the one on the instructions, I tried it out, lying flat on my back, surrounded by the white box of netting. I had the strange, slightly discomforting feeling of being interred. It cannot, however, have been that discomforting, for I promptly fell asleep.

I sat up with a start, as sometimes happens when you wake up somewhere unfamiliar like a hospital or a police station, and wrestled my way out of bed. Out the window a fat, pink sun was slung low in the sky and the evening's shadows crept long across the village clearing. Suddenly a child's voice called out. "Mr. Will go swim now."

Go for a swim—now? Well, I had not planned to, but I supposed I could. Anyway, it appeared to be a direction rather than a question. I looked out of the house. At the bottom of the steps stood a boy of about six or seven. He held an aluminum saucepan and a small piece of soap. "Come," he said.

I was mystified but, grabbing a towel, followed the instruction, and we set off down into the trees. Along the way we met a steady line of villagers coming toward us, dripping wet, the water sparkling in their hair. Piles of washing were balanced regally on their heads, and each carried a small aluminum saucepan and a bar of soap. I smiled as I passed, but each time I did so they lowered their eyes, carrying on by without a word.

"You white man," said the small boy elliptically. We walked for about ten minutes between towering trees, parrots squawking in the high, scarecrow branches, until we came into a clearing, a narrow valley in fact, of carefully cultivated and maintained gardens in which grew a great variety of plants that I had never seen before. Many had huge, green, shiny leaves. I rubbed one between finger and thumb as I passed.

"Taro," said the small boy, whose name, it turned out, was Stanley. I was none the wiser. At the far end of the garden, a bright stream wound its way through the roots of trees, the last evening sun reflecting warmly off the surface. Knee-deep stood a beautiful young woman dressed in a lava-lava—a bright red and blue cloth wrapped about her waist. Her eyes closed, she was pouring water over her head with an aluminum saucepan. She became aware of our presence and looked round slowly with one eye. When she saw me she jumped out of the stream without a word and went careering off down the slippery mud path as fast as her wet feet would carry her. Stanley chuckled and pointed at the water. "You swim."

I pulled off my T-shirt and stepped into the water in my shorts. It was not warm. Some people like to tell you how wonderful cold water is, how refreshing, how bracing. I do not. I tipped water over my head in the approved fashion and had a scrub around with the soap. A fish darted between my legs, gagging on the suds as I rinsed myself. Better get used to it, I thought, stepping out again. As I dried off, a flight of huge dark forms whooshed overhead and I shivered in the dusk of the forest. The water had really been quite chilly.

By the time we returned to the village, it was nearly dark, but a blue kerosene storm lamp burned brightly on the table outside my house. I thanked Stanley and went up the steps into the house to change. When I emerged, a bowl and spoon had been laid on the table. There was no one about so I approached cautiously. I looked in—a fish and a potato or, at least, the head half of a fish and a potato or, to be absolutely precise, the head half of what looked distinctly like a large goldfish and a potato. Ignoring the fish's rather accusatory eyes, I picked up the spoon. I had not eaten that day but had curiously little appetite. The fish was fine if you moved the lamp away a bit. The potato was sweet and had all the consistency of tiling grout.

I was manfully chomping my way through it when a group of women and children bustled into the light of the lantern. They arranged themselves around the table.

"We are one big happy family," they sang. "You are my brother." They pointed. I smiled and thanked them. Without a word, they disappeared into the night.

"Evening, Mr. Will. Everything good?" asked Luta as he slid onto the bench opposite me.

"Very all right, thank you very much, but just call me Will."

"Look, I have brought something for you to see."

From under his arm he pulled a large picture frame and turned it toward me. Black and white and water-stained, it was a photograph of a group of children that might have been any of those I had seen that day. In their midst stood a lone white man. Although the deerstalker, mackintosh, and hairy nose were gone, replaced by a sun hat, smart shorts, and altogether more youthful features, it was unmistakably the Commander who gazed out, relaxed and smiling.

"This small boy—me." Luta pointed to the bottom left, where he stood leaning on the shoulder of a friend. "And this Commander, he was best man. With him we worked for many years. Always good times, but then he was old and had to go back to England."

Reminiscing, he tapped the Commander heavily on the chest. "Twenty years this year he leaves us, and then we hear in a letter that he passed away. We were all sad, but now you have come to visit us and we are all very happy. He would be pleased that you are here."

With this, he slipped off the seat, wished me good night, and vanished into the dark.

What a wonderful place, I thought as I made my way into my bedroom carrying my hurricane lamp. Who would want to be anywhere else? Of course, I still had to think up something "useful" to do, but then I had been here only a day. Certainly it would be better to get a feel for the place before making any decisions.

Despite my siesta I felt tired. I put my flashlight under my pillow, climbed under my net, blew out my kerosene lamp, and closed my eyes. It was quiet in the village, and I could hear the water lapping at the shore. A gentle breeze blew in through the window, lifting the thin curtains and bringing with it a shadowy moonlight. What a wonderful place.

Then I heard it.

Then again.

It was scurrying, and it was inside the room. I was sure it was. Yes, it was. One of the six varieties. I looked up into the near dark. No, no, probably imagined it. I listened again. Nothing. Honestly, you silly sod. I squeezed my eyes shut.

With a trampoline bounce, something landed on the top of my mosquito net, and it was definitely alive.

Right . . .

So, what action do you take when an unidentified living object lands on your mosquito net in the middle of the night? I had no idea. I had never owned a mosquito net before. Reaching under my pillow, I pulled out my flashlight. I aimed it and fired. Whiskers, two teeth, and a twitching black nose made up the front end of the biggest rat I had ever seen. I shot out of bed, landing on all fours on the floor.

Oh, come on, it's only a rat.

Only a rat! What do you mean, only a rat?

I jumped up and waved the beam of my flashlight at it like a demented duelist. It did not budge but just stared at me and wiggled its whiskers threateningly.

I picked up the first thing that came to hand—a bottle of suntan lotion—and hurled it. I missed, the bottle hit the wall, the top flew off, and a great spray of white cream caught Mr.

Rat full in the ear. This time he did budge, disappearing through a hole between the roof and the wall. With a final wave of a disgusting pink tail, he was gone.

Some considerable time later, I climbed back under the net. Tucking it carefully under the edge of my toast-thin mattress, I pulled the sheet up to my chin and closed my eyes.

It had all been the most terrible mistake.

Terrible.

⤜⤛

CHAPTER 5

Brave New World

Daylight restored something of my balance, and I peered up at the warming sky with new enthusiasm as I shaved in a bucket that Stanley had delivered with a cheerful "Morne!"

I tried to catch sight of my face in the surface of the cold water but every time I ventured my head over the edge a drip fell from my chin to spoil the reflection.

I shook my head, astonished at my new reality, but a stinging nick to my earlobe and a drop of blood that blossomed in the water below convinced me that this was no dream. Absentmindedly, I shook the plastic razor, and a few suds flecked an irritated lizard, who scuttled bandy-legged under the house to clean himself up. I was here now and, as Grimble would no doubt have said, I was just going to have to make a proper go of it.

The church bell started to ring. I had leapt into my clothes with a speed practiced over many years of trying to make it to period one on time and tumbled down the few steps to greet Luta as brightly as I could manage.

"Service now if you like—in the church?"

"Yes, great. Service, good!" I bumbled after him.

To my embarrassment, I discovered on entering the church that in front of the pews, on the right-hand side, had been placed a single chair. To my greater chagrin, once I had been unwillingly guided to it, a damp, mildewed Bible was placed on my knee. A small piece of paper was attached to the open page with a rusty paper clip. It directed me, as I stood with the rest of the congregation, to read the first lesson. Inevitably, the passage was composed of a list of utterly unpronounceable names. Who in their right minds would call their children Zurishaddai, Amminadab, and Kohathites?

On the nod from a smiling priest, who was conducting the service with admirable gusto, I burbled my way through the list. I need not have been so concerned because, as I looked up and closed the book, an air of semiconsciousness hung over the congregation. Most of the women seated on the left of the aisle and nearly all the men on the right were resting their foreheads on their arms on the pew in front, perhaps in silent reflection. There was a familiar order to the short service, and although I did not recognize most of the words, when the priest (after hawking from a great depth and spitting thickly out of the window) had said a few lines as he made the sign of the cross, I knew that the proceedings had come to an end. We wandered outside, and I was about to make my way back to my house when the preacher came rushing over in his robe. "Mr. Will, I think?"

"Will, yes, just Will. Hello."

"My name Dudley Small Tome. Very nice to meet you." He panted.

Small Tome was, as one might expect, slight, but his hair,

combed upward into a towering rock 'n' roll quiff, added significantly to his height. I would soon learn he was irrepressibly
enthusiastic, his infectious grin adding an extra dimension to
even the most mundane of tasks. As self-instated chaplain, he
organized the church services in the absence of the official
vicar, who visited only once a month to celebrate communion
and pat the children on the head. A lay priest, or catechist as he
described himself, Small Tome carried out his duties with such
joie de vivre that his Sunday worship service became more than
just "church." He transformed the service into a theatrical experience, a sparkling spectacle. His swooping, singsong delivery,
his soul singer's "Let us pray!" and his seemingly endless
wardrobe of bright ecclesiastical garments, painstakingly
embroidered by his wife, would have enlivened the most dismal
of churches, the dreariest of days.

We walked along together, and he asked me whether I had
enjoyed the service. Yes, yes, I assured him. In fact, I thought I
had recognized a lot of it.

"Oh, yes. True one. Our church is Church of Melanesia,
one kind of Anglican Church. Your church I think, Mr. Will?
Church of England?"

I assured him of my allegiance.

"Bishop Patteson come bring us God 1866 but some
Solomon Island man kill him. Me sorry about this one," he
added ruefully. "Time before, too many people like to eat man.
Very bad."

He glanced up at me, his forehead lined by a frown. Yes, I
agreed wholeheartedly, very bad.

"Black man him rubbish man."

"Oh, well no, surely. . . . No, no, you're not, I mean . . ."

I had no idea how to answer this assertion, but I was suddenly aware that some of my most closely held convictions were
in for a rough ride. Luckily, Dudley Small Tome was already in
full flow on the history of the Church of Melanesia.

From the middle of the nineteenth century onward, missionaries of every Christian denomination had arrived en masse, keen to convert the heathen. The islanders were already well used to the coercions of the white man, who had appeared some years earlier in the form of slavers, the cynically named Blackbirders, who used to tempt the village men onboard their ships with baubles, mirrors, and drink. Then they would lock the "blackbirds" in and transport them to the sugar fields of Northern Australia. With this in mind the islanders had stoutly defended their homes and traditional way of life from all newcomers, including the men who arrived bearing crosses. Normally they just killed and ate them. For many years this had proved to be an extremely effective way of repulsing the invaders, and it was regularly agreed among the various groups spreading the Word across the Pacific that the Solomon Islanders would be the last to crack.

Eventually they did, and it was therefore unfortunate that just as Bishop Patteson had finally succeeded in turning the last unruly tribe onto the path of Jesus, he had been killed by a loose spear. Whether he was subsequently consumed was uncertain, and I did not think it diplomatic to inquire. His death was not in vain, however, for the Solomon Islands remained one of the countries most resolutely Christian in its allegiance.

At that moment Stanley, who, it transpired, was Small Tome's son, appeared with a woman, her hair carefully braided and her face and breasts tattooed in spiraling swirls. She was carrying a plate and bowl, which she put down on the table in front of me.

"Mi Ellen," she whispered, her eyes downcast.

"Nice wife for me!" exclaimed Dudley Small Tome, proudly. "Nice lady for cook food for Mr. William!"

As she was my next-door neighbor and because I had no kitchen of my own, she offered to cook for me in exchange for the few English recipes that I could remember from a "Survival

Cooking" course that I had once pursued while at university.

So we spent many happy afternoons in Ellen's smoke-blackened kitchen, slaving over a hot open fire, which one of the children would stoke between our legs, as it were. Once we'd put the finishing touches to "typically English" "yam and parrot fish stir-fry" or "squid fritters" (which were delicious), Ellen would accost passersby on the path that ran behind the house and, like a Dickensian nursemaid, force a couple of spoonfuls into them. As they swallowed involuntarily, she would stare intently at their faces, gauging the reaction. It was, more often than not, one of surprise.

Ellen was an attractive woman, and she cared a great deal for her appearance and that of her eight, nine, or possibly ten children, whom she would often admonish for ruining good clothes, having dirty faces, bringing live fish into the house, or one of any number of other daily misdemeanors. Such is the common cause, I suppose, of the united forces of worldwide motherhood.

However, her often austere appearance disguised a sharp sense of fun, and she would take great pleasure in pretending to chide me for some forgetfulness or incompetence. Throwing her hands in the air, she'd announce that supper was canceled and that there would be no hot water for a week. Not until she had flounced away to sit on the steps of her own house would the laughter bubble up, bursting out as she threw her face into her lap and her arms round her legs, gleeful at my mock dismay and contrition.

Ellen watched me eat with interest as Small Tome bombarded me with questions about life in Europe that ranged from the pedestrian "So what exactly is a train?" to the more fanciful "Do you have any problem with wild lions in your garden?" On this last point, I was quick to set his mind at rest, although in truth I had only rarely been in my garden.

"Some people tell me tin meat it got some human inside.

True one, Mr. Will?" Small Tome asked me with great interest.

This was not something that I had heard widely advertised. I told him that I was unsure. Small Tome nodded inscrutably.

Later, as Ellen was clearing away the substantial remains of another aquarium fish and sweet potato, around the corner swung a figure who was to loom large in my new life.

As he came shambling over to join us, he was an amazing sight; his huge afro hair moved as if it was divorced from him entirely, a separate entity floating above him. At the back of his head there hung down a number of neatly plaited pigtails. It came as no surprise, therefore, to discover that his nickname was Hair and Tassels—Tassels, for short. (I discovered several months later that his real name was Edward, but he used it only on official occasions, of which, in the village, there were next to none.)

His gangling, swinging, bowlegged gait, the heavy tattoos around his eyes, and the thick shell earrings that had stretched the lobes into loops gave him a fearsome, almost warriorlike appearance—that of a latter-day pirate. His teeth, one could see when he smiled his gaping grin, were largely missing, and the remainder, stained and crooked, was a dental catastrophe. Yet, when his mouth broke open to release a smoke-choked laugh and his eyes sparkled, it was easy to see why, wherever he went, he was followed, as he was now, by a swarm of children skipping to keep up behind the colorful ribbons that hung down from the plaits onto his shoulders.

Whenever Tassels heard his name mentioned, he would cry out, "Yes, please!" Whenever a plan for the following day was mooted, "Why not?" was his automatic response. His life contained no hurdles, no dilemmas, no concerns or worries: vegetables and fruits were plentiful, and his expert fishing skills provided him with enough surplus to paddle to Munda and trade against tobacco and tea, both of which he consumed avidly with the deep satisfaction of the true connoisseur.

In many respects he epitomized the islanders' approach to life, a life that was lived from day to day, secure in the knowledge that he had sufficient to keep body and soul together, that between the sea, the land, and the community around him he would be well provided for. With no need to plan for the future, the passage of time was inconsequential. To a very great degree it appeared that, apart from the introduction of Western clothing in the form of bundles of cast-off T-shirts and shorts donated by modest white people and some plates and bowls purchased at the store in Munda, life remained much as it had been for centuries. Untouched by consumerism, Tassels, like his fellow Solomon Islanders, lived his life at a pace that had been handed down from a time before history became a recognized concept.

One day sometime later, after we'd become friends, we went fishing just off the point of the village and, chatting to pass the while, I asked Tassels how old he was. There was a long, thoughtful silence as he peered down into the water, willing something to take his bait, and then, over his shoulder, he replied. "Thirty-five . . ."

There was another lengthy pause as he bobbed his line up and down. "Maybe forty-five."

He said this with no guarded modesty, no knowing wink, just a passing suggestion that it was not really that important. He really could not have been any more specific if he had wanted. Solomon Time has cast its long shadow across memories, confusing the passage of the years, causing people to forget their own ages, if, indeed, they had ever been aware of them.

"How old are you?" he asked.

"Thirty-three." Six months and three weeks. Getting on, in fact.

Tassels, the bad boy, the ne'er-do-well, had never married, but he had, it was rumored, a number of lady friends throughout the islands. He liked to play his old, battered guitar or dive for fish when the mood took him, and in keeping with his carefully tailored image he never liked to do anything too quickly. So now, when Luta suggested that he take me "walkbout" in a canoe for a tour of the neighboring islands, Tassels quickly volunteered two attendant boys to be my guides. He would, he assured me, be there when I got back.

It transpired that one of the boys was Stanley, who was to become an ever-present, ever-affable companion, and his friend Dudley Small Small Tome—not Dudley Small Tome but Dudley Small Small Tome.

Solomon Islanders, it became apparent, had a curious habit, not only handing down whole names from generation to generation as Americans often do (Chuck A. Shovelburger III, et cetera) but also seeming to hand whole names to different families. So in Mendali there were four George Lutas of differing ages and specifications. This was of course a recipe for profound confusion so, to differentiate between them, an adjective was employed: Tall George or Old George. Unfortunately, there was already one Dudley Small Tome resident in the village, so his junior, with no other visible distinguishing features apart from his smallness, became Dudley Small Small Tome.

Of this, however, sadly, he was unaware, for he was deaf and dumb. Yet he was a happy child. His cheeks—each patterned with the motif of the rising sun, which had been repeatedly engraved into the skin with the sharp spikes of a coconut palm by his loving parents when he was a baby—creased into a smile when he saw me. He bounced up to shake my hand and squeaked an unshaped, unintelligible greeting.

After an hour or two of "getting ready," which seemed to consist of little more than leaning against their wooden canoe, stroking and admiring it, the three of us, Stanley acting as translator and responsible group leader, set off on my orientation course.

Boarding the little boat, I wobbled amidships, then waved my paddle absentmindedly as the two youngsters powered us through the still lagoon. We rounded the next point, pierced the camouflage of graying, brittle leaves that hung far out over the transparent water, and slid secretively up a hidden river. It teemed with ancient fish, their gormless, gaping mouths adorned on either side with dangling mustaches. Beside them giant, lazy mud crabs, sloping sideways in the approved fashion, occasionally poked above the surface and snapped idly at us with their finger-length pincers before sluggishly raking around in the ooze, digging about for an invertebrate breakfast.

Propping the canoe's prow up on the rich humus of the riverbank and breaststroking our way through the curtains of creepers that dangled down from the sky, we ventured deep into the bush. I quelled an itching desire to grab one of the furry vines and swing across the narrow dip of the river, opening my lungs to release my jungle call before disappearing into the undergrowth with a terrible crash. We pushed on.

It was in the jungle that I started to understand the enormity of the events acted out in this corner of the world some half a century before. For the Solomon Islands had once been the center of one of the great battles of the Second World War. First the Japanese, then the Americans had pushed through here in their enthusiasm to destroy one another. Nature, so rudely trampled in the 1940s by boots produced in the great footwear factories of Arkansas or Okinawa, was only now crossly resuming its normal cycle of decay and regeneration. Now and then we halted to examine the remains of an ancient tank, lorry, or jeep. One of the boys would jump onto the metal skeleton of the driving seat and recklessly swing the steering wheel, while the other, wriggling out of sight, would reappear from a turret or behind a mossy, corroded machine gun. Tendrils now crept in around windows, and orchids poked delicately out of radiator grilles. Rubber had perished, crumbling to black dust, and sumps and engine blocks, finally rusted through, bled their contents darkly into the earth. Like a curious metal totem pole, the rear section of an airplane's fuselage stood vertical in a small grove of teak trees. Flakes of gray paint lay among the rotting leaves, but no markings remained to suggest who had suffered this disaster. Nor, curiously, was there any sign of the front half of the plane.

In their haste to push back the Japanese from Munda and northward back to Japan, the Americans had left a great deal of litter or trash. Tin water bottles, some pierced with painful-looking holes, and helmets, some pierced with fatal-looking holes, piles of green ammunition and empty six-fluid-ounce Coca-Cola bottles, the name of their state of origin stamped on the base, were strewn through the jungle. Wherever I traveled throughout the Solomons, I was to come across the remnants of a battle that, more than any other, had swung the war in the East toward its final outcome.

Back in the canoe, chased by the persecuting sun, we skimmed from one tiny island that fringed the reef around Randuvu to the next. Stopping at one, we disembarked and, among rusting oil drums filled with crumbling concrete, I was proudly led to inspect the remains of an old latrine. The walls, worn away by tropical rains and passing cyclones, had left a few brittle, rusting rods to be dissolved by the elements, but the cement footprints were set in the coral for posterity. Small Small Tome took up position for what I feared, at one moment, might be a practical demonstration.

"Merika bigman hemi usim dis wan, kinidi, kinidi," insisted Stanley, accompanied by forceful nodding from the squatting Small Small Tome. I nodded, mystified. It was only later that I discovered this had indeed been the wartime "comfort station" of John Fitzgerald Kennedy on this island—Lumbaria—and heard the full story of the mission that very nearly cut his life even shorter than it eventually was.

Back on Randuvu, Stanley and Small Small Tome led me deep into the vibrant jungle, where they had built dams and secret hideaways. They showed me honeycomb made by termites and how to eat it without being eaten myself. They cracked open soft ngali nuts and expertly smashed the shells of the crunchy cut nut. Tying their ankles together with vines to better their grip on the trunk, they shimmied up coconut trees to fetch the fruit, which with a swipe of a machete or bush knife whistled down to thud on the ground at my feet. The boys held each nut in the palm of one hand and with terrifying accuracy would split them in half with a single stroke of a whirling blade. We sat under the tallest trees in the world, staring up at the distant spots of white daylight and, using spatulas sliced from the smooth green husk, scooped out the sweet jelly inside.

All this, I failed to realize until our return to the village, while the boys were supposed to have been at school.

Sneaking out of their canoe, they disappeared behind the houses, leaving me to wave awkwardly at the imposing figure of Ethel, Ellen's sister, the kindergarten teacher, as she stood at the threshold of the schoolroom.

Luta came to my rescue. "Come, I show you the plantation. Where we worked before."

So off we set along a track that ran past the swimming stream and on further for what was, for my guide, a trip down memory lane. Soon we found ourselves among regimented rows of coconut trees, the ground under which had once been laid to grass "like an English garden." Now an impenetrable mass of undergrowth grew well above head height and crowded our way from either side. Down at ground level, among the snarled vegetation, I could make out the brown shapes of rotting coconut, some of which had sprouted and taken root, the young saplings fighting their way toward the sun.

"This." He pointed sadly at the single-track path we were following. "This was the main road. Commander's tractor use this road."

I gazed into the green and tried hard to imagine any form of transport that would have been sturdy enough to make its way through this tangle of unruly nature. Some five hundred yards farther on, we came to a slight promontory.

"House blong old man."

As we approached through the trees that sprouted along the water's edge, I made out the sharp angles of a man-made construction, the wooden frame of a house. It was in a sorry state, stripped bare of its cladding, its roof caved in. Stripping away the foliage in my mind's eye, I imagined in front of me a bungalow built of whitewashed boards, set back from a private jetty, and surrounded by a garden that was hedged with hibiscus and bougainvillea. In the garden grew mango and banana trees shading the low roof, and dotted around what had been a tidy, if not spotless lawn were carefully planted shrubs and flowers, their cultivated neatness in strong contrast to the jumble of jungle that grew up the hill behind it. So it was here that the Commander had called home for nearly thirty years.

We walked through the doorway and leaned on the shabby window frame that looked out over the flat sea to where an elderly man sat motionless in a canoe holding a fishing line. Quietly, fondly, Luta described the "time before," a world that came from history books, that was the stuff of adventure stories: the time of the Commander.

He had purchased the plantation, some two thousand acres of coconut trees and cocoa bushes, from the soap-sud magnates named the Lever Brothers. They had been forced to abandon it when the fighting had broken out and had not been keen to return.

The estate had been in a lamentable state when he had first arrived, but living in a tent erected on the site of his future home and with only a box of books and a case of gin for solace, the Commander had set about returning it to full operation.

He quickly engaged a workforce from outlying islands, and by the early 1960s he had created his own private kingdom, which was to prosper for the next twenty years. A daily regime was instituted that, if inflexible, was efficient and ordered. Work parties went about their allotted tasks: maintaining the trees, collecting their fruits, drying the kernels and beans, packing them into sacks, and finally loading them aboard the small, shallow-draft steamer that was moored at the jetty near the village. The boat would sail once a week to deliver its cargo to the white buyers in Gizo, the provincial capital. They, in turn, would ship the coconuts to Europe, where they were crushed for cooking oil and soap and the cocoa beans turned into chocolate bars for the delectation of schoolboys, dentists, and purveyors of acne remedies.

The Commander presided over the smooth running of this process from his office next door to the house, and from here too he would pay his workers their weekly wage. Every Friday, at the end of the day's work, the islanders would queue to collect their pay, and for those who wished to see some of their earnings put by, he operated a "bank," which offered moderate interest. Additionally, he ensured that a percentage of the profits funded pensions and provided for the maintenance of the church, a small first-aid post, and a sizable school building. This was run by a Mr. Thomas, who succeeded, unimaginably, in teaching two classes of forty youngsters at once.

The Commander was intensely protective of his world and resented the unannounced arrival of outsiders. It soon became understood that if anyone had business at Mendali he would be well advised to arrange an appointment in advance. If not he risked taking a shot across his bow from the powerful brass cannon that stood on the seawall in front of the Commander's bedroom and that he had no qualms at all in using. Luta laughed as he recollected the retreat of an American "lootenant" who had ventured incautiously into the bay looking for a safe anchorage. Signals in Morse and pennant had no effect on the salvos that came humming across the glinting water, and the patrol boat hurriedly extricated itself—full speed astern. When eventually the young officer came ashore alone in a dingy, he was given a short lesson in saluting properly and then sent back to his ship to put on a tie. He decided to find an alternative location to overnight.

"Commander not friendly with American and Australian people." Luta laughed.

He had concentrated instead on his private world and the people that, in his own idiosyncratic fashion, he had come to view as his family. Although he lived slightly apart from the village, a few hundred yards away across a natural harbor, he always attended church on Sunday, marriages, baptisms, and funerals, keeping a watchful eye on the boisterous young ones, solicitous about the welfare of the more senior. He could be harsh in his castigation of laziness or carelessness but was generous and genuine in his praise, offering small gifts or prizes to those who had done well. Luta was immensely proud of the decorated clock that, although it no longer ticked, still hung over the door to his hut.

The Commander seemed to have been totally immersed, perfectly happy in this remote hideaway. It was, however, an undeniable truth that certain mainstays of a civilized existence could be found only in London. Every three months a number of wooden cases would arrive at Gizo and be ferried back to Randuvu, where, among great excitement, they were unpacked on the floor of the sitting room. The islanders marveled at the shiny pairs of pigskin brogues from Loakes, bottles of brandy from Harrods, boxes of cigars from a tobacconist in Mayfair, and jars of Oxford's Orange Marmalade—thin cut. Occasionally, but only very occasionally, the Commander returned to his country of birth, presumably to settle his accounts. I thought suddenly of Stevenson and the fancy of a visit home. Here, at least, was someone for whom this was more of a chore than a pleasure.

Once, when he returned from picking up his latest consignment, there was consternation in the village when out of the steamer, under a parasol held gallantly by the Commander, stepped a young white woman. Miss Elizabeth was coming to stay and must be looked after with great care.

So while four boys from Liverpool were shaking the world eight days a week and the man who had once been resident on the strip of island across the water was making his ticker tape way toward the Oval Office, Miss Elizabeth would appear each morning from one of the two doors that gave onto the front lawn of the old man's house on the point at Mendali. Sitting at a garden table, she would take up her carpetbag and quietly knit or sew a garment for one of the newborn in the village. A while later the Commander would appear at the other door to smoke his first cigar of the morning. She was very nice. How long had she stayed, I asked, astonished by this revelation. Oh . . . Luta thought hard, a few weeks, maybe six months or a year. The precise nature of the couple's relationship remained concealed behind the mosquito netting of the whitewashed house and the natural discretion of their generation.

"In the end she wants to go back home to England. She said that he must decide between her and Solomon Islands. He stayed here with us . . ." Luta trailed off, frowning, his voice filled with puzzled, convoluted emotion.

After Miss Elizabeth had left, life returned to its normal course, and the plantation continued to prosper. There had, of course, been difficult, sometimes dangerous times. On one occasion, the cargo boat, leaving the Vonavona Lagoon off Munda on its return journey to Randuvu, had run into a sudden, destructive storm. Blown onto reefs, its bottom opened up on the sharp coral and it foundered. The crew, swept onto an island, survived, but the boat was lost. Fortunately, it had not just picked up a delivery from England. It was some months before a replacement arrived.

"Long time paddling," Luta commented, still weary at the memory.

One night, the Commander had woken to the beating of drums from the village across the water; rhythms intermingled with the screams of women and the angry shouting of the normally even-tempered men. Dressing quickly, he had grabbed a torch and his old service revolver and set off down the path to discover the reason for this bedlam. Suddenly, running toward him, came Jack, the Commander's foreman, half-dragging, half-pushing a terrified, babbling islander. He was covered in blood. The man, Jack explained, had had a spell cast upon him by the people of a different village and in his perturbed state had been convinced that the only way to rid himself of his demons was to kill someone. With a view to getting the whole nasty business out of the way as soon as possible, he had snatched up his bush knife and staggered into the village clearing. Apologizing briefly to the young daughter of his next-door neighbor, he had grabbed her by the hair and cut her head off. This accounted for his gory appearance and the none too understanding reaction of his neighbor.

At that moment a number of wooden canoes bumped hollowly along the jetty wall. With the aid of his gun the Commander managed to convince the war party, who had paddled the short distance across the mouth of the harbor, to stay in their boats, and eventually it was agreed the man should be handed over to the authorities in Munda. For three days, the villagers waited by the jetty, while the Commander paced his house. The cursed man crouched, terrified, in a corner, convinced that he would be killed at any moment.

The police finally arrived, and the man was sent to prison for twenty years. Rather sensibly, he never returned.

This kind of emergency, however, was the rare exception, and life would perhaps have continued indefinitely in its normal pattern. But in 1978 the Solomons followed in the footsteps of the majority of Britain's former colonies and protectorates and achieved its independence. The Commander was not the type of man to take his orders from anyone and, after lengthy disputes with the new government, decided it was time to leave.

But, although his governance of the plantation had been autocratic, his control total, his word final, his decision to leave was his most difficult. Finally, not able to bear saying farewell to his "people," he rose before dawn on the morning of April 1, 1981, ordered his boatman to ready the new steamer, and slipped away across the lagoon. He could not look back.

There was a heavy, uncomfortable silence as Luta followed that last journey with his eye. As I watched him, I was suddenly stunned by the realization that at the same moment that this little vignette was being played out on Randuvu, Margaret Thatcher was busy handbagging her way across Britain, the Sex Pistols had just stopped appalling my parents, and I was attempting to enjoy my first cigarettes, wondering all the while if my voice was ever going to break.

"Yes, every day a strict routine but happy time."

"But, Luta, what's happened? Why's the plantation closed down? What happened when he left? Did nobody take over?"

"Government buy the plantation, but when Commander leave us then nobody came. Nothing happened. Nearly twenty years nothing happening in the plantation."

"So now you have gone back to the traditional life," I said brightly. People were always doing that in England, it was very popular.

"Yes, but time is not the same now. Not like time before.

People want different things. Kerosene, petrol, soap, and cooking oil, and now the church is very bad. Sometimes in a dry time the water in the tank is finished, and then we've got to go round the island in the canoes to the river along the coast. We want to make some improvements, but it is very hard."

And it was true that even if the islanders seemed to be living a utopian idyll, the outside world had eventually discovered them. Inevitably, even though the thought made me hurt, the islanders wanted the opportunity to discover the material world. If they spent their money unwisely, "squandered" it on "rubbish," then it was clearly their choice to do so. Heaven knew, enough of my own money had gone up in smoke or down the drain—in fact, in exactly those two directions.

The paternalism of the Empire, despite its clear failings, had at least put in place some legal and political infrastructure that might go some way to protecting them from other more unscrupulous foreign intervention. Now it was time for the Western world to remove its cosseting hands and, while remaining willing to assist, allow the islanders to make their own decisions, even if, from a perspective of greater experience, they might be deemed unwise and I was certainly no Commander.

Much later I was told the story of a neighboring chief who, having saved over several years the proceeds of his sales of shells and carved bowls, had flown to Honiara. He returned with a television, video recorder, and a selection of ultraviolent videos from—interestingly—America and Japan. He was suddenly the most popular man on Randuvu, canoes scrunching to a halt on the beach in front of his house, but unhappily it was not to last long. A few months later the supplies of petrol for the generator ran low, often lasting only the length of the trailers and, in the wet tropical heat, the videocassettes reacted by sprouting a green, foul-smelling mold. Eventually the generator seized completely, and its various heavier parts were removed to be used as canoe anchors. The television set was converted into a solid table, and the tapes, too, had proved useful, fluttering as they now did from tall sticks planted in the garden to frighten away the birds. . . .

The old man would no doubt have been livid to hear this story but, no, I was certainly no Commander who could tell anyone what to do. However, repairs to the church and a water supply, extending the school and perhaps providing electricity to light the early nights of the Tropics seemed like worthwhile ventures. I decided then that it was the moment to act.

"Yes, we will try and organize some moneymaking projects. We must try. But I wonder what would be the best thing?" I asked probingly.

Luta only shrugged as we turned toward Mendali. We walked back in silence, and I suddenly felt a weight of responsibility land on my shoulders. Outside the kindergarten was now standing, presumably by way of punishment, the not greatly chastened Stanley. He waved gleefully when he spotted us appearing from the jungle. Small Small Tome had, it seemed, made good his escape. Standing between the church and the meeting place, where the horrible murder had taken place that bewitched night, the school building was low-sided, open at the top to let some breeze through and fenced in leaf at the bottom to thwart escape attempts. A blackboard on an easel supplied Ethel with a writing surface and something to rap with a stick should order need to be called. The stick she used to point and to underline but never to chastise.

Ethel did, however, have a fairly thankless task as she, like Mr. Thomas before her, attempted to teach two classes at once. The older ones would sit on the fine sand floor at the front of the room to copy out numbers and letters on slates with small bits of soft coral. This completed, they would recite their alphabet and times tables. The younger ones, meanwhile, would sit anarchically at the back and throw wooden building blocks at each other and any unsuspecting passersby. Hardly a week went past without a nasty cut or a mild concussion. At eleven o'clock school was "out." They sang a final rousing version of "Old Mac-Donald Had a Farm," taught to them by some passing min-strel—excluding the verses about the cow and the sheep, two animals no one had ever seen, let alone heard. Then, like chil-dren the world over, they ran, screaming their relief, from the school "gates." Then, in the absence of a park, sweetshop, or television, the children shot straight up trees, throwing off their clothes as they went, and hurled themselves out into the warm waters of the lagoon, where they would play for hours.

As I watched them happily splashing, Tassels appeared from the shade of some palms, yawning extravagantly. "Now you me go fishing little bit and catch stack of nice fish."

With that certainty explained, he set off to find his fishing line, leaving me to admire his dugout canoe.

Dugout canoes are awe-inspiring creations, cut and carved by eye with a hand adze. A tree and a hatchet and enor-mous skill produce a canoe that is perfect in line, dimension, and finish. They ranged, depending on the size of tree, from one to forty seaters. This does not mean of course that they do not wobble—a great deal. But after only one outing I was consider-ably more relaxed and confident. Now I hardly had to grip the shiny, sloping sides at all, and only occasionally was I convinced that we were going to capsize. If I sat absolutely motionless, I was sure that I would feel confident, comfortable enough to participate in our fishing trip.

Fishing is as much a way of life in the Solomon Islands as is driving a car or getting stuck in a traffic jam in the developed world. It is something that you grow up with from the earliest age and that becomes an integral aspect of everyday living. The sea teemed with an astonishing variety of species that ranged from the magnificent to the monstrous, and every male villager from toddler upward was adept at attracting their attention.

I was fired with enthusiasm. Just off the point of the rectangular Pao Island, where the coral reef gave way to the deep ocean, it was with the pleasure of the enthusiastic amateur that, supervised by Tassels, I paid out the line from a smooth wooden baton until it ran some hundred yards straight down. I stared down into the blinding blue of the water and tried to imagine what sort of interest was being taken in the white squares of squid that were attached to the large, indigestible hook—and by whom.

Breezes blew considerately over us, and I relaxed as much as it was safe to, gazing thoughtfully at the outlying islands that had been sprinkled along the coast of Randuvu.

Nothing happened.

We chatted awhile, small talk much as one might make on the way to the shops, killing time before getting down to the really pleasurable part of the trip. Tassels asked me whether the Queen was well. I remembered then that, although this was an independent country, she was still the head of state. She had visited the islands when he, Tassels, had been a small boy. The Commander had sent Old Obadiah, the boatman, to Gizo, where her big ship was anchored, with a letter of greeting. Just as he was handing it over to one of the crew, who had come down the steps to receive it, he had dropped it into the water. Obadiah had jumped in and rescued it, but when he finally handed it over the ink was dripping from it in light blue drops. He had never dared to tell the old man, but they often wondered whether she had been able to read it.

"Did you see her recently?"

Only on the television, I replied.

"Hmm, television very nice one, I think?"

"Well . . ."

"Ah, something now," he announced confidently as he lit another roll-up. How he knew I do not know, because he had no line himself and was lying on his back with his eyes closed. I was ready, however. I licked my lips with anticipation and inadvertently slurped up a gobbet of suntan cream. I managed to avoid swallowing it and was repositioning myself to spit it over the side discreetly when there was a tractor tug on my line. Lurching like an inexperienced water-skier, I struggled to remain inside the boat.

"Tassels, Tassels, quick, quick! Blimey, it must be enormous!" There was clearly something of almighty proportions down there. Bracing myself against the sturdy timber, I readied for the battle.

In a show of superiority, the leviathan below me yanked again like a burly bell ringer. The opaque cheese wire of the line sliced deep into my finger. Fortunately there was a bone in the way, but as I had no real desire to witness my fingers pop off one by one like so many chipolatas, I let go. I tried not to imagine them slowly sinking downward, pointing accusingly upward before they were gobbled up like so many party snacks by various grotesque creatures. I shuddered and stuck my injured digit into my mouth to salve it with exotic-tasting lotion.

So concerned was I about my wound that I had forgotten about my tackle. Fortunately Tassels sat up and grabbed the spinning stick just before it went jumping out into the sea. Standing, he heaved and wound, heaved and wound, as the canoe rocked and slopped. Quite calmly, I gripped everything hard and hunched down to allow Tassels to better see the line that now ran taut from the stern. I decided against turning around in the tight space, so instead I squinted up at Tassels's grinning face. The scrubby stubble on his chin, bristling with excitement, was silhouetted against the sun.

"Oh, nice one, Mr. Will, very nice big one." He heaved again, but then, suddenly, his expression fell as the dripping, vibrating fishing line went slack. Ten, perhaps fifteen turns later something skittered and splashed along the surface of the water beside me before flicking into the canoe. I stared down at the large, neatly severed head of a puzzled-looking tuna. Matching its surprise, I looked back up at Tassels.

"Well, where's the rest of it?" I demanded.

"Oh, bad luck, bad luck. Devil come take him." He sighed, his face surprisingly grave. "Devil now."

"Devil?" The sun seemed to have been turned down several notches. "What kind of . . . err . . . what kind of devil would that be then?"

Tassels sat down with his back to me, dejected. "Sharki, big one I think."

"Sharki, where? Here, sharks?" I leaned forward and tucked my elbows in.

"Staka 'long here."

Staka? Stacks—lots?

Just at that moment there was a powerful swirling below us, and the water slap-slapped on the resonant wood.

"What was that?"

This it turned out was a superfluous inquiry because, with a hissing slice, the surface of the sea opened up and the answer became only too obvious. A shark's fin, a real one just like in the films, rose perhaps a foot above the water. Moving with extraordinary momentum, it ran the length of the canoe. So little was our freeboard that water splashed onto my upper arms and we rocked violently as it disappeared out of sight below our bow. Reappearing, it ran along our other side, and I could not help but make out its unmistakable, vicious outline in the clear water. Perhaps fifteen, twenty feet long, it was certainly a good deal bigger than our canoe. Suddenly, silently, it twisted away and was gone. For the time being.

We made very good time back to the village. I was completely exhausted as I crawled ashore and stamped a few times on the ground to get some feeling back into my numb legs.

"Oh bad luck now!" exclaimed Small Tome when he saw our

catch. I was much surprised at this reaction. I was very much under the impression that good fortune had been on our side.

Grimble had, needless to stay, also encountered sharks. Whenever I consulted his book, it seemed that he had always done something just that little bit better, more exciting, or dangerous than anyone else. Some of it was so obviously made up. Mind you, he had not liked the sharks much either. What was more, when he had had his lucky escape, the islander with him had actually jumped into the water—poor mad fool. "He [the islander] slid overboard and paddled around waiting to be noticed." *Waiting to be noticed!*

He soon was. The fin began to circle him and then shot forward like an arrow; the head and shoulders of the brute broke surface, rolling as they lunged. My friend flicked aside in the last blink of time and shot his knife into the upswinging belly. As it surged by I saw the belly rip itself open like a zip-fastener, discharging blood and guts. The tiger [shark!] disappeared for a while, to float up dead a hundred yards off. That kind of single conflict used to be fairly common. It was rather like a nice score of fifty at cricket in England; the villagers applauded but did not make a great song of it.

Grimble was clearly in charge of a village for the criminally insane. I had no intention of going back on the water for quite some time—let alone in it.

I collapsed in my hut, sorely in need of a rest and a couple of large whiskeys (which I did not have). Unfortunately it appeared that it was now lesson time. Imp, a serious but kindly man, who had been sent by the Commander to a Roman Catholic college on an island some miles north of Randuvu and was considered to be the wise man of the village, was also a fearless educator. As I sat in my house in a pale sweat, fanning myself with a limp *Robinson Crusoe,* he came to tell me that he had decided that, from this day onward, I was to receive instruction in how to "tok-tok Pijin."

For an hour between prayer and supper, I was to learn how to speak this strange, corrupted form of English. It had first been gleaned from the sandalwood traders and whalers who had arrived in the late 1700s and had now become the lingua franca for the hundred different tribes that spoke ninety-odd different languages in this wide scattering of islands.

I was keen to learn because Grimble had managed it— although he seemed incapable of preventing himself from adding "Old Man" or "Old Boy" to the end of every phrase. R. L. Stevenson, being a bit of a bright spark, had actually learned one of the local languages, but I convinced myself that Pijin would be more useful, as I would then be able to speak to everyone regardless of tribe. Robinson Crusoe obviously hadn't had to learn anything.

Initially, it all seemed very straightforward. All I had to do was to read out loud the seemingly unintelligible spellings that Imp wrote down for me in his beautifully crafted handwriting and, after a couple of attempts, words and phrases would magically appear in a wonderful, muddled up, anachronistic version of English. Sadly, like so many of life's pleasures, it was quite straightforward to learn the basics, more difficult to master.

Every evening, however, from that day on, adopting fictional characters, the two of us would conduct imaginary conversations, Imp writing the scripts as we went:

"Goodfella mornen long yu. Yu oraet?"—Good morning. Are you well?

"Me oraet."—Very well, thank you.

"Watkaen day blong week him now today?"—What day of the week is it?

"Me no savvy. Station blong polis hemi wea?"—I really don't know, but whereabouts is the police station?

"Yu like for payim disfala [this feller] kokorako?"—Would you like to buy this chicken?

"Come narawan make me lookim. Mi no like pig-pig."—Perhaps you could bring another one for me to have a look at. I'm not very fond of pork.

"Oh sori him old tumas."—Sorry, but it is very old.

(*Tumas*, it transpired, trickily, meant not "too much" but "very." So the statement "Commander hemi go back long England. Hemi old tumas" meant that, although he had been getting on a bit, he was not necessarily past it.)

"Oh sori me gotim belly run."—I'm really sorry but I am suffering from diarrhea.

"Him orate. S'pose me lender enjin blong you?"—Please don't apologize. Could I borrow your engine?

"Oh sori, him buggerup finish."—I'm afraid it has irreparably broken down.

And so in this way, the conversations, becoming more and more surreal, drifted on into suppertime to the general confusion of everyone else.

Over the first few weeks of my stay, my progress was steady and my teacher seemed pleased with his pupil, who, in turn, found this reaction pleasantly novel. So, eventually, I decided to round off my education with a few lessons from Stanley and his friends. They leaped at the chance to reveal some important secrets to me.

Sitting in a row in the shade of one of the beached canoes, the little boys and girls solemnly imparted to me a snippet of mysterious but priceless information that had been divulged to them by a "man weewee blong sailin bot"—a French man in a yacht. Unless one employed a "plastik blong push-push," a condom, whatever one of those was, the inevitable outcome, for some reason, would be a "bubbly Mary"—a pregnant woman. The circumstances under which these precautions should be put into practice were unfortunately unclear, but I thanked them very much all the same. Useful information indeed.

I wondered whether Grimble had known about "plastik blong push-push"—I doubted it. Robert Louis had been far too frail to contemplate anything so energetic, and presumably Robinson C. had had no reason to progress any further than the contemplation stage.

After I had thanked Imp for my first Pijin lesson and he had impressed upon me the importance of practice and of completing the homework that he had left me, Small Tome arrived in great excitement clutching a hessian sack.

"Nice present for Mr. Will!" he exclaimed as he hopped from one foot to the other and reached inside. Slowly and carefully he pulled out a sleek, mischievous-looking ginger cat. "Very nice one for rat!"

"Fantastic, thank you." And my thanks were heartfelt. "What is his . . . her name?"

"Name?"

"Well, in England we give animals names."

"Why?"

"Well . . . we just . . . err . . ."

"What name then?" Small Tome asked curiously.

"Well . . ." I noticed a couple of mangoes that one of the children had left on my table. "I shall call her Chutney."

"Sutni?" Small Tome stumbled over the word but shrugged and charged on to his next great idea. "Now, I have a nice something for you this evening, Mr. Will. Tonight we play cards and I want you to be on my team!"

Much flattered, I readily agreed, although I made sure he understood that I was not a great player.

"No wariwari," he said, his bonhomie inexhaustible. "You follow me."

Only too late did I discover that Dudley Small Tome, my new partner, was incurably incompetent.

Nevertheless, that evening and almost every evening from

then on, after everyone had eaten, six of us players, crowded by assorted onlookers and teams of advisers and supporters, met at the table outside my house. Sustained by pints of steaming, sweet black tea that was ferried endlessly from Ellen's eternal fire, we played an idiosyncratic version of whist, the arcane and seemingly flexible rules of which left me often confused and Small Tome permanently floundering. George Luta and Hair and Tassels plus Imp and Henry Fatty (who might once have been a chubby child but was now a cheerful and friendly man mountain) were our two pairs of adversaries.

Games were played at a lightning pace. With enormous enjoyment and great good humor, the cards were thumped down with such a tremendous crash that the children, who were seated on the ground under the table playing their own game with imaginary cards, shrieked with excitement and the tin teapot rattled.

Imp noted down and added up the scores on a gray piece of card, while Luta rolled endless cigarettes from greasy sticks of black tobacco and strips of my much admired airmail paper. We played long into the night, but when finally yawns took the place of words and Small Tome and I had been soundly thrashed, Luta shaped up the worn cards and slid them back into their packet.

"*Rodo diana.* Good night!"

Our group dispersed, and I climbed the steps to bed, confused, exhilarated, and extraordinarily tired by this first full day in Mendali. Chutney flashed her road-marking eyes at me from the roof ridge, and I smiled as I heard my partner talking earnestly to Ellen. He just could not understand how we'd lost that last hand. What about all the other hands, Small Tome?

Smiling, I climbed into bed with Arthur Grimble.

❧

An Innocent Encounter

Soon, much sooner than I had expected, the nature of my days in Mendali developed a perfect normality. Weaving my way up the corkscrew root to my "smolhaus," attempting to catch my reflection in the top of a bucket, unwrapping a banana leaf to reveal a whole cooked fish that I ate with my fingers, and washing in a stream with an aluminum saucepan and a slip of soap became actions that were in no way out of the ordinary.

This was a happy, gentle existence, but I will admit now, lest I give the impression of an entirely perfect world, the food was awful.

The islands spread themselves lazily across the Tropic of Capricorn just a few degrees south of the Equator. All year round the temperature remained constant, the rain fell with refreshing reliability, and the seasons needed play no part in the gardener's diary. Sow and, in these conditions, pretty shortly you should reap. The choice of vegetables, however, was limited—depressingly so—because here food was treated, perhaps quite correctly, not as a means to demonstrate financial or intellectual superiority ("Isn't she so very clever in the kitchen? Does wonderful things with the foie gras. I have it flown in *on saysonne, voo savay* . . . Know a little chap just near us in the *Perrygorrrd*—he sorts us out.") but simply as fuel to be consumed.

These vegetables and fruits had sustained the islanders and their ancestors for many hundreds, possibly thousands of years. Quantity was, of course, a priority. Variety, sadly, was not, and the diet of the islands soon became depressingly predictable, reliant as it was on three or four indistinguishable root vegetables that required Herculean amounts of mastication and copious flushing with water before they could be swallowed—a little like trying to consume a bar of soap but with none of the flavor or the foaming qualities. Used as I had been to enjoying the cuisine of any corner of the world whenever I chose (or at least its Anglo imitation created on an industrial estate in Middlesex), my taste buds were now in revolt. Previously they had enjoyed nothing more than touring the fifteen aisles of the out-of-town supermarket, lingering at the delicatessen and asking sensible questions about new cheeses. Now they were hiding food under their spoons, accidentally spilling it, or sneakily feeding chunks to the cat, passing children, and the tropical fish. On two occasions, they had folded their arms and refused point-blank to eat even if they had to stay there all night.

It seemed from my readings that I was not alone in my gastronomic disappointment. Grimble had also encountered the ubiquitous tubers "whose unhallowed starchiness no treatment under heaven was ever known to exorcize." Fortunately, he did, on occasion, receive deliveries of tinned food. These, though, were no cause for great excitement either. "With the honorable exceptions of asparagus and beetroot, which always seemed to retain faint memories of their better selves, the vegetables doomed to canning in 1916 entered their iron cells bleakly determined to betray every sweetness of their early promise. When they emerged, the eye dared hardly dwell upon their livid looks, and the taste of one and all—celery or onion, pea, cabbage, cauliflower, bean or potato—was as the taste of iron filings boiled in dishwater."

Even the uncomplaining RSL noted that "an onion, an Irish potato or a beef-steak, had been long lost to sense and dear aspiration."

Crusoe, of course, had had no problem at all in creating a superbly run market garden organized, cultivated, harvested, and consumed single-handedly. His island was, by "great good fortune," "a pleasant, fruitful part," and he was, to my great irritation, always contemplating "with great pleasure the fruitfulness of that valley and the pleasantness of the situation." Well, there was nothing wrong with Randuvu and—if he thought he was so bloody marvelous, I would show him—I was not to be outdone. Although I possessed no greater gardening experience than beans and paper towels at primary school, I was spurred on by the rumblings of my stomach and set about the creation of "Garden blong William."

Early on I had discovered some dusty packets of seeds in the small store in Munda, and for my own interest I planted a small vegetable patch on the edge of the villagers' gardens. Soon in the damp, warm climate rows of seedlings—tomato, eggplant, pepper, and cabbage—sprouted in green lines out of the soft, brown earth, and every day after church I took a simple pleasure in seeing how my garden grew.

One day, as I was returning with Stanley, my assistant, from a morning inspection, he pointed out a tree. "Jam fruit. Nice one."

Sweet, dark red, and shiny like a cherry but containing pips rather than a stone, the fruits might well make delicious jam. They also looked rather like grapes, so I collected as much as I could carry in the front of my T-shirt and, when I returned to the house, poured them into my large plastic drinking bottle. Mashing the fruit with the handle of my toothbrush, I added some sugar borrowed from Ellen and filled the flask up with water. The lid fitted tightly, and I replaced the cap on the drinking straw. By the time I looked at it again in the evening, it had popped off and the fizzing inside was audible. The smell that it gave off, if not reminiscent of any of the great vintages, proved beyond doubt that it was doing what nature had intended. Within a few weeks I had purloined a huge plastic bucket with lid and had all the makings of a fine cellar.

Different but no longer strange, my new life surprised me only when I realized how easily I had adapted and how little I missed. No longer did I fumble for light switches or reach out for the tap, cold drinks were no longer indispensable, not being able to watch the news seemed to have made no great difference to my effect on world affairs, and I had not bought a new gadget since I had arrived. Apart, of course, from the half-size bush knife that I carried wherever I went, probably more as a fashion accessory than with any useful purpose in mind.

Effortlessly Robinson Crusoe had managed to outstrip his own usually substantial levels of pomposity when he too considered what he had gained by his enforced isolation: "It was now that I began sensibly to feel how much more happy the life I now led was, with all its miserable circumstances, than the wicked, cursed abominable one that I led all the past part of my days."

Although I did not share the same qualms about my former behavior, I did recognize the attractions of a lifestyle in which there was no routine to be followed, no order of events laid down to which I was expected to adhere: no expectation, no condemnation. It was quite acceptable to do nothing but simply enjoy the natural beauty of the world about me and the genuine, nonjudgmental friendship of the sweet-tempered villagers.

In fact, I really had no complaints, no complaints at all, which made it all the harder to decide what it was that I might do to "help." But Luta's words echoed about me, and I believed that if we could use the funds available to create an income from which the community as a whole might benefit, then we would be going some way to fulfilling the Commander's wishes. Anyway, I was ready for action, ready to get down to business. What then was this wonderful income producer to be? I still had next to no idea.

"Have a meeting," suggested Geoff.

He and Gerry had become my secret advisers on the other side of the lagoon. Under the guise of having to post a letter, I would covertly sneak over to see them if ever I were in need of information or advice.

"Solomon Islanders love meetings," agreed Gerry.

This proved to be only too true. One evening, after Small Tome and I had suffered another crushing defeat at the card table and he was having one of the more complex rules explained to him again by Imp, I suggested to Luta that we should call everyone together to discuss what we might do. He became most excited, nodding enthusiastically and volunteering to organize the time and the place. Everybody would come, he was sure.

So one Sunday morning after the church service, we convened in the shade of the old ngali nut tree at the edge of the clearing. Everybody did come—although not all at the same time. Nevertheless, within an hour or so we were ready and I, who had been sitting on some old sacks with my back to the tree, stood up to open the meeting. The audience settled, looking up expectantly as if the lights had dimmed for the latest blockbuster at the cinema.

Rolling cigarettes and lighting them from an ember that smoldered in a half coconut shell, the men chomped happily on the mildly intoxicating but unbelievably bitter betel nuts and leaves, which they mixed into a red paste in their mouths and spat copiously on the ground. The third ingredient, lime powder, was passed in a pot from hand to hand.

Perhaps a little more aloof but still curious, the women sat separately, sometimes breast-feeding, sometimes stroking the hair of naked children who were themselves ruffling scraggy, long-suffering cats that they held firmly by the tail. Some of the women were arranged in groups of four. A daughter lay with her head in a mother's lap while a sister knelt behind her and another stood in turn behind her. Slowly and methodically, as they listened, they searched for the small, onyx-black bugs in each other's hair, killing them neatly between their teeth as they plucked them out.

Despite the fact that this assembled crowd was considerably more interested in what I had to say and certainly more generous in allowing me to say it than any class I had taught in a former life, I was still less than confident—I knew that yet again I was ill-prepared. Earlier, I had tried to write a few notes on a piece of paper and had even planned to brandish it to underline my points. Finally I had decided against it, as I did not really have any points to make. I started uncertainly, but Crusoe would have been proud of me, as pomposity prevailed.

"Your good friends in England would like to assist you in the organization of some profitable and sustainable ventures."

That sounded like a reasonable, almost professional start.

"So, we are gathered here today to have a talk about plans for the future."

From the blank looks of my audience, I surmised that this was something of a new concept.

"By sustainable, I mean projects that do not require complex machinery that is difficult or expensive to repair and which will be relatively quick turnover and high yield."

Now I was getting into my stride.

At this point a little boy of perhaps three pottered into the proceedings. His name was Innocent, and never has anyone been more aptly named. His great, nut-colored eyes gazed out from beneath his blond-tipped cloud of hair in astonishment at this extraordinary world, his mouth half open at the amazing sights and sounds of everyday life. He was the most delightful baby and, had it been any other moment of the week, I would have whiled away half an hour in his company, regressing as adults do when they talk to small children. Today, however, was different. I was at a vital meeting discussing matters that could shape the futures of these villagers' lives. I could not be, would not be, distracted from this important business. Innocent, on the other hand, was totally enthralled by the curious sight of two thin, white legs covered in fine blond hairs poking out from a voluminous pair of army surplus shorts. I felt a tickle on my shin and then a small stroking on my kneecap.

"It is our hope that we can help you to provide something of lasting worth for your community." I tried a small jiggle in a hope that the wandering hand might be dissuaded, but Innocent was not to be deterred from further investigating this amazing discovery.

"We shall try to work together to create a regular income that may benefit all your future community projects." To my relief, Innocent, one hand on his bare tummy, wandered away. Out of the corner of my eye, I saw him reach down, bending bowlegged at both knees, and pick up a stick, which he threw with practiced ease at one of his sisters. Eventually the wails subsided and I pressed on.

"We are hoping that any suggestions will come from you and that we will be able to act upon them soon." A gentle stroking heralded Innocent's return. Reaching down, I made a subtle flicking motion with my fingers. All eyes were now leveled at knee height.

"I wonder, does anybody have any suggestions?"

Everyone was spellbound. A slight tug should have been warning enough.

"Perhaps someone has some ideas? Please feel free to say what you— Ow! Ow! Ouch! Ow!"

Innocent had grabbed as many hairs as his small grip could hold and yanked for all he was worth. He seemed disappointed that only a few came away. In reaction to the sharp pain I stepped back, caught my heel on a root and, arms flailing to regain my balance, fell backward, producing a peculiar noise that suggested that something sharp was sticking through the sacks on which I now found myself sitting.

This was all too much for my audience, who until then had made a supreme effort to keep a collective straight face. Now, they fell about as I ruefully rubbed my leg. Yes, I suppose it was funny but not really that funny.

The laughter carried on long after I had casually lit a cigarette. Small Tome recovered just long enough to gasp, "We think maybe you had better decide and then we can help you."

Great.

⤞

CHAPTER 7

Worin Island

"Creeeeeak! Eeeeeeeeaaaaaw!" the yacht howled as it was dragged inch by excruciating inch backward off the spiky reef. The water boiled under the twin outboards of Geoff's yellow-and-blue diving launch, and the towing ropes squeaked and groaned, but slowly it came clear of the ridge of coral and at last floated free. The skipper was sitting head in hands by the mast, not daring to go belowdecks to inspect the depth of the impromptu spa bath that was foaming up through the hull into his forecabin.

We'd watched from the guesthouse jetty as a schooner, as Geoff had described it, had tried to negotiate the narrow passage between Hopei and Hombupeka. Rust-colored sails above a clean white hull trimmed with teak, it had looked magnificent against the graded blues and greens of the sea and had been just close enough for us to see the midmorning sun spark against the polished brass of the portholes and the anxious skipper hunched over his wheel.

His progress had been much hampered by dozens of children paddling in circles around the boat, shouting encouragement and waving bunches of bananas at him.

"Him all right, him all right. No wariwari, no wariwari! Yu like for payim banana? Banana blong mifala nice tumas."

Now we could see him desperately trying to work out from his instruments and snatched glances overboard how soon he would run aground. Whether his calculations had been right or wrong, he had not had to wait long before, with a resonant *boom* and a slithering, smashing noise that emanated from inside the cabin and gave the impression that it contained a comprehensive china and glass department, the little ship ground to a halt.

"Ooh, sori now, sori now. Dis one him rubbish rock, ooh rubbish. Yu badluck man!"

Before the collision had even taken place, Geoff had started up his engines and we were on our way to the rescue.

Now that the boat was free from the reef, we loosed our lines and swung around to her bow before towing her toward New Georgia. When the nearest suitable beach appeared, Geoff pulled away to our left, leaving the injured boat to drift under its own momentum until it gently scraped to a halt on the sand.

"There you go, boy," he called cheerfully as we drifted a little way offshore, motors idling. "Just wait for the tide to run out and you can have a look at your damage. You fin or bilge keel? Hey? Oh well, you'll have to prop her. Good luck!"

"Stupid bastard! He should never have come in here without a pilot," Geoff muttered as he wheeled the boat around. We left the sailor wondering how he was going to salvage the situation while he did his best to turn down the amazing discounts that were now being offered by the persistent banana salesmen.

Soon we were thumping our way across the light chop to Munda.

"How did your meeting go, Will?"

Self-pity enveloped me most comfortably as I outlined what had happened and told him what Small Tome had finished by saying. "Which is really very little help at all. I'm bound to come up with some harebrained plan that will be no use to anybody."

I could see that Geoff was loath to disagree with me, but instead he made a suggestion. "Perhaps you should try and provide something there is a lack of here?" He cut the engines, and we gently nudged the pontoon.

"What would you suggest?" I asked despondently as I tied up at the wharf and we headed into the shade of the leaf house.

"Oh, I don't know." He paused. "There must be loads of things."

"What sorts of things?" I pressed.

Geoff groaned and cast his eyes round. He was an immensely practical man, who I was sure was endlessly irritated by my "green" questions, but his nature was so generous that he was always willing to help out. I was and remain very grateful to him.

Outside the three guesthouse rooms a pair of bantams, two down-at-heel troubadours in their gaudy but tattered finery, were strutting their way toward the market.

"Look, what about chickens? Why don't you do chickens? That'd be a good idea. You can never find a decent chook here. They're all those scrawny, bony old village ones. You'd sell them hand over fist."

"Chickens? I don't know the first thing about chickens."

"Well then, perhaps tell me something you do know the first thing about and then we can discuss that," Geoff suggested, with a broad grin.

"Well, yes, I see your point. . . . What about these chickens then? What do you have to do?'

Geoff looked up at the sky and breathed in deeply before letting the air out through his teeth. "Oh, for . . . look, you're trying to find something relatively straightforward, that is fairly quick turnover, something that you and your guys are not going to get bored with—that is relatively risk free—and that provides a good profit. You presumably are looking to find something that the guys can take over reasonably easily whenever it is that you move on. Right?"

"Right."

"Right, I think the best thing you can do is go and see my mate Warren up in Gizo. He's got a chicken farm up there. Makes a fortune. I'll tell him you are going over. Look, I've got to go and tidy up." He stood up and set off down the path.

"How will I find him?" I called after him, but he had gone.

Chickens! Well, there was something I hadn't thought of. Chickens.

Pecking their way back home, the colorful couple returned, the cock waiting every few yards for his lady wife to catch him up.

So, if you wanted to "do" chickens, what exactly did you "do"?

Three days later I took the up-down, ten-minute flight to the provincial capital, Gizo. To my surprise the airport was not actually in Gizo but on a different island altogether. Waiting for the flight, a fast aluminum boat was moored alongside the runway, and once all the other passengers and their staggering quantities of belongings were onboard, the driver, with a twist of the wheel, swung the boat in a white arc. Opening up the throttles of the two hefty outboards, he dropped a pair of pink sunglasses from his forehead onto the bridge of his nose and we thundered toward the town. Inching my way toward the bow, I clambered over baskets of fruit and vegetables, an incongruous

Swiss fondue set, and the inevitable bundles of yam. Grabbing knees to steady myself, I finally reached the short handrail by the wheel and asked the driver if he knew Warren. There were so few white people living in the islands that they were all known by name and by profession. Geoff was "Jef, man blong dive," Gerry, "Jeri, man blong boat," and Warren, sure enough, was "Worin, man blong kokorako." The man nodded as I caught a mouthful of salt spray. "Time yumi arrive, me showim yu office blong him."

Good, that would save a bit of time. He appeared unconcerned about me retching in the bottom of his boat.

"Him long there." After we'd disembarked, he waved his arm generously at the town to our right. "Him no long way tumas. Name blong office blong him Santo."

This turned out to be quite true if not totally precise; his office Santo was not that far at all, only about three hundred yards away down a narrow side street off the main strip of tacky tarmac. About half an hour and three sets of conflicting directions later, I was standing outside the shanty-style construction. Its wooden front seemed to be held together by thin strips of tin nailed in a patchwork across rough boards. A dusty sign with the name of the business and a picture of an ailing bird that appeared to claim direct descent from the dodo hung at a jaunty angle next to the slatted front door. I knocked, and immediately a pair of eyes appeared at one of the gaps.

"Right. Umm . . . me like for . . . err, story with Warren. Him . . . err . . . stop here?"

Blinking, the eyes pulled at the door and, with a nudge of my shoulder, it opened on an uneven concrete floor. In the fetid room, a skinny man sat back down on a stool. On the floor at his feet was a pile of triangular pieces of thick, gray cardboard.

"Worin, him go back long house blong him."

"Where is his house? I mean . . . um . . . haus blong him."

The man came to the front of the shop and pointed down

the lane and across the lagoon to a distant island. "Hem stop long der."

I thanked him and set off to look for a taxi.

"Hey, mista." He waved me back with one of his triangles. "Yu like payim somefala fin blong sharki? Him nice tumas for soup."

He wafted it under my nose, and I smelled the bile-inspiring odor of old, dead fish. Politely, I declined.

Down at the oily dock I found a crab fisherman who agreed to take me over to the island and wait for me while I had the secrets of "doing" chickens revealed by "Worin." We were quickly back into the bouncing sea.

As we came inside the sheltering crest of "Worin Ilan," the taxi driver, who had embarked on an enthusiastic monologue from the moment we'd pushed off from the wharf, tapped me on the shoulder. Two or three hundred yards to our left he pointed out a low island, almost a sandbar, a couple of lopsided coconuts sprouting from its middle. "Island, dis one, yu lookim? Yu lookim?"

I assured him that I could see it.

"Kinidi, Kinidi— Big man from Merika him stop long this one."

Here it was, he went on to explain in the mildly conde-scending tones of the tour guide, here it was, on this very reef— imagine the scene if you will, August 2, 1943, the war raging—that "Kinidi fall down inside sea."

At two-thirty in the morning, Lt. John F. Kennedy had been at the wheel of his patrol boat, *PT-109*, most of his crew asleep below him. The night was clouded dark as they cut back through the lagoons to the base on Lumbaria, off Randuvu, at the end of a reconnaissance tour of the northern islands.

They had become separated from the rest of the flotilla just after sundown, but the young officer was confident, despite the poor visibility, that he could navigate his way back home.

The powerful engines hummed smoothly below him as he steered his first command through the maze of waterways, excited to be at last getting a piece of the action.

He was presumably less thrilled, however, when suddenly the shadow of the giant Japanese destroyer *Amagiri* appeared without warning from the humid gloom and implacably smashed into the midget craft, cutting it neatly in two.

"This is how it feels to be killed," JFK later remembered thinking—as did possibly two of the other seamen, who actually were killed.

The massive ship plowed on through the night, its skipper unaware of how close he had come to changing the course of modern American history. The sailors in the water clung to the wreckage of *PT-109* for the rest of the night. At dawn, they spotted the island alongside which we were now motoring. JFK, in suitably heroic fashion, towed one of the wounded men to land with a rope that he clenched between his teeth.

Two days later some passing islanders discovered the survivors. They were uncertain whether the castaways were friend or foe, but after an impromptu performance of "Stars and Stripes Forever" from the Americans, complete with salutes at attention and no doubt a tear in the odd brave eye, they agreed to take a message back to the base. Provided with writing materials in the form of the inside of an old coconut and a sharp piece of coral, Kennedy inscribed the historic message: "Native knows posit he can pilot 11 alive need small boat Kennedy."

The natives, solemnly holding the shell, paddled away. Four days later the crew were rescued and returned to Lumbaria for some well-earned R and R and the luxury of the privy that Small Small Tome had pointed out on our first tour.

"Yu lookim?"

I did—Kennedy Island.

We pulled up alongside a neat wooden jetty on the larger island across the water and, leaving the self-appointed tour operator still muttering to himself, I climbed a zigzagging path worn into the steep incline of a low, chalky cliff. As I craned my neck back I could see the roof of a spacious and well-appointed leaf house with outstanding panoramic views of the Coral Sea and Gizo beyond. I reached the level top and approached. All seemed quiet, so I tentatively called out, "Hello, anybody there? Hello? I've come to have a look at your chickens."

This was ridiculous. Stepping onto a wide veranda, I called again.

"In ya come, mate" came a voice. "Make yerself at home. Wait till I get me strides on and I'll be right with ya. Yeah, sorry, mate. Old Geoff got me on the radio, said you might be coming. You must be the fella that wants to start up some chooks."

"Well, yes, that's right, but I am not sure if I know how to go about it," I said to one of the walls of a corridor that ran the width of the house.

"Yeah, he said you didn't have much of a clue. Piece of piss, mate," said Warren as he came round the corner doing up his fly. "Sorry about the wait. Just havin' a quick root with the missus."

I heard a yawn from inside.

"Oh, oh, no problem, no problem. I could have, I mean, yes, I could have waited until you'd err . . . well . . ."

Solid and stocky, he was quite certainly the hairiest man I had ever seen; tufts of black curls sprouted in every direction. Innocent would have had a field day. Covering every square inch of his body apart from his smooth blue chin and a thin strip between a thick rug of curly, dark hair and his extraordinary eyebrow, which swooped out in a single line, the dense matting gave the impression that he was already dressed.

"So what do you need to know, mate?" He pulled a shirt unnecessarily over his head. Hairs peeked out unruly from collar and cuffs as he bent down to pull on a pair of crinkled boots.

"Well, just about everything, I'm afraid."

"Okay then, mate, let's start from the beginning." He pulled two chairs to the edge of the balcony, and we sat looking out over the lagoon, shaded from the caustic sunshine by the overhanging roof. From this height I could see the beach of Kennedy Island shelving away deeply in the invisible water far out beyond the surf.

"Right, rule number one. Which came first, the chicken or the egg? Neither, mate. The chook food. No good you go getting a whole load of chicks and you ain't got any feed. Yeah?"

I nodded in agreement and, peering over, he inspected the notebook that I had opened like an attentive secretary. He seemed satisfied that I had taken his first lesson in this highly specialized art onboard. He rattled on as I turned the pages furiously. Suddenly he stopped.

"Okay, you better come and see the little bastards."

We set off down a hill behind the house. In a clearing stood three sturdy, leaf-roofed houses, their sides enclosed with fine mesh wire. In the shady inside a colossal amount of eating was taking place, so much in fact that there was hardly a flutter or cluck.

"Four hundred in each one. That's twelve hundred of the little bastards." "Little bastards" was clearly a term of endearment. "Built the houses here so we don't get too much of the smell up at the house. Of course if the wind does change and we get a bit of a whiff of shit, I think to myself, Warren, that smell's the smell of money, mate."

So all that afternoon I followed him around, disciple's pad in hand, and learned about the whole process, "from hatching to hatchet" as he described it. In fact I did not need to worry about the hatching because, according to Warren, I was going to buy the day-old chicks direct from Australia; they would be flown into Honiara and straight on to Munda. It all seemed straightforward enough.

The lesson continued. I learned where to build the house

so it would be cool enough. I was told of the importance of clean water every day and regular feeding times. Warren took me through the niceties of slaughtering, delivery, and the state of the market. His assured manner filled me with confidence. It really did seem that it was going to be a "piece of piss." We stopped by a large metal drum. I peered in. It was full of pink, protruding rubber fingers.

"When you really get going," he said with a matey slap on the back, "you can get yourself one of these."

He threw out one arm in the manner of a variety show presenter.

"A plucking machine!"

I looked suitably impressed.

"And it makes a great little sex toy too!"

I turned my head upside down to better imagine how this might be.

Walking back down the path to the sea, we looked out across the lagoon, postcard pink and orange as dusk began to fall. It was a staggering sight and filled me with a feeling of energy and enthusiasm for this new project. Yes, I too was going to enter the realms of the few. Together we would form the Solomon Islands Poultry Growers Association, Western Province (SIPGAWP). The future was feathered.

I shook Warren firmly by the hand. "Thank you, Warren, for having shown me around."

"No worries, mate, no worries. Good luck to you." He winked kindly.

Wiggling the big toe of the driver who had fallen asleep in the bottom of the canoe, he helped us to cast off. I climbed in and turned to wave good-bye as we chugged out backward.

"Oh! Only one thing I forgot to tell you, mate."

"What's that?" I asked, walking forward in the boat to better catch this last morsel of information.

"You won't get any day-old chicks delivered to the Solomons! Not a fackin' feather!"

"Oh, right. So why would that be, then?" I attempted to conceal my dismay.

"Plane's broken down in Brisbane and the company says it ain't got the money to repair it! So there's no more deliveries!" He turned on his hirsute heel and disappeared up the path muttering. "Not a fackin' feather!"

Suddenly, as we pulled away, hot disappointment swept over me; I sat down on the bench seat of the canoe and closed my eyes. I had already visualized the island waking to the sound of hundreds of cheerful "cheep-cheeps." Smiling villagers in striped aprons and straw hats, Purveyors of Fine Poultry. Announcing first-year profits under the spreading ngali nut tree. I rubbed my knee. Expansion, refrigeration, exports, container ships, brand names, logos, "for services to industry." I lowered my head slightly. It was all possible.

And the food . . . God, the food! A gastronomic dream had been served and consumed in my imaginary dining room; my table groaned with roasts, casseroles, hot pots and fricassees, coq au vin, chicken biryani, chicken liver risotto, chili chicken, poulet tropical, and chicken Maryland—whatever that was. The choice was endless. Now it was all being whisked away from me by a shadowy figure dressed in a gorilla suit. No more deliveries. No chicks to be had in the whole of the islands. . . . Not a blooming feather.

"It's a great idea," I explained to the other players over the card table the following evening. "Nice and easy to look after, and we could sell them really easily at the market in Munda and at the rest house. You only have to grow them for six weeks and then you just have to kill them and pluck them. We can get the feed sent by ship to Munda and go and pick it up in the canoes and Bob's your uncle."

Henry and Tome looked a bit perplexed.

"The only problem," I finished gloomily, "is that we can't get hold of any day-old chicks."

"Well, perhaps we can get the little chickens from somebody else," said Tassels positively.

"Every coconut falls down one day," added Luta, wisely. "Your deal."

Sighing, I handed round the cards. A whole country with no chickens. I shook my head. Unbelievable. There had to be some somewhere.

Later, as our game drew to another dismal close, we saw Gordon, Imp's right-handy man, punting across the calm water outside my house. His ghostly form lit by the kerosene lamp on the prow of his canoe, he was making his way back from crayfishing. He and his friend Moses would dive, like madmen, into the dark waters lit only by the lamp and root out the shy crustaceans from underneath the ledges and rocks where they attempted to hide.

"Any luck?" I called out.

"Ooh, staka nice one tonight."

Out of the gloom came hurtling a dark object, which landed like a knight's gauntlet on the table and slid to the far end. Deep blue, fringed with brown, he was a handsome creature about a foot long with a graceful fanned tail. He sat looking stunned by this mistreatment and waiting for the next outrage to be performed upon his person. He did not have to wait long, because hardly had he had a chance to collect himself than Small Tome jumped up, scooped him up, and set off in the direction of Ellen's kitchen.

A few minutes later, Small Tome returned with the handsome creature, who was now a deep red fringed with yellow. In quiet contemplation we ate him, and I pondered the chicken conundrum again. Perhaps we could buy some eggs and hatch them ourselves? I wasn't sure if you could do that. I would have to find out from Worin. He really was the most extraordinarily hairy man.

In the sophisticated, automated, communicated Western world, the creation of such a small project would have presented insignificant complications, indeed would hardly have been worth reporting. It would have required nothing more taxing than picking up the telephone, flexing a credit card, checking the diary, sitting back, and watching it prosper. Or so I imagined, never having done anything remotely similar anywhere. But here, in the isolation of the vast South Pacific, in a country that possessed only the most basic of infrastructures and where even a straightforward venture could at any minute turn into an unbridled adventure, it was certain that I had set myself a challenge. At that moment, as I cracked another claw and sucked noisily, I had no idea that it was to be one of Olympian proportions.

CHAPTER 8

Wuni and the Wantoks

At the service the next morning, it seemed that some of my problems had been given some special attention. Back at my table, I had just finished off my breakfast of pancakes, a recipe that I had been given by Marlene and that had now been perfected by Ellen. (Unfortunately, we'd had to make do without butter, milk, eggs, or baking powder. This said, they certainly filled you up for the day and quite often for some days after that.) I was washing them down with inky black Papua New Guinean tea and watching Stanley fishing for bait.

Day in, day out, a huge school of translucent fish sat at the end of the jetty, feeding on the peelings and scraps that came flying out of the window of Ellen's kitchen. Throwing a triple hook out into the middle of the shoal, Stanley left it to sink for a few moments before pulling it back with a few sharp tugs. If he was lucky and a fish was not, one would be snagged on one of the three sharp barbs. He was depositing them, still wriggling, in a battered kettle full of water a step or two behind him; live bait made a much more appetizing lure twitching on the end of a line. Unfortunately, unbeknownst to him, every time he dropped one in and turned his back in search of another, Chutney would shoot out from my house and scoop it out with a paw. Grabbing it in her mouth, she would belt back into the house to eat it, hidden from view under my desk. After an hour or so, when Stanley was ready to go fishing, he turned to pick up the container. To his consternation he discovered that it was empty but for an inch or so of water in the bottom and not, as he had imagined, brimming with indignant small fry. He looked around suspiciously for a culprit but could see only Chutney basking in the sun, a picture of bloated innocence, and me sitting at my table, an unwilling accomplice staring guiltily at my pancakes. Shaking his head in disbelief, he started back to his task. Chutney opened one eye.

Over Stanley's shoulder I could see, across the bay, the inimitable figure of Tassels paddling toward me, his hair bobbling from side to side like a small bush in a storm. Tassels had mastered or possibly even invented the technique of self-bailing. Often the older canoes had developed cracks and splits along their lengths from standing too long in the direct glare of the sun. Sometimes these were unsuccessfully plugged with old strips of cloth, but more often than not the water just trickled gently in. Tassels, sitting cross-legged in the stern of his one-man canoe, was slooshing the water out over the side with the sole of his foot as his paddle rhythmically propelled him along. He pulled up at the side of the jetty and with astonishing agility leapt out. Reaching down into the canoe, he plucked out a fish about three feet long. Two bloodied fingers stuck through the gills and poked strangely out of the sharp mouth.

"Kingfish for William. Him number-one good one." He slapped it down, shining and sleek, beside my pancakes with such a thump that it spilled my PNG tea.

"Nice tumas," very nice indeed, I wholeheartedly agreed as I admired the spectrum of colors concealed within the silvery scales. There were some fish that were delicious to eat, the majority passed muster, some were hatpin boxes of bones, and a significant number were downright inedible—something like trying to consume your own shirt. Most had passed in front of me since I had arrived. Kingfish, or Spanish mackerel as it was sometimes known, had firm white flesh, remarkably few bones, and was usually big enough not to be squabbled over.

"Perhaps Ellen will cook it for lunch?" She had recently been practicing a new recipe that involved lime and ginger, both of which grew in abundance in the jungle; it was superb. "You'll have lunch with me, Tassels?"

"Why not? Mi gotta onefala nice story butta me rest first time."

Time it was for his mandatory midmorning snooze; I was just going to have to wait for the exciting piece of news he had to impart.

He took his nap on one of the narrow benches outside the house. Here he lay, stretched out fully, his head resting on the soft cushion of his hair. Soon he had gently begun to snore, remaining impervious to a gang of boys who appeared shortly afterward. They clambered up around him and onto the table to watch with total absorption as my pen formed the imperfect words of a letter home. Their arms around each other's shoulders, they shared glances full of an inexplicable thrill at observing this exercise. Occasionally one or another would silently practice writing his own letter to an imaginary friend far away, marking out fanciful forms and shapes with a shy finger on the smooth surface of the table.

Only when we were enjoying the moist fillets of the kingfish, uninterrupted by the ingratiating Chutney, who was slumped feeling mildly unwell on my bed, did Tassels divulge his "nice story," and nice it certainly proved to be.

He had been fishing that morning round the point at Kukurana on beyond Pao.

"Mi fish little bit, mi pullim disfala kingfis. Then me lookim onefala wantok blong me."

"Won tuck? What's a won tuck?"

Tassels sighed at this interruption to his tale, and Ellen smiled indulgently as he set about trying to explain this most integral of all Solomon Islands institutions. He paused occasionally, his decorated face sincere with a desire that I should properly understand. He was quite right to presume that this was going to be a difficult concept for me to grasp. A *wantok*—a "onetalk" in the corrupted English of Pijin—was someone with whom you shared a language. As there were close to a hundred different languages and dialects in the Solomons and perhaps half a dozen different ones on Randuvu alone, a *wantok* was really a relative by language, although he or she might live in any part of the islands. Now perhaps this was not, in itself, too surprising: a recognition of an accent in England is often cause enough for two people to discover an automatic, often misplaced camaraderie. What was more surprising was what this wantokship entitled you to. Simply put, your wantok could expect through custom and local etiquette to make use of however many of your belongings he or she might require.

This was, of course, open to some breadth of interpretation. Many a village store had closed down as a result of the arrival of the wantoks one sunny morning, and many Solomon Islanders had no real incentive to work for the future, as the wantoks could be counted on to handle their hard-earned pay for them. A license to scrounge, you might call it, and perhaps another reason, as well as the sheer lack of necessity, that no one looked for work, everyone contenting themselves instead with the subsistence lifestyle that revolved around gardening and fishing and games of cards. According to Geoff, only 10 percent of the population were in formal employment at any one time.

Inversely, of course, a wantok was an immediate friend, savior, and protector in times of hardship. After a cyclone struck, canoes would arrive full of help and advice, everyone ready to assist with the repair work. Should a garden fail, woven baskets of abundant produce would be delivered to the door of the family in short supply.

Wantoks were the most reliable means of communication. Going out of their way to deliver news from the capital of a child's exam success to proud parents or the return date of a wife, away visiting relatives, to a despairing husband, they were far more trustworthy than the Chinese whispers of the bush telegraph or even the snowy reception of Old Obadiah's antiquated battery-powered radio. (Having said that, I must note that his set seemed to be permanently tuned to Radio Netherlands, and its announcers, who spoke irritatingly good English, rather than to the service messages of the Solomon Islands Broadcasting Company.)

Tassels, satisfied that I had grasped the essence of this institution, went on with his story. So, where had he got to? Oh, yes, that was right. So, there they were, chatting away over a couple of fishing lines, leaning on the sides of their respective canoes, and Tassels mentioned to his wantok Jeremiah that they had an *araikwao*—a "waetman" in their common language—living in the village. For some reason he wanted to get his hands on some day-old chicks—"somefala small kokorako." Well, that was very interesting, because it just so happened that Jeremiah had heard tell only the other day of a man who was breeding chickens up north. He would probably be the guy to go and see. He lived up in the Marovo Lagoon, near where Cousin Zephaniah had married that girl. What was her name? That was right,

Tassels knew just who he meant and pretty much where they lived. Well, that would be the thing to do, pop up and visit him, and it would be a nice chance for a bit of "walkbout."

"Yumi twofala go lookim, Mista Will. Name blong him Wuni. Him nice man tumas. S'pose him savvy helpim yumi?"

A very nice man called Wuni? Still, if it got us any closer to our intended goal, then there could be no harm in trying.

"Why not?" I replied, and Tassel's eyes twinkled. "But how are we going to get there?"

"Use canoe with injin blong iumi."

I knew there was a catch.

Traveling any distance farther than paddling would physically allow was difficult in the Solomons. Most people, especially those who lived in the hinterlands, away from the shore, had no form of motorized transport and relied on passing traffic. Consequently it was with some trepidation that I made my preparations for the long journey the following morning, particularly as the precise location of our destination seemed to be in some doubt.

In charge of logistics, Tassels had decided that we would leave sometime in the morning, as it would take a long while to get there. When he was asked to be a little more specific, he said it was about thirty miles away. Small Tome thought it was more like five. Old Obadiah, who was bumbling past as we pondered the answer, further muddied the waters by declaring that if it was five paces less than two hundred miles then he was a whiteman. Whatever the truth, we would have to stay the night in "somefala place" and go to see Wuni the following morning. This would probably leave us with enough time to make it back to the village before nightfall, thereby missing only one game of cards.

I packed a few belongings into a waterproof bag and went to bed early to prepare for the early start. Chutney, however, had other plans. She was in the habit of patrolling my room at night in pursuit of any creature that, as a result of an oversight on her part, had been left alive. This had been, until now, the recipe for a much-improved night's sleep, as I had heard nothing more from the rats apart from the odd crunched bone. Certainly I had not seen one since Chutney's arrival—I had occasionally found bits of them in my bed, but any still alive had fled.

That night, however, she must have been more vigilant than usual, because at four o'clock in the morning she launched herself onto the roof of my net. Chutney was a fair degree heavier than the rat had been, and my double grannies (I had not stayed in the Cub Scouts long enough to do knots) couldn't support her. She landed bodily on my chest. I do not know who was more surprised, but I do know that Chutney planted her claws deep into my shoulder to break her fall before racing out the door. Half an hour of stinging disinfectant later, I abandoned any attempt at resurrecting my net or any thought of going back to bed. I dressed and waited by my window for the sun to rise over the lagoon.

To pass the time, I pulled Grimble down from the shelf. He too had had the occasional problem sleeping in the Tropics and had spent the odd night sitting up and writing. From at least one description of the sun rising over the islands—"At noonday, the lagoon colors are sheeted flames of cobalt and viridian, agate and emerald so fierce they sear the sight."—I could only imagine that he'd a thesaurus in one hand and, more than likely, a bottle of Scotch in the other.

CHAPTER 9

＜≈＞

Keeping My Head

It was true that in the hour before dawn the village was at its stillest and even the waters of the horseshoe bay seemed to have taken a brief rest from their constant movement. The stars were so numerous and varied in their intensity that a clear light lay across the shadowy village and the silvered sea.

Of course, this peace on earth was shattered the moment the town crier cockerel awoke and decided that as he was up so should everybody else be. With a blatant disregard for his own popularity, or even safety, he would keep up this performance until he was confident that his message had reached every corner of the village. So irritating was he, so snide and so self-important, that had I had the knowledge or the wherewithal, I would have reduced his status from cock to capon very shortly after my arrival. Even the sun, rudely awoken, was forced to appear above the trees, an irascible giant peering in to discover the reason for this commotion.

When Old Obadiah, by some distance the most senior citizen of the community, could no longer bear the noise, he would grope for his paperweight-thick glasses, tie the ill-fitting frames to his head with a length of bootlace, and emerge from his house. Shuffling his way to the vestry behind the altar of the church, he would sit on the ground in front of a round, hollowed-out log and beat out an intricate reveille. Imperceptibly the gathering of houses then began to stir.

The water was at its clearest now, unsullied by the traffic of the day, and the resident angelfish swam delicately to and fro, wondering vaguely what they had planned for the day. Not until later would the trevally come scything in; these murderous predators with their armor gray scales snapped up their prey with violent, rushing attacks that splashed pinkish water up through the stones of the jetty, only then to flip around and cruise swiftly back to the safety of the deeper blue.

From my window I watched blearily as the daylight filtered down through the water, coloring the corals with their true shades of yellow, purple, and green. Among them royal blue starfish twinkled dreamily, and thousands of fish—shiny magnetic shards each the length of a pocketknife blade—moved in precise unison, flicking this way and that across the underwater landscape.

We left the tiny bay of Mendali and crossed out over the Blanche Channel. Like overofficious wardens, dolphins rose and dived at the bow of the boat, rose and dived along our two sides, as if to ensure we kept to the correct route. This particular morning there seemed to be more than usual. Perhaps they recognized that this was a proper journey, an adventure. I certainly did; I had brought my life jacket.

Up ahead a slender garfish rose, its swordlike nose piercing the surface of the sea, the bones of its weird green skeleton visible through its translucent body. Through some dynamic that I did not understand, it hurled itself fifteen feet into the air, followed from a much greater depth by the sleek steel of a king-fish, exploding with power. It followed the garfish in its mighty arc and, just when it seemed that the greater fish would seize it between its slicing jaws, the smaller one managed to flick its way out of danger as the two crashed back into the water. The dolphins left us when we reached the safety of the reef's edge on the far side of the lagoon. Their slick gray forms rose one last time before diving as they turned back to the cooler waters.

Tassels watched them go and smiled. "Time for hunting again soon."

"Hunting? What, not the dolphins, surely?" I said, voicing the concerns of a generation brought up on friendly tins of tuna and episodes of *Flipper*.

"Why not?" He looked at me with genuine curiosity.

"Well . . ." I would have to give this some thought.

As we entered the Roviana Lagoon, I discovered that the view from the sea was deceptive. Inside the lagoon there was a mass of islands. Some were large, forested, and inhabited, the villages sprinkled carelessly along the shores. Others were tiny and bare, covered with nothing more than a scattering of shrubs or a few coconuts. One island consisted of a solitary tree and just enough room to lay out a towel. The Solomon Islands, I realized with a sudden, selfish thrill, must be one of the last places on earth untrammeled by the flip-flops and hiking boots of the holidaymaker and his down-market, less hygienic friend, the traveler. Watch them as they gate-crash the private parts of the planet, unwittingly or negligently causing yet another part of the real world to be subsumed into a nonstop, Disneyified Coca-Cola carnival.

There was something secret, almost enchanted, about these waterways as we pushed on toward the hills of Mahimba and Vangunu, something timeless, as if nothing had ever been different, something that was so hidden that it could never be found. Could never be spoiled. This thought, though, I knew to be not just simple fantasy but straightforward delusion.

As we snaked through a silted channel between two points, Stanley and Small Small Tome, who had decided to join us, presumably to avoid the rigors of "Kindi," sat up from where they had been lying in the bow and pointed excitedly to our right.

Tassels grinned. "They want you to look in this island."

"Great." I laughed the laugh of someone who suspects that he may be about to be the butt of a practical joke.

We beached the canoe, and Tassels yanked up the engine, cocking it out of the water. Leading the way, the two boys, their bare feet springing over fallen logs and branches, headed into the bush. I followed. Under a canopy of trees, which allowed just a few shafts of sunlight down to play on the forest floor, we came into a perfectly circular clearing. In its center was what appeared, at a distance, to be a white, tooth-shaped rock protruding from the earth, a weird geological anomaly in these coral islands.

As I strode toward it, I noticed that the others were hanging back on the rim of the circle. Confused, I smiled at them and stepped closer. Juddering, a series of images flashed before my bulging eyeballs. Piercing stares from empty sockets, lipless, gumless, gaping mouths, a garish orange moth taking flight from a cavity where once the flesh of a nose must have been, and teeth, teeth were scattered like so many ngali nuts around the fringe of a pyramid of thirty human skulls. I tried not to take a step back, but as I did so a stab of light cut across me.

On all sides figures dashed and darted between the trees, disappearing, reappearing. As they closed in, I could hear the panting whoops of the headhunters. I stood with my back to the shrine, the brim of my hat drooping miserably over my ears, until I was surrounded.

Dragging a whimpering old man into the circle, a warrior, his black skin shining against the white war paint daubed on his near naked body, wrenched his victim's head back by the hair, laying bare his wrinkled neck. With a downward slash of his knife, he decapitated him. There was no sound but a dull *tok* as the windpipe was severed and an "Oh!" of surprise from the lips before they drained of blood.

Holding the head aloft, the painted figure let out a scream of joy as the drumbeat of the feast started up noisily in the jungle mountains. My eyes were swimming, pricking with the sweat that ran into them from my forehead. Wiping my face, I looked again, and there swinging in front of me, dripping with red ink, was the severed head of Robert, my former student. He somehow succeeded in looking as smug as ever. "Sir, my mother wants to know—"

Suddenly everything began to swirl.

"Everything all right, Mr. Will?" asked Stanley with a smile.

"Err . . . yes, of course, absolutely fine, thank you. Well, this is all very interesting. Yes, excellent. Do you think, should we be getting back to the boat?" I said, heading off in the wrong direction.

"So where do those, err . . . where do they come from then, Tassels?"

"Smolboy laek for mekem yu fright li'l bit!"

"Oh, yes. I know, ha, ha! Shame it didn't work, eh!"

The skulls were the remains of respected ancestors, preserved to be honored. Although Christian burial had now replaced the shrines, they'd been left as a sign of respect to the dead. There must have been a time, however, when skulls were as ubiquitous as the coconuts that littered the bush; for it was believed that by decapitating a man and taking his skull home with you, you would acquire his power. Very often an enemy's head was brought back alive—that it is to say that a head was kept connected to its owner and the whole imprisoned in the village until such time as food stocks ran low. This system cleverly sidestepped problems of refrigeration in a sweltering climate.

Only as recently as 1892 was the terrible head-hunting Chief Ingava, who would think nothing of paddling more than a hundred miles for quality produce, eventually killed. His fortress had been built on the fringes of the Roviana Lagoon, where now we found ourselves. Head-hunting and cannibalism were eventually sidelined by the missionaries and the colonial powers in the 1920s, apparently dying out completely after World War II.

Robert Louis Stevenson, on the other hand, could hardly talk about anything but "long pig," the cannibal term for human flesh. He had been taken aback when given directions by a man who was nonchalantly chewing on roast arm of boy—apparently the best cut—and had been doubtful of the motives of a chief who had played host for him and his good lady wife: He was "an incurable cannibal grandee. His favourite morsel was the human hand, of which he speaks today with an ill-favoured lustfulness. When he said goodbye to Mrs. Stevenson, holding her hand, viewing her with tearful eyes, he wrote upon her mind a sentimental impression which I try in vain to share."

That said, he may have been wrong, because there was a photograph of the good Mrs. Stevenson in the frontispiece of my copy of In the South Seas and, although the picture was a little blurred, I could not believe that even in the flesh she had been remotely appetizing.

RLS considered, however, that on balance the cannibals were acting from a principled standpoint. "They were not cruel; apart from this custom, they are a race of the most kindly; rightly speaking, to eat a man's flesh after he is dead is far less hateful than to oppress him while he lives; and even the victims

of their appetite were gently used in life and suddenly and pain-
lessly dispatched at last."

I found the whole concept more difficult to accept and
Robinson C., not much recognized for his enlightened
approach, "discovered much abhorrence at the very thoughts of
it and at the least appearance of it." So when he came across
"three skulls, five hands and the bones of three or four legs and
feet and abundance of other body parts," he made a policy decision there and then to shoot any suspect cannibals on sight.
They were, after all, "poor ignorant creatures."

I was worrying the various rights and wrongs about in my
mind and praying that I was not going to have to resolve this
moral dilemma for myself when we arrived back at the canoe.
Inevitably, we discovered that the engine was on one of its
perennial breaks, refusing point-blank, despite Tassels's less
than delicate ministrations, to start. Apart from the whirring of
the spring and the occasional cough, the motor expressed no
interest in reapplying itself to its designated task. Small Small
Tome, who had disappeared, came back with some bananas and
ripe papaw. I got back out again. Sitting on the trunk of a
coconut tree that grew flat out across the sea, we dangled our
feet in the water and ate the fruit as Tassels pulled on the starting rope time after time. Standing in the water to his waist, he
was running with sweat. When it became too much, he simply
sank down below the surface for a few seconds, to reemerge
with a fizzing shake of his head and set back to his task only a
little less bouffant than before.

"No worries." Tassels laughed, and Stanley began to gig-
gle. Small Small Tome, recognizing the humor of the moment,
joined in with his own curious expression of mirth. I was not at
all sure how they could always take such a carefree approach;
we needed to get on; there was a great deal to do, and we were
straying off target.

Nevertheless, it was certainly true that one of the excitements of life in the Solomons was traveling by boat. Hardly a sea journey went by without some sort of incident, small or downright disastrous. One of the biggest problems was the invention of the outboard motor. Presumably it was a cheap, efficient, and quick mode of transport; one yank of the starting cord and you were slicing through the waves, the spray in your face, the sun on your back, and the wind in your hair. But this was, sadly, an image confined to advertising brochures. In reality, hours were spent with the engine cover off and bits of dismantled engine held precariously from sinking into the clear blue by fingers and teeth. I can only presume that many months of research in the workshops of engineering factories around the world had been required to design an engine that would compliantly start when you wanted to set off, only unfailingly to break down the moment you were out of sight of land or the weather worsened.

Had we been followed by a support ship loaded with spares and qualified mechanics, things might have been a little less wearisome. However, in a country where a screwdriver was a luxury item and a wrench that fitted was just as rare, there was often little to do but sit and bob. Flagging down passing boats was also problematic; waving normally elicited only a wave in response as the occupants of the other boat zoomed past.

If various clunkings, grindings, backfires, and ominous silences formed the soundtrack to my boating nightmares, petrol became their fuel. It was expensive, and we were always running on empty, half a gallon scrounged here, half a gallon siphoned off there. Petrol also had a remarkable propensity to mix itself with seawater, which mysteriously seemed to lurk at the bottom of every tank.

Boating, however, was never a lonely occupation. I hardly ever traveled in a canoe (as all boats, large or small and irre-

spective of their construction, were called) that was not dangerously overloaded. Our present trip was a roomy luxury.

When the women came back from the market in Munda,
where they had sold their sweet potato and cassava, it was not
unknown for there to be twenty-five people plus assorted
babies, pineapples, stacks of bananas, and sacks of rice on
board one dugout canoe. On one occasion Tassels, the official
driver, set off with a hair's width of freeboard only to experience
the novelty of driving a canoe that was actually underwater
although the raised engine was still running. The contents
swam back to the marketplace, and the whole operation, minus
a couple of sacks of soggy rice, was started again.

Only rarely did I remember the inflatable life jacket that I
had been given back in England, compliments of one of the
world's airlines. So, when the engine broke down or the petrol
ran out and the tide was thundering along westward, pursued by
malevolent gusting rain clouds, I often wondered how much
more of my life on the ocean wave remained.

Still the engine would not start. After a while I, too,
resigned myself to searching around for a funny side to the situation but, just as I was beginning to despair of finding one, the
engine coughed asthmatically, cleared its throat a couple of
times, roused itself, and started to putter. We hurriedly pushed
off, lest it should have a change of heart, and picked up speed as
we headed for the islands of Vangunu and Nggatokae, ahead of
us to the east. Behind us I could see distant islands disappearing, obscured by swaths of dark mist.

Then the first drops began to fall. The sea that had been as
smooth as blue glass quickly lost its shine as if smeared by a
giant, invisible rag. As the rain fell harder, the surface of the sea
turned a milky opaque, the drops falling like a million tiny beads
that seemed to bounce off it as if off tarmac. Still harder it
came, and the surface began to smoke with the ferocity of the

downpour until I was under the strange impression of being trapped inside an inverted novelty ball in the midst of a swirling, artificial snowstorm. I was as wet as I was ever going to get, and the fall on my back felt like a warm, therapeutic jet at a health spa. The two boys curled up where they sat, their foreheads almost touching their toes, and hibernated. At the helm Tassels, holding the blade of a paddle above his eyes to protect them from the drops that now stung like buckshot, smiled and stuck doggedly to our course. When the deluge could get no harder, it did, and visibility shrank to the bow of the canoe.

And then it stopped. I watched the clouds overtake us, moving on ahead, soaking everything in their path. Soon in the heat of the sun and the wind, clothes dried, fingers, puffed and white, uncrinkled, and Tassels regained his normal effervescence.

We threw out a fish-shaped lure, which I had bought as an extravagance from Geoff. It wiggled most realistically as it was towed in our wake. "You can't fail with this one," he had promised. "You'll rape the ocean."

I did not really want to do anything quite so drastic, but up until today I had not had so much as a nibble. Mindful of the devils lurking below, I handled the line gingerly.

"Yu bad luck fisherman," said Stanley, taking it from me.

I willed him not to catch anything but inevitably, a short while later, he yanked hard. Slowing the engine, Tassels and he started to pull, boy's hand over man's, filling the bottom of the boat with tangling spools. Out of the water leaped the flashing red and purple spots of a coral trout and, with an expert flick, the little boy brought the handsome fish on board. He grinned up at me as he disengaged the hook from its panting mouth. "Stanley good luck fisherman."

"You know, in my country many people go fishing, but they sometimes put the fish back in the water."

"So why do they go fishing, if they just put them back?"

asked Stanley after he had signed this extraordinary behavior to the incredulous Small Small Tome. It was, undeniably, a good question.

The sun was sinking reluctantly below the horizon behind us as we chugged along the coastline of one of the larger islands until we came to a beach, the size of a volleyball court, sheltered by a steep hill and protected from the wind by a rocky outcrop.

"Yumi rest here. Nice water for drink but swim first time." Solomon Islanders were fastidiously clean, and going to bed without washing off the grime of the day was unheard of. I could quite happily just have had a bite to eat, rolled up, and gone to sleep, but instead we tramped off, following a stream up through the bush until we came upon a bathtub pool. We took it in turn to wash ourselves in the puckeringly cold water that gushed out of the hillside before returning to the shore to dry off in the last gleams of sunlight.

Tassels chopped down a number of saplings and, constructing a frame, which he covered with coconut leaves fetched down by Stanley, he built a bedroom on the sand while I ineffectively cleaned the fish. We cooked it on an open fire, ate it with some sweet potatoes packed by Ellen, and washed it all down with coconut milk.

Stanley and Small Small Tome fell instantly and deeply asleep. Tassels and I chatted quietly about the coming day and smoked one of his head-numbing cigarettes, cut from his stick of gooey black tobacco and rolled in a bit of exercise book paper, which he had somehow preserved from our drenching. As I gazed out across the Pacific, the ticking in my head slowed. I had been wrong. There was no need to be in a rush—ever.

As the last embers of the fire blacked out one by one, I lay down, tucking my life jacket behind my head, and closed my eyes.

Ten minutes later in they came, low over the water, hundreds of them, wave after wave, all coming directly for me, their high-pitched whine a forewarning of the impending attack—mosquitoes like MiG fighters. Their meat-seeking equipment was finely tuned and, unerringly, they found their target. With a degree of satisfaction I splatted the first one that buried its hooter into my leg. In the moonlight I could see the dark stain of blood—mine, most probably—but soon the onslaught was too great. Their presence at night was nothing new, but without the bomb-shelter protection of my net I was at their mercy. For a moment I even considered inflating my life jacket and spending the night bobbing in the protection of the sea but decided instead to cover as much bare flesh as possible with the few articles of clothing that I had brought. It seemed to me deeply unfair, as I stumbled around in the dark, morally wrong in fact, that this blitzkrieg was concentrated entirely on me. My companions slept on, unscathed.

With a spare pair of shorts on my head and my legs and arms wrapped in my plastic anorak, I tried to sleep. As I drifted off, I smiled contentedly. All the curious jigsaw pieces that had brought me to where I was lying now were falling into place; all those pieces of sterile information I had been given before I left were developing resonance and hue.

Before my departure, I'd no idea how I would fulfill the Commander's intentions, but now I had an excellent plan, and tomorrow we were going to take the first step toward putting it into action. I felt a tingle of excitement and a painful sting on the top edge of my right ear. I readjusted my shorts.

CHAPTER 10

Crown Derby

From a distance, the rock formation that towered above us resembled the head and hunched shoulders of a grumpy ogre striding over the crest of the mountain. His gigantic hands clenched in his double duvet pockets, he was stomping toward us, his massive lace-up boots scuffing sourly along, wiping out a few hundred acres of forest here, a few hundred more there; soon he would be splashing about in the lagoon, swamping the small group of seaside houses.

"Mountain man, him rubbish man," pronounced Stanley as the two lads looked up fearfully at the advancing figure.

Fee, fi, fo, fum, I agreed. I was, after all, an Englishman.

At his feet, on the strip of gold thrown down between the green and the blue, stood a handful of unremarkable huts casting their spindly shadows down among those of the fringing, unruffled palms, but in front of them the water was foaming with activity. The entrance to the shallow bay had been ringed by canoes in a line, prow to stern, and men of all ages were beating the water with the blades of their paddles, the flat slaps audible above the sound of our engine.

Suddenly, as we approached, one of them leaped to his feet, balancing for a second or two as he followed the movement of something below the surface. Extending his arm far behind him and with a protracted scream, he hurled his many-pronged spear down into the water with a surprising ferocity. It had clearly found its target because, rather than sink out of sight, the lance waved and waggled furiously.

Following his lead, other men jumped up, throwing, stabbing, and shouting until there must have been thirty or forty wooden shafts twisting violently this way and that in the thrashing water. Their ammunition expended, many of the men jumped into the water to wrestle with these unseen adversaries, their empty canoes spilling out and away from the tight band that had prevented their prey from escaping into the open sea outside the cove. Now that the cordon was broken, we could see the awful reason for this intense excitement.

As we grew nearer, a burly villager staggered out of the boiling red sea in a strange, horrific embrace with a dolphin. The duo managed a couple of steps of the Charleston on the beach before the man, losing his balance, toppled over on his partner and blood squirted in a thick paint jet onto the sand. Here it collected briefly before it soaked down among the fine grains to leave a dark slick, above which the flies immediately congregated with a buzz of excitement.

Unabashed by his clumsiness, the eager dancer capered back into the water, leaving the dying creature to be inspected by a group of curious children, who squatted down closely around it. As its heart weakened, the creature bled in fainter and fainter surges, and its skin, normally the smoothest gray, began to dull and blacken.

We drove around the fringes of the melee and pulled our canoe up onto the beach. The other three rushed over, and I followed. By the time I had reached the crowd, the village had been turned into an impromptu abattoir—men, women, and children busying themselves over the carcasses, their arms bloody to the elbow, their feet leaving gory footprints as they worked. Turning away, forewarned by a certain salty keenness in the back of my mouth, I found myself gazing at a woman who, seated on the sand with a cheerful smile, was prizing the teeth from a decapitated dolphin's head that rested upright on her lap. As each one was successfully extracted, she dropped it plinking onto a metal plate at her side.

Making my way back to the canoe, exercising firm control over my rebelling insides, I sat down in its shade and sucked in deep breaths of sea air. At least I was not the first white man to have found his sensitivities prickled by the occasional barbarity of these simple islands.

Crusoe had struggled at the moment of his discovery of partially consumed human remains. "I turned away my face from the horrid spectacle; my stomach grew sick and I was just at the point of fainting, when nature discharged the disorder from my stomach; and having vomited with uncommon violence, I was a little relieved."

Even the stalwart Grimble had suffered a similar fate after a giant octopus had stuck itself to his face, which, it appeared, was not an uncommon event. He had "left hurriedly for the cover of the jetty and was sick." In the shade of the canoe, I was not at all sure I was not going to follow in these gentlemen's venerable footsteps.

Stanley beamed when the others returned. "Staka nice teeth." I had seen the tiny, sharp, gory slivers, and they had not been particularly enticing. I mentioned as much.

Stanley shook his head and explained that Solomon Islands "kastom" decreed that a boy must buy his bride from her parents, and although now this price was often paid in hard cash, no checks or postal orders, very often still part or whole was paid in "kastom" money. Depending on your island and indeed your village, this might come in a number of forms. Dolphins' teeth here, however, were, as I had witnessed, much prized as the common currency.

Shell money, on the other hand, is favored out in Malaita Province. Braids as thick as one's forearm, several yards long, are made up of thousands and thousands of tiny shells, each about half the size and twice the thickness of a button, as which they had once also been used. Several of these ropes, weighing some ten or fifteen pounds each, are worn as decoration by the bride at her wedding. When Small Tome's youngest sister, Ruth, had married, she had staggered into the church, supported by a couple of friends, and after the ceremony, which had taken place wih her seated on the ground, she had had to be hoisted upright by her new husband.

Lighter, altogether more practical, and very popular with the ladies in Temotu Province was red feather money: long garlands of plumes, plucked from the much sought after red, sweet-toothed scarlet honeyeater bird, plaited, coiled, and used to buy a wife from her father. The good news for the scarlet honeyeater is that he is only trapped, to be released later a little balder and probably none the wiser but still alive. I wondered whether perhaps there was any way of doing the same with the teeth: Just whip a few out and then let the dolphin go. Probably not.

While I pondered all this, Tassels, with a sharp hiss, attracted the attention of a young girl, staggering under the weight of a huge slice of oozing meat draped over her shoulder, which she was lugging home for lunch. Did she know, by any chance, the way to Wuni's house? With a jerk of her chin and a jabbered instruction, she dripped on down the beach. We all turned to look up the hill, toward the goliath who, now lit from behind by the glowering sun, looked angrier than ever.

"So, everybody ready? Shall we go?" I asked as positively as I could. Stanley and Small Small Tome were tracing crosses in the sand with their toes and looking anything but thrilled about my proposal. Tassels's natural enthusiasm, however, came to the rescue. "Why not?" he answered cheerfully as he set off. Sighing, we three started walking.

"Mountain man him cranky tumas," moaned Stanley as he simultaneously translated, fist-clenching and snarling his impression. I had to agree that the rock was looking pretty cantankerous.

As we climbed away from the shore, the vegetation grew in over our heads and the path became mercifully shady. Despite this, the humidity hung so heavy in the air that within ten minutes sweat was sluicing down my back and legs, and my feet slopped in my boots. Before long the others, who looked as if they were going for a Sunday morning stroll in the park, quickly left me behind, chatting happily as Tassels swung his bush knife easily in front of him. He cut back the odd branch or swiped away the spiders' webs that had been thoughtlessly constructed across the way. On the few occasions that I caught my face in one, being a little taller than the others, I could feel it press into my skin like a bank raider's stocking, or rather as I imagine such a stocking would, before it eventually broke free from its attachments. I had to claw it off like glue, hoping it had not come complete with its proprietor.

Nearing the top of the incline, however, I experienced the curious sensation of someone lightly laying a hand on the top of my hat. I stopped and slowly peered up. I could see nothing but the underside of the rim. I carefully removed the hat and, keeping it upright, lowered it to inspect. On it sat a spider so colossal that, had it been sighted in Europe, it would have been reason enough for the evacuation of a medium-size town. "G'day. Nice hat!" it leered sarcastically.

Automatically, I flicked down, sharply. Swinging like an

abseiler, the creature sailed out on conker-string thread to land on my shin. Its legs were certainly as hairy as my own. Hopping around energetically, a one-man cancan show, I kicked hard to dislodge it as it gently began to stroke. At last I watched, with a burst of sweaty relief, as it came loose and flew into the trees. When Small Small Tome, sensing some disturbance, turned round, I gave him the most convincing thumbs-up I could muster.

We eventually arrived on a small plateau overlooking the village and the sea. I stopped to catch my breath, which the view and the climb had combined to take from me. From here we could see the whole broken, mad maze of islands, the blue leading the unwary into a million equally confusing, equally isolated, identical byways. In the farthest distance to our right, on the hazy horizon, I could just make out the smudged outline of the peaks of Randuvu.

Now a stern breeze was pushing wavelets along the shore and whipping white horses across the bay. Smoke from various fires whisked over the top of them and disappeared in the sky above the lagoon as the villagers below readied themselves for their feast. Fortunately none of the smells reached us, as my senses had suffered quite enough assaults for the time being.

Up to our left we saw the steely reflection of a galvanized tin roof. "Up there, I think." I nodded

A few minutes later we found ourselves outside a smart wooden house painted a bright yellow and red. From within came the distorted blaring of a portable radio. "If ya think I'm sexy and ya want my body," a static-bound singer was croaking.

"Hello," I called. "Hello, is there anyone there? I am looking for Mr. Wuni." I felt as self-conscious making this approach as I had done at Mr. Worin's.

A woman stuck her head out of the window at the gable end of the raised house. "If ya think I'm sexy and ya want my body," she sang stridently along as she punched the air above her head like a victorious boxer.

"If you think I'm sexy and you want my body," she repeated.

Unkind though it might sound, on both counts, I did not. Anyway, it was much too hot. I smiled up at her.

Her face was covered in an extraordinarily intricate tattoo, which as she waved us to approach I saw was replicated on the whole circumference of her dark brown arms and even down the lengths of her fingers. Unlike the other tattoos that I had seen, these were not outlines but more a broad print that covered the whole skin like diaphanous cloth. I learned afterward from Tassels that she was from the minuscule Lord Howe Atoll, Luaniua, which was so remote and so limited in its range of activities that there was nothing for people to do but tattoo each other. The woman turned and called back into the house something in her own language that I did not understand.

"Darling, there are some strange people to see you and one of them is white! Try not to be too long as I want you to go and see if you can get hold of a couple of those delicious dolphin steaks later. I haven't got anything for this evening." Or at least this was what I guessed was her general drift.

Slowly, clambering down the steps one by one, came a dwarf. If he was not technically a dwarf, then he was certainly challenged in terms of height in the most exacting possible way. Hardly taller than Stanley, he barely reached my waist. He was also extremely elderly, his gray hair knotted in a ball on the top of his head, but his brown face, crisscrossed by a thousand wrinkles, crackled into a wide smile when he spotted us and waved us to approach.

He was dressed only in a lava-lava, tied with precision round his middle, and a leather pouch was slung over his shoulder and across his stomach. From it stuck the stem of a much-chewed pipe. His bowed legs and a slight stoop did not prevent him from exuding a rather military air, and his sturdy bare feet came to rest at a sharp right angle as he waited in the shade of the overhanging roof. He supported himself with the aid of a long carved stick some length taller than he, and this too added to his dignified appearance. Certainly, however, his most prominent feature was the fact that he had only one eye. It blinked at me, the other socket covered by a strip of dark cloth that was tied around his head.

"Goodness gracious. What on earth have we here? Great Scott, you're not an Englishman are you by any good fortune?"

I nodded dumbly. His pronunciation was perfect, his accent, public school and the gentlemen's clubs of St. James's.

"Well, what a simply super surprise. Dearest, there's an English chap come to see us. Isn't that nice?"

His wife, who had momentarily retreated from the window to turn off the radio, reappeared. "Lovely, dear," she replied as if she was standing in a rose garden holding a pair of secateurs.

I was dumbfounded.

"Mister, Mister Wunner, Wuni?" I stammered.

"That's right, old boy. 'One-eye' at your service," he replied with a mock salute.

The others looked as startled as I was sure I did, and I sensed that Stanley was trying not to laugh. I attempted to regain my composure. "We are interested in some chickens."

"Chickens, by crikey. It's chickens you're after, is it? All in good time, my dear fellow, all in good time. First let's have a cup of jolly old tea. We'll make ourselves comfortable in the shade of this marvelous tree."

He leaned against a towering mahogany and spoke to his wife in their native language. She quickly withdrew her head, and from inside the house I could hear the clattering of china. Wuni gestured to an upturned car battery. "Not much, I am afraid, but better than the ground. Can't have guests sitting on the ground."

He sat at my feet and peered up at me monocularly.

"You don't know Lord Ravenscroft, do you? He stayed on

the plantation once. He was a friend of the Boss, you know."

The Boss?

"Yes, the Colonel, used to own the plantation here after the war, y'know? Bought it from the Lever Brothers. I was his foreman. Thirty-five years, don't y'know."

Colonels and commanders.

"Is that how you learned to speak such good English?"

"Oh, I'm a bit rusty now," he said with ease. "Don't get the chance to practice much these days."

He was, however, clearly planning to make up for lost time and continued without hesitation. "So, where are you from, old boy? Don't tell me you are from Dorking. That's where the old man came from, or at least that's where his parents lived. Wouldn't that be fun if you came from Dorking too?"

I was just about to disappoint him when he went on. I had the feeling that this was going to be a long cup of tea.

"So what brings you all the way out from old Blighty?"

"Well, that is actually a very good question—"

"The Colonel used to start the day at six-thirty prompt. British military discipline, you know. That's how to get things done, he used to say."

He smiled at the others, who nodded mystified. Tassels, I sensed, clearly believed that our host was a couple of bananas short of the bunch. From the signs that Stanley was covertly flashing to Small Small Tome, I guessed that he was of much the same opinion.

Formal introductions were now made, and I through some misunderstanding suddenly became Wilf. Muriel, Wuni's wife, put down a tray to shake hands. On it were set out some very smart, if slightly chipped, teacups and saucers, a teapot, a plate of biscuits, and a silver sugar bowl. I could see Stanley eyeing the biscuits. Disappearing into the outside kitchen, Muriel reappeared with a blackened, steaming kettle, holding its wire handle in a wad of leaves.

"You be Mother, please," Wuni said. Presuming that he was talking to his wife, I smiled at her but, looking up, I saw him, his head cocked on one side, staring at me with his one eye.

"Oh, yes, of course," I said, trying to remember my manners and praying that I would not drop something.

"Present from the Colonel. Finest Crown Derby, but you probably knew that, Wilf," he said as if he had read my mind.

"Yes, the old Crown Derby," I said cheerfully, although I wouldn't have known it from Royal Doulton.

Tassels was looking more and more baffled. The boys, by contrast, had overcome their inhibitions and were halfway through the biscuits.

"Of course, I was here during the war, Wilf."

With this inauspicious introduction, he embarked on an account of his war record with all the enthusiasm of an after-dinner speaker who has just recovered from losing his voice. "You see, the Japs attacked in forty-two."

At this stage in the story, Muriel, acting, no doubt, from experience, made a tactical retreat into the house.

The Japanese had arrived in huge numbers, bringing with them all the paraphernalia necessary to wage war. It was the first time that Wuni, who had in fact been James at the time, had seen an Oriental, let alone the huge quantities of planes, guns, trucks, and equipment. "We'd no idea that there was a war on, old man. Some of the islanders thought that they had come from the moon or from the Devil, can you believe it!"

Initially the Japanese had taken little notice of the local population, busy as they were setting up camp, but as soon as they expanded their operations and required more space, they trampled through the villages, destroying them. The villagers fled inland, up into the bush, while the battles against the Americans raged above and below them.

When the smoke cleared and they returned to the shore, they found a very different scene. Gone were the setting suns and the Zero fighters, replaced by the Stars and Stripes and some pretty buoyant GIs. The Americans were friendly and only too happy to introduce the locals to some of the cornerstones of their great culture. For the first time Wuni and his family experienced the pleasures of sitting around while smoking Marlboro cigarettes and swigging warm Coke.

"Ghastly muck, the Colonel used to say. I thought it was a drop of good stuff." Wuni laughed.

The villagers had acted as guides and scouts, showing the Americans shortcuts and paths through the bush. The young James, or Jimmy, man, as he had now become known, was as keen as any of the other island boys to befriend these strangers. They had boxes that talked and magazines full of pictures to look at. Jimmy, who had heard about the cold countries where the white men lived, was surprised to discover that their women wore as few clothes as Solomon women and in some cases even fewer. He and his friends enjoyed partaking in the strange social ritual of placing a soft, white strip or a sweet, pink cube in their mouths. These they then chewed, following their new visitors' lead, while talking fast and loud out of the other side of their mouths. This was all something quite new to the quiet, often shy islanders, who looked in amazement at these strange white men, so different from the English colonials, who until then had held sway.

"And some of these American fellows were black, you know, as black as you and me. Somfala blak," he divulged for Tassels's benefit. Sadly, the refreshments had weighed heavy, and the trio were sound asleep, their backs to the tree, their legs fanned out around them. Undismayed, Mein Host continued.

One day Jimmy and a young American corporal ("NCO, pretty green, didn't seem to have much of an idea, I'm afraid") were sent out to search for a Japanese pilot who had crash-landed at the incensed giant's feet farther up the hill from where we were now sitting. To their surprise they found him very quickly. He was still alive, dangling from his parachute, which, in turn, dangled from a branch high up in the rain forest canopy. The American instructed the pilot to "Come down this minute, y'hear," but the unfortunate man, with the best will in the world, was powerless to comply.

"Goddamn!"

For want of any better idea, the soldier ordered Jimmy to shoot. Jimmy refused, and after a bit of "You shoot him," "No, you shoot him," Jimmy admitted that he did not have any bullets in his gun. Nobody had shown him how to load it. Eventually, after a lengthy dither, the young American decided to fire a warning shot. Pulling out his own pistol and taking unsteady aim, he fired. There was a roar that shook the forest and a noise like rushing wind as a colony of a thousand giant fruit bats took fright and wump-wumped their way through the forest to find a more peaceful spot for their inverted siestas.

When the three of them opened their eyes, the Japanese flier was still hanging there, looking down miserably. Blocking one ear, the soldier squeezed the trigger once more. In his efforts to dodge the bullets, which he was now certain were aimed directly at him, the pilot was wiggling his legs like a cyclist in the Tour de France.

This action dislodged him from the branch to which he was so insecurely attached, and like a winged cockatoo he spiraled down, landing on Jimmy and the inept corporal, who in an attempt to take evasive action had run into each other. The three adversaries were knocked out but so, unfortunately, was Wuni's eye. Despite the ministrations of a U.S. army surgeon in the field hospital, there was nothing that could be done to save it.

"The two fellows came out to see me here last year. We've kept in touch over the years, y'know. Of course they're getting on a bit now; might be their last trip," he said, as he wiped his ancient eye and eventually paused.

"Yes, well, thank you very much for telling me. Nice story. Very interesting."

So absorbed had I become, I had failed to notice the hour slip by. The sun was now high in the sky, and it was time to get down to business. "Now, I wondered if we could talk chickens for a moment?"

"But of course, what would you like to discuss?"

"Well, my friends and I . . ." I glanced over to Tassels, who was snoring very gently. The two boys were now lying out full stretch on the ground. "Well, we are interested in buying some chicken feed and some day-old chicks."

"No problem," Wuni replied thoughtfully, "no problem at all."

Standing and picking up the tray in his wide-stretched arms, he clambered up the high steps back into his house.

Wonderful. This was easier than I had thought it was going to be. We might even be able to take some today—except we did not have anywhere to keep them. I was sure we could overcome that. We could give, say, a dozen to each family to look after for a couple of days. No, that probably wasn't too practical. My mind raced. We could sort something out.

Shortly he returned, holding a square of white card. "Here you are, this is the place to go." He held it out.

"I, I'm sorry. I don't under— Could you just say that again? I thought you had—"

"No, I gave up doing chickens about five years ago. Well, it was all getting a bit too difficult. You know how it is?"

I did not.

"But I thought you said no problem?" My disappointment was leaving my politeness behind.

"Well, there is no problem. Just go and see this chap." He proffered the card again.

Taking it, I turned it and read the inscription:

MR. WU
HONIARA

Wuni, leaning heavily on his stick, his pipe clenched firmly between his teeth, looked up at me as I read it.

"Mr. Wu. He can help you, but he won't give his chickens to just anybody, y'know. You absolutely must say that I sent you, and then he will make a nice price for you."

"Oh, I see. Well, that's great; so where will I find Mr. . . . err . . . Wu? Do you have a phone number or an address or anything?"

"No, but go to Chinatown and ask for him there. Someone will be able to lead you to him."

"Right, so I just go to the capital and ask for Mr. Wu and then someone will tell me where he is and then I will buy his chickens and come back with them." I fear at this stage I let a note of sarcasm creep into my voice.

"What other choice have you got, old boy? What other choice?"

"Yes, well, I see."

I woke the others and, yawning, they thanked him for tea.

"Do pop in again anytime. So interesting to talk to you, Wilf."

I looked back and waved at Wuni and Muriel, who dwarfed him now as she stood at his side. They raised their hands in farewell. As we meandered back slowly to the sea, I shook my head in disbelief. The whole thing was farcical. Did he really think that I was going to hike all the way to Honiara to try to find a Chinese man on the off chance that he might have some chickens for sale? It was ridiculous. He must think I was stark staring mad.

"Come on, old boy!" Stanley laughed from farther down below.

Coming, coming, old man.

CHAPTER 11

⌘

The Television
Personality

O kay. So, how do I look from this soide? Any better? Yeah,
this soide'll be the go. Move that loight a bit, would ya,
mate? It's shining roight in me oyes."

There was lot of shuffling and adjusting taking place at the
far end of the bar at the guesthouse. From the other end of the
long room, I watched as heaps of electrical equipment and coils
of cable were rearranged around the corpulent figure astride the
barstool.

"Who's he?" I asked Gerry, who had just joined me at the
table, which was tucked under one of the conch-shell lamps
and where I was writing a letter home in the fond but remote
hope of getting one in return.

"Oh, some Australian television presenter feller; can't
remember his name right at the moment. They're making some
program about fishing. How did you get on, on your trip?"

"Huh, well . . ."

I had come to town to buy a sack of flour, for pancake-making purposes, and to visit the post office for a chat with Silas the manager, who as a result of the dismal trickle of letters that made it through to Munda from Honiara, was relaxing in one of the greatest sinecures since politics was invented. Tassels, who had come with me, had run the canoe down the coast to take some sick folk to the hospital and, with time to kill before their return, I told Gerry all about Wuni and showed him the card that he had given me.

"And anyway he seemed to think that I was just going to go to Honiara and see if I could track this Mr. Wu down."

We both laughed loudly, which elicited a scowl from a crouching cameraman.

"So, what are you going to do instead?"

"Hmm?"

"Well, how are you going to get some chickens? I suppose it all depends on how much you want them. If you do, you don't really have much choice but to see if you can get hold of him."

"But I'd never find him!"

"Honiara isn't exactly Mexico City," Gerry pointed out. "Everybody knows everybody else. Particularly in Chinatown. Go on. Give it a go. Try your luck, why don't you?"

He chuckled as he saw me staring out toward Randuvu, hopelessly bogged down by my indecision. Gerry's happy-go-luck-of-the-Irish approach seemed to fit much more comfortably in the islands than my nervous concern. I made a mental note to try to adopt his style.

"You should know by now that trying to get anything sorted out here is never gonna be that easy," he added.

I nodded in agreement and sighed. All right, so now I was going to go. Or was I? Well, perhaps. Anyway, if I did go, how was I going to get there?

"So, how am I ever going to—?"

But Gerry had already gone.

The easiest way to go was by plane, but unfortunately it was also the least affordable. My savings were still roughly intact, but not robust enough for jet-setting or even taking one of the island hoppers. The trip to Gizo had been expense enough. I did not want to spend any of the "Fund" unnecessarily, as the expenses round the corner were still hazy. The only alternative that I was aware of was to hitch a ride aboard the MV *Iuminao*, a dilapidated cargo ship that steamed in perpetuity round the islands and took a night and day of extreme discomfort to make the journey from Munda to Honiara.

Romantic though the idea of sea travel might have seemed, the *Iuminao* had sometime before entered what the French call, with charming euphemism, its *troisième âge* in terms of looks and, it was generally considered, seaworthiness. Despite this, the ship was always grossly overloaded with both goods and passengers, which meant that the facilities, such as they were, rapidly filled to overflowing and would then sluice their contents across the deck on which you were fitfully sleeping. Apart from this malodorous inconvenience, Gerry was convinced that it had "gotta sink one day." Considering my present run of luck, it would come as little surprise if that one day was my day.

To be sure, nothing was at all straightforward. Oh, well, I would have to give it some more thought. But then, to my great surprise, the solution to my problem came from an entirely unexpected quarter. He was sitting on the other side of the room, a cold beer in his hand.

"Okay, Barry, mate. That'll do, won't it? I reckon we can do the rest back in the studio. What d'ya reckon?"

The bearded presenter grinned at Rachel, the shy girl who performed every role from barmaid to cook in the rest house.

"So what special something are you going to be serving up for us tonight? Something noice and sweet loike yerself, I hope. Give us a beer, love."

The short but wiry cameraman cast his eyes heavenward. He was obviously used to his presenter's natural, easy lasciviousness. He began to pack away his equipment into customized flight cases, snapping the catches closed. The presenter called across to me. "How are yer?"

"Fine, thank you." I answered cautiously and leaned over a little to see if there was any sign of Tassels on the path.

"So what brings you out to the arse end of nowhere?" He rubbed his beach-ball belly in anticipation of his evening meal.

"Well, I live on that island over there." I pointed out of the open doors.

He took a cursory glance before taking a swig of his beer before looking disapprovingly at the bottle that was engulfed in his hand.

"So what do you do out there?" he asked distractedly, as he winked at the passing, blushing Rachel.

"Well . . ." I took a deep breath. "Well, we are trying to raise chickens."

"Is that roight? So how many have you got out there?"

I knew he was going to ask that.

"Um, none right at the moment."

Actually, I need not have worried. If my answer had been three and a half million, the reaction would have been exactly the same. "Oh, yeah? Roight. Well, we're here making a documentary about fishing. I'm pretty, well, y'know, very experienced. Yeah, I've been fishing all me loife. Pretty much everywhere. What's that?"

I checked to see whether I had asked anything. No, nothing.

"Yeah, well, that's roight, all over the world. We've caught some great fish out here. Foight like crazy but we've been pretty much onto them. What sort? Oh, the usual, snapper, rainbow, wahoo, mahimahi, all the classics, that's pretty much what you would expect. Course, you're roight, I brought all me own stuff out with me, sponsored, see. Equipment out here's not up to much, but you can't be too surprised. They're pretty backward out here, eh?"

"Well, I'm not really too much of an expert—"

"Well, I suppose I am used to the best stuff back in Oz. Listen, gotta go, mate. Noice to meet ya. What did you say yer name was?"

"Will."

"Bill, that's it. Good on yer, Bill. Yeah, loike I said, I've got to go and get ready. We're flying back to Honiara tomorrow. Chartered a plane to take all our stuff. Got a lot of equipment, see. Yeah, that's roight. Film crew, see."

"Honiara? Did you say Honiara?"

"That's it. It's the capital, mate. Leaving at ten tomorrow. Got to get packed up." He made a move for the door.

There was no subtle way to go about this, but then I was not sure that that really mattered. "I wonder . . . do you think it might be possible. . . . You see, the thing is that I was hoping to go to Honiara myself. There wouldn't be any chance of catching a lift with you, would there?"

He looked surprised, then what passed for thoughtful, and finally, suddenly magnanimous. "Well, I don't see why not, mate. No, I reckon that should be pretty much alroight, but you won't be able to bring too much stuff with you, mate. It's all done on weight and we're a film crew so we've a lot of . . ."

Yes, yes, I knew.

"Thank you very much. That's great. I'll be at the airfield at ten. That's really kind of you. See you tomorrow."

"Yeah, well, no worries. See you tomorrow."

Hoisting his jeans up by the belt loops, he made for the door. As he did so, Tassels, who had tied up the canoe at the guesthouse jetty, walked in, bestowing upon him a toothless, creased grin. Starting slightly, the television personality quickened his pace, glancing over his shoulder as my friend sat down beside me and imparted the good news that only three of the ten villagers that he had taken to the hospital had tested positive for malaria.

My turn next, I supposed.

On our return to Mendali, I told Small Tome and Ellen of this lucky coincidence.

"How long will you go for?" asked Small Tome.

"I don't know," I replied. "I suppose as long as it takes to find Mr. Wu."

Ellen leaned over to Small Tome, her dark, tattooed face grave, and muttered something in their local language.

"Ellen says there are some very bad women in Honiara. She doesn't like you go around with them, and you must come back soon!"

I promised that I would be back as soon as I could and that I would make the most strenuous of efforts to stay clear of any of the honeytraps of feminine charm that the capital might have to offer. Ellen seemed placated and went off to her kitchen. "You live with us so we must look after you," declared Small Tome solemnly.

Arriving at the battered airport a few minutes early, I was carrying the very discreetest of bags. I had no idea where or, for that matter, for how long I would be staying or how much I would need to take, but above all I did not want to run the risk of being overweight. I was even willing to jettison a few items if the need arose. In the departure room was an enormous pile of cases and bags. The Australian presenter, dressed in a snappy safari suit and hat, was sitting puffing on one of the benches while an assistant, probably a key grip or best boy, checked the luggage off against a list.

"Yep." He looked up. "It's all here."

The wiry cameraman sipping on a water bottle stood up. "Right, everyone ready?"

I nodded, and we all walked out onto the frying pan of the tarmac. Shimmering, our plane awaited. It was about half the size of the one that had delivered me—a six-seater known as an Islander. The luggage was loaded in first, a lengthy and perspiration-inspiring procedure, and finally we all clambered in on top of it. The Australian presenter lay almost supine, wedging me securely into a small corner by one of the rear windows. The assistant climbed in next, followed by the cameraman, who was holding a professional-looking camera with proper black, dromedary humps. It was only at that point that I realized the door of the plane had been unbolted and stowed in the tail.

"We should get some great shots of the Vonavona Lagoon from up there," he said as he clipped one end of a mountaineer's carabiner to the metal frame of the seat and the other to his waistband. The Australian presenter groaned and closed his eyes.

"Doncha reckon we've got enough footage already?" he mumbled weakly as drops of sweat dribbled into his beard.

The pilot, a cheerful Solomon Islander, jumped into the front seat. "Everybody ready for takeoff?"

I was sure that I noticed the slightest shake of the presenter's head.

The pilot flicked a switch, and the starboard engine fired into life, quickly reaching the deafening hum of full revs. He flicked the port switch, and the propeller blades started to swing round like a lazy fan, but that was all. No roar, no puff of black smoke, just a gentle rotation.

"A problem, I think," said the pilot simply. "Let's have a look." He switched both engines off.

By the time the presenter had extricated himself, with no small amount of pushing from me and pulling from the best grip, and we were all back on the runway, the pilot had stripped off the engine housing. He was standing looking at the offending machine with his hands on his hips. "Anyone got any tool kit?" he asked breezily.

The presenter paled visibly.

Just at that moment, Gerry's mechanic, who worked pretty much full-time on broken down outboards in the area and whose name, uniquely, was Nob, came walking by. He was dispatched to his workshop on a bicycle borrowed from Silas, the postman, who had managed to find time to offer help and advice. About half an hour later Nob came pedaling back holding a small box of tools. In next to no time he and the pilot had unscrewed all six spark plugs and were blowing on them enthusiastically, polishing them on their shirts under the direction of the postmaster.

"No wari." Nob laughed over his shoulder. "Oh, me no lookim any engine like this one. Him nice tumas."

"Well, maybe we could stay another day," suggested the presenter. "We can always charter another ploine."

"One that works," he added darkly.

The pilot, who was not going to have his craft talked about so rudely, responded robustly. "No good you say this one him rubbish one. This one him nice plane. No wariwari."

So we all squeezed back on board. This time both engines fired first time and, with a thumbs-up from the pilot and polite applause from the onlookers on the ground, we taxied away from the terminal building. Takeoff was smooth, and soon we were high up above the mountains of New Georgia. The cameraman edged toward the doorway. "Fantastic!" he yelled over the wind noise.

"Fuckin' lunatic," muttered the presenter, and he closed his eyes again.

We soared over the lagoon, and as I peered through the plastic window and down past the wing strut, I wondered whether Wuni would look up and see the small plane, a white man hanging out of the door.

An hour later, we touched down on the runway at Henderson Airport and tumbled out. My traveling companions offered me a lift to the town center, which I gratefully accepted, and we started to load the innumerable bags into a waiting minibus. As the last cases came off, two men appeared from the shade of the terminal building and advanced toward the plane. Reaching in with a simultaneous groan, they pulled out a cardboard coffin from just below where the fat presenter had been sitting. It was easy to tell from their puffing and staggering that it was not empty.

They lugged the coffin in the direction of a truck that had just pulled up, swirling in diesel smoke and dust. With a one, two, three, heave they attempted to hoist it onto the back, but just as it reached the right height a handle at one end snapped, the coffin hit the ground headfirst, the top sprang off, and I closed my eyes.

After what I thought was a respectful while, I opened them again and watched as the two pallbearers darted here and there to pick up the five or six dozen coconuts that were now rolling and spinning around on Runway One. I laughed out loud with relief and turned to the others. The fat presenter had his hands clapped to his face, one over each eye.

"Oi, mate, you can come out now." The cameraman sighed as he turned to get into the bus.

Slowly the pudgy fingers parted.

By the time we arrived at the crew's hotel, the fat presenter was in the midst of a funny turn. In fact he must have been suffering quite badly because he went to his room without a beer, complaining loudly that he was going down with malaria and would someone please call a doctor. The cameraman smiled unkindly and offered to buy me a drink. "To celebrate!" He winked.

I declined. I had to find Mr. Wu.

CHAPTER 12

~ॐ~

The Big H

Honiara, as I quickly discovered, is the unsightly boil in the navel of the otherwise dazzling, seductively beautiful Solomon Islands. Fortunately, however, it is little more than a minor blemish because, as Gerry had pointed out, the capital, sitting stupefied in the heat of Guadalcanal Island, is no Mexico City. In fact, it is more reminiscent of the cardboard set of a low-budget spaghetti Western.

Slouching like a hungover vagrant against the foothills of Tandachehe Ridge, Honiara gazes blearily out across its one main street to the sea and the marine breakers' yard that is the wreckage-strewn stretch of water running between Guadalcanal and the Florida Islands. In 1942, this had been the stage for some of the biggest sea battles in history.

Local intelligence had informed the Americans that the Japanese were building an airstrip at Henderson Field on

Guadalcanal as a springboard for the further invasion of Pacific islands including New Zealand and Australia. The U.S. Navy decided it was time to act. The subsequent Battle of Savo on August 9, 1942, proved to be one of the greatest defeats in its naval history. Subsequent counterattacks here and in the Western Province, on the islands surrounding Randuvu, did finally force the Japanese back, and the terrible bloodshed in this quiet corner of the world proved to be a turning point in the Pacific campaign. Seventy warships and more than a thousand planes were destroyed, but the loss of life was so great that the actual number of casualties is meaningless. Suffice it to say that this now quiet piece of ocean is known as Iron Bottom Sound. Ironically or fittingly or perhaps both, construction of the present-day international airport was financed in 1996 by the Japan government.

Mendana Avenue, the main strip in Honiara, served as an unsurfaced obstacle course for the convoys of battered imported cars and pickup trucks jolting and jouncing through the dust that hung permanently over the town like a comic-strip fart.

Arching my back, perhaps a little like a matador, I managed to avoid the gray splash of a puddle thrown up by the wheels of a bulging minibus. It groaned on, hooting asthmatically, through the crowds that had chosen to come to live and wheeze in this grimy metropolis, in search, no doubt, of wealth and fortune and the heaps of cheap plastic crap that were emblematic of much admired Western prosperity. Dick Whittington, despite exhortations to give Honiara a second chance, would have taken one look and run.

"Get down to the yacht club," Gerry had advised. "There's always loads of people at the bar. Sure there'll be someone there who'll be getting you pointed in the right direction."

Leaving the shade of the hotel entrance, I had successfully negotiated the main road and set off down a side street, which led toward the docks. Ahead of me were open metal gates, and I could hear the hubbub of noise inside as the members of the Point Cruz Yacht Club assembled for lunch. I signed my name in a visitors' book and went in. The clubroom had, it seemed, been designed by someone with qualifications in aeronautical architecture and opened at one end to the tepid sea. Fans stirred an atmosphere of outdated exclusivity and wafted the smell of stale tobacco and narrow-mindedness over almost entirely white heads.

Down one side ran a lengthy bar, at which sat a dozen men, each with a glass or sometimes two in front of him. Not wanting to look out of place, I ordered a beer. As I waited for it to be poured, I smiled and muttered hello to the gentleman who, dressed in shorts and socks, both knee-length, sat on the next stool. Turning, he looked at me as if I had just asked whether I could purchase his daughter at a substantial discount. With something between a snarl and a snort, he slid from his seat and made his way unsteadily to the other side of the room.

"Bloody man just came up to me and started talking. I've been a member here for nearly seventeen years. Seventeen bloody years, and he just starts talking to me. Jesus!" he complained loudly to a deaf waiter.

I paid for my drink and smiled weakly at the man who sat on the stool to my other side.

"Ahh, y'down wanna lissen to him. M'serable ol' bugger. Alwez m'serable," he said kindly if a little incoherently. "Jus' arrive?"

"Well, yes, just this morning."

"Don, m'name's Don." He wiped a moist hand on his shirt-front and stuck it out. His head, shining from ear to ear under the few strands of black hair that were scraped over his scalp, wobbled slightly as, with no small effort, he raised his eyes to meet mine. He belched and some little while later put his hand over his mouth. "Juss ask me anything yer need t'know, anything, an' I'll tell yer."

"Well, as a matter of fact, I'm trying to get to Chinatown."

Only when he reached for a pile of beer mats and began to lay them out with the utmost concentration on the counter did I realize my mistake.

"Right, Shinatown, right. So thississus—the yoclub." He stabbed at one of the cardboard squares, which went spinning away onto the floor.

"No, shorry thississus." He managed to pin another one down. "Where didju say you wannid to go? Shinatown? Yushed Shinatown?"

This was a disaster.

"Excuse me, it's Will, isn't it?"

From the floor, where I was making an escape attempt under the guise of looking for the errant beer mat, I looked up at a friendly, attractive woman and a smiling, shaven-headed man.

"You don't remember us, do you?"

"Oh, hello!" I said, dredging my memory. "I . . . umm . . ."

Then, fortunately, it came back to me. "Yes, yes. It's Jane and Nick, isn't it? We met at the rest house. How are you?" I asked a little too effusively.

"Shinatown . . ."

"Good, good, thanks."

Jane was an agricultural adviser who worked for one of the bigger aid agencies. Nick, her husband, was the skipper of a trawler but was on leave and along for the ride. They were both from New Zealand, and I had enjoyed meeting them in Munda, where Jane had given a series of workshops about growing vegetables.

Unlike most of the other charitable types who wandered through, she exuded an air of efficiency and knowledgeable professionalism. She had also seemed to be more interested in making progress than in making purchases in the guesthouse's tiny gift shop, which seemed to be permanently abustle with young men in ponytails and sandals and earnest girls in long floral dresses, murmuring in awestruck tones, "Mom's just going to love this," or "Honey, he says he doesn't take U.S. dollars. Can you believe that?"

I managed to extricate myself from Don, who was staring uncomprehendingly at his map, by assuring him that his directions had been excellent. He nodded in serious agreement and set about the not inconsiderable task of getting his glass off the bar and some, at least, of the contents into his mouth. We retreated to an unoccupied shelf that surrounded a pillar in the center of the room.

Jane and Nick waited patiently as I somewhat long-windedly explained what had brought me to Honiara. "But I could have done without the dolphin hunting," I finished, feeling queasy at the memory.

Jane laughed. "I tried to set up a village-based beef cattle project in Makira, but when it came to slaughtering them, the villagers had become so fond of them that they had given them all pet names. They refused, point-blank, to allow anyone to get near them. Eventually, they knocked down the fences of the paddock and let the cattle go in the middle of the night."

You say tomato and I say tomato.

"Right, we better get going," she said as she scooped up her keys from the ledge. "Where are you staying, Will?"

"Well, I am not quite sure at the moment," I admitted, and so with a generosity and hospitality that the English find overwhelming as well as slightly odd, they both immediately said that, of course, in that case, I was to come and stay with them.

"We'll sort you out. Let's head on up to the house." Jane jumped up enthusiastically.

"We'll go to the gas shop, tomorrow," Nick said enigmatically as I clambered into the back of the white four-wheel-drive pickup, admiring the pink, swirly artwork on the side that read

SOLOMON ISLANDS WOMEN'S AGRICULTURAL ADVICE SUPPORT GROUP. I bounced about as we rattled up and over the deep ridges that ran down from the crest of hills that encircled the town. As we rounded a bend I caught a glimpse of the interior of the island, of flat pastures and leafy villages. Nick gestured out of the window with a flick of his thumb. "See that? That's GRA territory."

If a day walking around the town was a tiring, depressing, and dirty affair with not much to recommend it, then it seemed that a day walking around outside the town was a worrying, risky, and on occasion downright dangerous affair with nothing at all to recommend it. Outside the city limits of Honiara was bandit country, ruled by the GRA, the Guadalcanal Republican Army, or one of its various guises—the young troublemakers changed their name every time they watched a new Hollywood action film on their stolen video player.

Initially they had banded together resentful of the influx of "immigrants" from different Solomon Islands who had come to Honiara. In order to prevent them spreading farther into the island, they had arranged roadblocks at either end of the town. The "immigrants," in order to protect themselves from these hooligans, had arranged their own roadblocks on their side, and the result was stagnant gridlock. Honiara, however, was, to all intents and purposes, blockaded, and deliveries of supplies could arrive only by sea. Now the GRA sat in the outback and waited for something to happen. So far nothing had, but they had contented themselves, in the meantime, with some fairly leisurely looting of abandoned outlying houses and a subsequent modicum of arson.

Equipped with homemade weapons fashioned out of rusting lumps of metal salvaged from World War II dumps and loaded with handmade ammunition, the GRA were to be considered dangerous more for their lack of organization and discipline than for their firepower. The situation was, nevertheless, still taken seriously enough for the double checkpoints at either end of the town to have remained in place. It goes without saying that it was within the confines of these roadblocks that I proposed to stay. Despite this, Honiara was, of course, a much safer place, in terms of risk to the individual, than the vast majority of European cities and, compared to any American one, it was a walk in the park, although admittedly a pretty scruffy one.

Pulling up on a circular drive, we climbed out in front of a brick villa built, rather precariously, over a sharp incline. Negotiating a guard dog with a shameless nose and a saliva imbalance, I followed my friends in through the front door. It was only then that I realized how long it had been since I had visited a "real" house. There were tiles on the floor, glass in the windows, switches on the walls, and, enshrined in an alcove of the open-plan living room, a television set. I felt slightly overawed.

"Here you go. This is where you are," Jane said, opening a door off the hallway.

Lit by a floor-to-ceiling picture window, it was a grand room furnished with cupboards, a dressing table with mirror, and a four-poster bed, which, draped as it was with a mosquito net that hung from its center, looked like a medieval caravan. I tested it, and the water-filled mattress wobbled like a huge jelly. Through another door, on the far side, was a bathroom, and in it were two hand basins, a bidet, a bath, and a separate shower. I counted. Ten taps. Nine more than in the whole of Mendali.

I ran my hand over the wooden and plastic surfaces, then looked out the window across the swimming pool to the sea. Much of the town was hidden from view by trees; Honiara suddenly began to look quite appealing.

"What a great place," I exclaimed as Jane took some folded towels from a cupboard and placed them on a chair by a trouser press, into which I had every intention of slipping my shorts at a later stage.

"It is nice, but it isn't ours. Actually it belongs to the deputy high commissioner. He and his wife are away on leave at the moment. All the people who normally look after the house, all the servants, are on holiday. We are just house sitting. Talking of which, I've been invited to a drinks party by one of the big aid agency bosses this evening. Would you like to come?"

Certainly I would.

"Unfortunately, I don't really have any clothes to speak of."

"Just borrow some of Nick's. They should fit you."

About an hour later, having showered off the dirt of the day and played around for a while with the bidet, which had a jet that nearly but not quite hit the ceiling, I squeezed myself into a pair of Nick's slightly too tight, very much too short, beige chinos. The four inches between five foot ten and six foot two represented a larger difference in size than Jane had imagined. Unfortunately, this made sitting difficult and bending over an impossibility. It seemed, though, that my sense of fashion, never a strong point, had slipped so far down my list of priorities that I happily zipped myself into a pair of borrowed gray, ankle-height boots with pixie points. If I crooked my legs slightly, they almost met the bottom of my trousers. I found some Indonesian aftershave in the bathroom cupboard (at least I think it was Indonesian—and aftershave—it certainly smelled pretty powerful) and gave my shirt a good dousing. Practicing a couple of dance moves in the mirror as I passed, I went out the door and without further ado was whisked off to the party.

With a crunch of spotless gravel we swept up in the Women's Agricultural Advice truck to the door of a grand residence. Nick rang the doorbell, and a Solomon Islander uncomfortable in waitressing uniform opened the door. It had been a few years since I had done any regular gate crashing, so I was feeling rather nervous. I crouched and felt the comfort of trouser meeting boot as we went in.

"Darlings!" whooped a woman dressed in a green velvet

dress and pearls. She held a champagne glass and a crumpled paper napkin in one hand and a cigarette, complete with gravity-defying ash, in the other. Crumbs of puff pastry peeked from her cleavage and dusted the sides of her heavily lipsticked mouth.

"Paula, we've brought a friend, Will. He lives out near Munda, you know?"

"The provinces, how wonderful." She planted on my cheek a kiss, which succeeded in being both wet and sticky at the same time. "God, I wish I could go somewhere like that. . . . Anywhere, in fact."

I straightened up, fearing knee lock. "I hope you don't mind me just turning up like this—"

"Mind, why should I mind? More the merrier." She grinned lopsidedly and fiddled playfully with her pearls. "Just hope *you* don't mind all the unbelievable bores that seem to have turned up tonight. Now where did I put that fucking gin?"

She steamed off in the direction of what appeared to be the lavatory, leaving a trail of ash and smoke in her wake.

"That's the wife!" Nick chuckled. "Just wait till you meet 'His Excellency'! Right Royal Ronnie, we call him."

We walked down a short, wide flight of steps, across a near empty room, and through some French windows out into a large garden. The air was heavy with airport boutique perfume and a strong scent of self-importance.

Just as people like to join clubs to reenact the battles of the English Civil War or dress up in 1940s clothes to dance the jitterbug, I appeared to have stumbled upon a reunion of the Colonial Debauchery Appreciation Society, whose members' aims were to talk at great length, generally on the fascinating subject of the person who was speaking, and drink the assembled company under the table. The meeting was really going very well.

Like Grimble's social world in the Gilbert and Ellice Islands, the expat community had always been small in the Solomons, which, being some several months of travel away from family and friends, did not feature in the top twenty popular far-flung outposts of the British Empire. Indeed for many years they were run almost single-handedly by Charles Morris Woodford, who had been appointed as the first British commissioner over the protectorate in 1896. For nearly twenty years, with only a couple of dozen men to help him, he had been responsible for 100,000 islanders, most of whom were enthusiastic headhunters. Drawing only a civil servant's wage and living in the most basic of circumstances, he had "governed" the Solomons until 1915, when he had retired. In all that time he had remained resolutely unarmed, attempting instead to convince the warlike islanders of the benefits of peace. He had installed a system of government and justice that was still in operation today.

How he might have enjoyed the lifestyle of the aid workers who had flooded the country since independence: the return flights home, the houses, the cars, the diving lessons, the health and pension packages, and, of course, the strings of zeros attached to the tax-free salaries. These were all, it seemed, basic requirements. Mind you, if he had had, as part of his job description, to attend many functions like this, he might have been less envious.

A stage overhung by bobbing trees was being set up for a performance by a local pipe band in traditional dress of leaves and shells. They were starkly in contrast to the guests, dressed in limp suits and damp, dated dresses. The drink appeared to have been flowing for a little while, and I was greeted by a number of strangers as they careered past. Most were already shouting. A pale South African brought us drinks. Grasping three glasses in one hand, he filled them to the slopping brim.

"Great party, yis, great party. You can always count on old Ronnie for a great party. You British, mon?" he asked me as he handed me a glass with a circular motion of his arm.

"I am."

"Well, cheers, old chap." He laughed, not unpleasantly, and raised the bottle of wine above his head before taking a swig from it.

Nick and Jane were quickly lassoed by some Americans that they knew, and I stood alone, surrounded by an ever-increasing barrage of noise, catching snatches of conversation.

"So why don't you let the dog use the front door and the house girl can just go round the back?" said a severely plucked woman, her lidless eyeballs swimming with burst blood vessels.

"I don't mind, but I don't want either of them using the pool," replied a man. His bottle black hair and gray roots shone in the loops of festive lights.

"You can buy real Italian mozzarella from that new store by the open market. They make it in New Zealand from yaks or something. Fly it in. It's pretty good the sort of supplies they can get in these days."

"When we next go on leave, Margaret says she is going to have a face-lift."

"'Bout bloody time too!"

"Yeh, but the worst of it is, I'll have to pay for it. No chance of getting that on overseas expenses, I suppose, eh? Ha, ha!"

From inside a smart-looking shuttered veranda came a gale of laughter and the wet smash of a dropped bottle.

"Naturally, our aid program is ze best in ze whole islands; it is—how you guys say?—bloody marvelous. Next year ven Dieter vill be taking his retirement I vill become Direktor—pretty good, huh?"

"Listen, mate, why do you think your program is so . . ."

"So who have we got here?" A voice boomed in my ear. "Who invited you then, friend?"

"Err . . . well, as a matter of fact . . ." I found myself looking at a crooked, skinny man in his fifties. His thin, cigarette
smoke hair was brushed straight backward, accentuating the
length of his nose. This extraordinarily long but lumpy
appendage was the color of the claret that he sniffed as he
swilled his glass. His watery eyes blinked as he cut me off in full
falter. "What's your name, young man?"

I told him.

"Well, I'm Ronnie, and it's good to have you on board. Let
me show you around, introduce you to a few people."

Did people really still talk like that?

Gripping my shoulders, he propelled me along, like a
shopper pushing his trolley, as we wheeled through the crowd.

"Susan, this is a new chap in town. Look after him and do
try not to be too miserable."

"Yes, Ronnie," Susan answered meekly. Susan's husband
was "in oil," and their three teenage children were at boarding
school in England. "I would much rather they were here, but I
suppose it's for the best. And, of course, the company pays for
everything."

I made a vast error of judgment in telling her that I had
once been a teacher myself. This prompted her to pull out a picture of her offspring and give me a tearful blow-by-blow
account of their academic progress or, in one case, lack of it.

"Freddy has never been that good at school things, you
know. Pretty good at all sorts of other things like . . . err . . . puz-
zles and that sort of thing, much better than me, you know; he's
not thick, I mean . . ." She stared at the photo thoughtfully. "I
was absolutely hopeless at school, and I don't think I'm thick,
although Gerald always says I am. Do you think I'm thick?
Sorry, what was your . . . ?"

The pipe band struck up, beating out rhythms on lengths
of bamboo and singing about goodness knows what. Nobody
looked round or paid them the slightest attention apart from an

automatic smattering of applause at the end of each song. Nick pushed his way through the crowd, making a face. "When you are ready to go just give us a nod. Okay?"

I nodded.

Jane was looking pained by a lengthy discourse on European involvement in the Solomons, which was being delivered by a fat Finn who was at least sober. She was delighted to get away. We'd just made it to the front door when we were stopped in our tracks. "And where do you young things think you are off to?" It was "His Excellency."

We made some excuses about having to get up early and having a busy day tomorrow. Ronnie made some deeply improper suggestions about the real reasons that we were leaving and offered to see us out. At the car we were poised to say our farewells when he suddenly turned an extremely strange shade of off-white, gurgled, staggered a few paces, leaned against a palm tree, and threw up copiously. We waited in embarrassed silence. He eventually came back, wiping his mouth with a handkerchief.

"Sorry," he whispered with a spittle-flecked smile. "Just had to clear my throat."

◂▰▸

Mr. Wu

Atop the sloshing water bed, I dreamed that I had been cast adrift on a raft circled by sharks dressed in white linen suits while the Commander puffed past me disapprovingly in his immaculate steamer. Later I feared that I would drown in a terrible sea of watery pancake mixture and dolphin blood presided over by Royal Ronnie, swigging all the while from a bottle in which he had imprisoned the tearful Susan. When morning came I was much relieved to be able to paddle my way to the edge of the bed and roll out, crashing onto the cool tile.

Nick and I thumped and bumped our way back down the hill into town. Parking in front of one of the novelty shops that sold limitless tat to those who had something to spend, we hurried down the road toward the gas shop.

Sunlight was doing its best to glance off the concrete, mock-leaf roof of the central market. The twelve stars of the

European Union were emblazoned over the front entrance, where they shone in a self-congratulatory circle. The open hall was teeming with people, and the stalls were ready for their inquisitive hands. Woven baskets full of sweet potatoes and cassava were piled up in dark, dusty pyramids, and cherry toma- toes were arranged on a baize of wilted leaves like uniform bil- liard balls waiting to be sold for a dollar a frame. In one of the farthest corners a shy man with a knife sat on a stool in front of a huge pile of coconuts. He would lop off the top of one of them, pop in a straw, hand it over to his thirsty customer, and accept the money wordlessly before sitting back down again, staring firmly at the floor. Children sat on the entrance steps chewing sticks of yellow-green sugarcane as their parents sold the previous night's catch out of big insulated boxes. Rummag- ing in the ice, they pulled out weird species, caricatures of nor- mal fish, and threw them into the purchasers' arms before taking the money in crimped, blue-black hands.

Pushing through the gathering crowds outside Honiara Bookshop, which advertised itself to be "Namabawan bookstore long Solomon Islan" and which sold an astonishing variety of garbage but, as far as I could see through the double doors, no books, we arrived on the doorstep of the gas shop. It was closed but, as it was not yet half past nine, we sat on the pavement and waited. After only an hour in the dripping heat, the door was unbolted from the inside. We entered in time to see the man- ager disappearing out through the back. Humming tunelessly, I inspected the stock while we waited for his return.

The shop was crammed with rice cookers, lamps, ovens and refrigerators, woks, boilers, kettles and stoves, in fact every gas appliance conceivable except, of course, fires and heaters. I noticed some small individual gas rings. I lifted one of the paper-and-string tags. They were extremely cheap and I was considering buying one for Ellen when the man came back.

"Oh, hello, I am looking for Mr. Wu." By now asking absurd questions had become second nature.

The man looked at me with some suspicion.

"Mr. Wu is not here. He does not come here anymore. He must stay at the farm."

"The farm, what farm?"

"The farm down at Red Beach, where he keeps the chickens."

"Chickens, he says he's got chickens!" I shouted at Nick, who did not look suitably impressed. "Yes, that's the one I want. Please, could you tell me how to get to Red Beach?"

"Down the coast about seven miles."

"Great, thanks, bye."

I hurried from the shop, and Nick followed, the man in the shop looking curiously after us. I turned to him. "Look, Nick, do you think there is any chance . . . ? Perhaps you're busy? I mean, if it's too far . . ."

"Well, if you want to risk the roadblocks, then I'm up for it."

"Err . . . well . . ."

Some bread, a tin of corned beef, and a few bottles of water were packed as provisions, although I am not sure why we bought the corned beef as we both knew it was disgusting—a sort of vibrant pink paste with gristly bits. We set off toward the roadblock at the ominously named Alligator Creek.

Wearing my bushwhacker shorts and boots, my explorer's hat and pioneering sunglasses, I was feeling quite the part as we drove down the road that straightened out of town. Somewhere very deep inside me and not in any great quantity I was discovering my spirit of adventure.

We rattled across a railway-tie bridge high over a mudflat riverbed. Mangroves grew thickly on the banks down below, and a trickle of water slithered its way across the ooze. Alligator

Creek and the roadblock. In any event, it was deserted, and we rolled slowly on down the road.

High in a pencil cedar to our left, a male frigate bird puffed up to an impressive display of courtship. (Although why we were being so honored, I was unsure.) As he stretched his glossy black wings wide, his pink crop swelled, I am sorry to have to say, like a giant pair of testicles. Nick pointed out the rare Sanford's eagle circling in a descending spiral directly over the road. To my untrained eye, it looked distinctly like a vulture and was certainly as menacing. Gliding across the sun, it was eclipsed into shadowy silhouette. Bobbing and whirring through the trees, a white-collared woodpecker followed the course of a nimble stream that sped round the roots of aged trees.

Up on our left was a sign partly obscured by foliage. RED BEACH, 5 KM. As we neared it, we could both clearly see that its tin surface was pockmarked with bullet holes. It could, of course, have been the woodpecker.

Passing a Japanese war memorial, we crossed through some ill-tended rice fields and entered a forest of pometia trees, their shiny trunks ghostly in the shaded light.

"We must be pretty close by now. Keep your eyes peeled."

Nick slowed down, hunching up to the steering wheel to see better through the windshield, which had now become a smear of dust, splattered insects, and the last couple of squirts of water left in the windscreen washer. A building shone whitely up ahead, an American-style homestead. A broken gate would once have opened onto a carefully laid front garden, which was now much overgrown. Immediately, I felt there was something not quite right, and then, of course, I realized what it was. The house had no roof. We pulled up and, getting out rather slowly, approached. As there was clearly not much point in knocking, we tried the front door handle. The door was locked. We followed the dwelling round and, as we peered through a shattered window, we could see dark marks scorched up the walls and smell the pungent reek of smoke and damp ash.

"I think this must have been the place, the place where old Ted Birch used to live."

A Yorkshire man with a ready sense of humor and a rough tongue, Ted Birch had brought his wife, Anne, out to the islands just after the war. In an old, reputedly pretty unseaworthy, wooden cargo ship, the *Blue Porpoise,* they had pottered in and around the islands of the Central Province as traders, delivering supplies to far-flung colonials, colonels and commanders, and to the fledgling village stores. Ted and Anne provided the kerosene, cooking oil, and soap that the villagers required and, rather than return to Honiara unladen, they took delivery of sacks of cocoa and copra, the dried kernel of the coconut, bound for the oil-processing plants at Yandina. These sat in the hold alongside the wooden ornaments and utensils that they bought from carver communities deep in the bush. Wrapped in calico, the lustrous ebony bowls and mythical rosewood figurines inlaid with shell remained protected from the elements for the duration of the voyage. Once returned to Honiara, Ted and Anne sold them to departing expats who would take them home as presents or mementos "of our time in the Tropics." No doubt, hidden away behind lace curtains, they still incongruously decorate the hallways and front rooms of carefully kept houses in Croydon and Crawley.

On one such trip to the Reef and Santa Cruz Islands, Anne had contracted malaria. Sick though she was, there was no real cause for concern because, just a couple of days' sail away in Honiara, treatment could be found. But then, just off Tinakula, the engine stopped. Although they had plentiful supplies of food and water, it took Ted three days to isolate the problem and repair the engine while Anne lay feverish in a cabin above him. By the time they got under way again Anne was dangerously, deliriously ill. As the *Blue Porpoise* came alongside the wharf in Honiara, she died.

Having no desire to carry on cruising without his shipmate of more than thirty years, Ted had sold the boat and come ashore, moving to a house in Red Beach. He had eventually retired and, although popular with the islanders and expats alike, he became a virtual recluse. When the trouble started, most of his neighbors fled to the safety of Honiara. He refused.

"Bugger tha'."

The inevitable happened. He returned one evening from his weekly trip to town to find a gang of young boys delighting in dismantling his house and destroying its contents. They were armed with homemade guns, spears, and machetes. Incensed, the Englishman strode into his castle and without a word disarmed a surprised twelve-year-old, grabbing him by the ear. His accomplices deserted their partner in crime and disappeared off into the gloom. Still holding on to the ear, Ted made radio contact with the police and asked them to come as quickly as they could. When they arrived, he handed over the youthful prisoner but was irritated when the sergeant made light of the confiscated weapon.

"These never go off, you know." He chortled as he roughly propped it in the corner of the room. There was promptly an ear-splitting explosion as the handmade cartridge detonated, nicking the sergeant's right buttock and blowing a huge hole in Ted's prized gramophone. Ted packed his remaining possessions into his truck and took off for town. The following night his house was torched.

I sniffed nervously. "Well, there doesn't seem to be anybody here much. Perhaps we ought to make a move."

"Where to?"

I wasn't terribly sure.

We climbed back into the pickup. I wasn't feeling quite as

gung ho as I had when we set off out of town. Apart from anything else, driving along in a women's self-help truck that had
pink squiggly writing on the sides rather deflated my macho
pretensions. What was more, there was a distinctly eerie atmosphere in this abandoned clearing among the trees, which
intensified as the vulture floated back into view.

Nick started up the engine, and we whined backward out
of the driveway. We had followed the road a little farther and I
was about to suggest that we turn back when Nick slowed to a
stop.

"Look, through there!"

I peered past him into the bush. Through a tangle of trees
and vines, I could just make out an oblong building. A slender
trail, quite overgrown but passable, led toward it. We pulled
over onto the verge. Foolishly, I took up the vanguard and, with
Nick close behind, I could not allow myself the luxury of second thoughts. Facing us stood a pair of large doors at one end of
a warehouse. To the right was a cookhouse, but no smoke rose
from it. Silence. And, however hard I strained my ears, I
couldn't hear any cheeping.

"Call out," Nick suggested. "We don't want someone taking potshots at us."

Very true.

Uncertain what to call under such circumstances, I
cleared my throat. "Hello, any chickens for sale?" We are
unarmed and come in friendship.

My voice should have been much louder, but the sound
did not seem to want to come. I tried again. "Hello, is there anybody there?" This was a better effort. Like Grimble's "my legs
began to feel more stick-like than they normally were."

We listened. Then with a slight creak one of the doors
opened a crack, and I suddenly found myself face-to-face with
Nick. Turned back around, I saw a blinking Chinese face peer
out.

"Wha' you wan'?" he asked, but not aggressively.

"Mr. Wu?"

"Yes."

It was he! It was Mr. Wu! I stepped out into the light.

"How you fine me?" Good question.

"Wuni sent me. He said you might have some day-old chicks that I could buy from you."

"Ah, ma ow fren Wuni. Cumminsigh." With that he pushed the door wider open and disappeared. Following him, we found ourselves in a room open to the rafters. It was dark, but a few shafts of dusty sunlight, like expensive spotlights, had pierced between the planks that walled the building. In one corner was a pile of copra sacks, which seemed to double as a bed, and at the back of the room were a gas ring, a gas bottle, and a few packets of food. On the dirt floor stood a wooden table piled high with papers and office paraphernalia. Suspended just above it by a long chain that ran from a beam high up in the roof space was an old-fashioned bronze scale, the lead weights divided equally on either side so that it balanced perfectly. It twisted slowly in the still air.

Mr. Wu was a man of indeterminate age dressed entirely in navy blue. He wore a cotton jacket that buttoned up to the neck, calf-length trousers, and a pair of slippers. His hair, neatly parted, shone, and his eyes gleamed in the gloom. When he spoke it was at great speed and with an almost impenetrable accent. For the greater part I had no idea what he was saying.

"No chicken."

This, by contrast, was easy enough to understand, although I tried not to believe my ears. I had not risked life and limb to get here only to be told "No chicken." I felt like throttling Mr. Wu or bursting into tears or laughter or all three simultaneously. Perhaps sensing some threat to his personal security, he added, "No chicken this wee. Ness wee. Egg hatch ness wee. This wee use ing yoo batter. So ready ness wee."

"Batter?" Ing yoo batter? What the hell was he talking about?

"Incubator," whispered Nick.

"Oh, yes. Incubator, of course, absolutely. Ing yoo batter, yes, yes, good." I hardly knew what one was.

"Cumeyeshoyoo." He ushered us through a door.

Laid out on the floor in a room similar to the first were dozens of square boxes with clear plastic lids. Underneath each lid I could see in grids about a hundred indentations, and resting in each one was an egg. Above them all hung strong lamps with aluminum shades. Mr. Wu saw me looking curiously.

"Owsae, Jenny Reya."

"He's got a generator outside," hissed Nick.

"I know," I hissed back. I would have got there in the end. We both smiled at Mr. Wu. Back in the front room, he sat at his desk.

"So how many yoo rike?" He fitted a pair of gold-rimmed half-moon glasses to his nose and pulled out a ledger from the pile.

"Two hundred, please."

"Derively where?"

"Err . . . Munda."

"Nine hundred fifty dollar." This he pronounced very distinctly. Almost exactly what Warren had forecast. I handed the money over in the green fifty-dollar Solomon bills, ominously decorated with sharks and crocodiles. He counted them carefully, turning them occasionally to make sure they were all the same way round, and then with a lick of his thumb he counted them through again with practiced ease. He wrote me out a receipt, signing it with a complicated signature in Chinese.

"Allive next Fliday." In about ten days.

"Morne fry." On the first plane, perfect.

When I explained to him that I wanted to order two hundred every two weeks, he looked most pleased and explained how to pay the money into his account at the bank in Munda. When he had received the money he would dispatch the chicks. He wrote an account number on the receipt and handed it to me with both hands.

"Do you sell feed as well?"

"Honiala" was his only suggestion. I did not mind. We'd achieved enough for one day. Thanking him, we made for the door. As we left I noticed a revolver hanging from a nail.

"Do you get much trouble here?"

"No tlubble. Anywa come, bang, bang!" He mimed firing off two rounds most expertly.

I ducked, and we jumped back into the truck, setting off in the direction of the town. The barrier still pointed heaven-ward, and there was no sign of life at the roadblocks, so we drove straight through and, with a last glance, I put bandit country behind me.

At least we'd not had to eat our corned beef.

~≈~

CHAPTER 14

Catching the Boat

"Two days we've been waiting for this feed—two days!" I grumbled as we sat on the edge of the wharf at Munda.

Just before lunch on the day after our meeting with Mr. Wu, I had at last tracked down some of the sacks of evil-smelling brown pellets that chickens, apparently, found so appetizing. Hurrying to the shipping office at the docks, before allowing myself the luxury of a flight home, I attempted to arrange their delivery. The clerk consulted his timetables ponderously.

"The ship will leave on Saturday."

"Great, so when does it arrive in Munda?" I asked, holding the door half open.

He consulted a number of different pieces of paper on the table in front of him and then, confused, some more in a pile on the floor.

"Monday," he finally pronounced, after a great deal of mysterious scribbling and crossing out on a notepad. Then, after a short pause, he added, "Or . . . maybe Thursday."

Solomon Time.

Waiting was a pastime that I prided myself on having adapted to well since my arrival. Never a devotee of deadlines, I agreed that if something happened a little behind schedule it was unlikely to have any significant effect. The world would continue to turn on its axis, if indeed that is what it does.

(Small Tome and I had discussed this at some length.

"How do you know it does?" he asked.

"Well, it does; everybody knows that."

"Well, I don't!" he said, triumphantly proving his point.

I blushed deeply.)

In any case, no action that I took seemed to have the slightest effect on anything, so, generally speaking, I was happy to relax and indulge in the pointless pleasure of hope.

Only a few weeks before, on a Thursday, we'd paddled to a football competition up in the Vonavona Lagoon, just along from Vella Lavella. I had been appointed manager and team coach, although I was not terribly well qualified for the job. Kickoff for the first match was to have taken place at eleven that morning. Nobody was quite on time, but by four in the afternoon all but one of the teams had arrived.

The Hutuna team appeared only the following morning because a wantok had borrowed the village canoe to go fishing. Striking a rich run of tuna, he had made a unilateral decision to return it a bit later than agreed. The team, when eventually they beached their boat at the nearest spot as the kurru kurru flew, had sprinted through a few surprised gardens and on up the road, changing into their uniforms as they came. This effort resulted only in individual injury and collective exhaustion. They need not have worried, as the organizers and referees had finished marshaling another competition only that lunchtime. By the time they had installed themselves in the officials' hut on the side of the pitch and set up their public address system, there was just time to announce that the competition would be delayed until the following morning. Unfortunately Saturday was the day of rest for the Seventh-Day Adventist teams and Sunday the Sabbath for everybody else. Accordingly, it was agreed to postpone proceedings until Monday at noon. Eventually, because of some further delays as a result of a couple of lost whistles and running repairs that had to be made to the ball in between games with a bicycle puncture kit, the final was played in the dusk of the following Wednesday. Fortunately, we'd been knocked out in the second round.

Some teams and spectators had, however, been camped at the pitch for a whole week, but all this without a word of complaint, without a murmur of annoyance. After all, what difference did it make which day anything took place? The weather was constantly warm, food and water were plentiful and, surrounded by family and friends, one simply lay back in the shade of the trees and savored the delicious anticipation of watching the Beautiful Game.

This aptitude for treading water as time ebbed and flowed around them meant that the islanders found my fretful impatience, which occasionally was impossible for me to subdue, extremely difficult to understand.

On the other hand, we'd now been waiting for just over forty-eight hours for the *Maoaoa*, the bloody cargo ship, to hove into view. Another morning had just risen over the post office, and I had already stayed two nights with my wantoks, Geoff and Marlene, while Small Tome, with Hapi and Luki (two of Fatty's teenage sons), had stayed with some of theirs in nearby Kokenggolo.

"I am going to radio the ship and see if I can find out

where they are," I announced, standing up. If it was still a long way off, then we could at least all return to the village and come back later. I turned on my heel and set off up the road.

"No wari, Will. He will come soon. Maybe we just wait here and keep lookout."

Small Tome gestured toward Kundu Kundu, a pair of islands that marked the passage at the edge of the reef that the ship would have to follow. A light onshore breeze fluttered the downy hibiscus and disturbed the drowsing flowers on the bougainvillea that shaded him as he sat with Hapi and Luki and fed pebbles to the myriad fish swimming to and fro at their feet.

Oh well, perhaps there wasn't any real rush, perhaps it was just easier to wait. Small Tome was right. The ship would come in its own sweet time, and there was nothing at all I could do to hurry it up. I stretched out on the sand by the jetty and stared up at a coconut palm, which was, according to Stevenson, "that giraffe of vegetables, so ungainly, to the English eye so foreign." He had clearly never been to Torquay.

In the upper leaves a pair of parakeets were engaged in a domestic standoff. Whether they were on nonsquawking terms because of some deep-seated dissatisfaction with their relationship or whether it was a temporary tiff was impossible to tell. Now, however, they were perched on separate branches and looking steadfastly in opposite directions. Despite this distraction, after about five minutes I began to fidget. I stood up again. "Right, I am definitely going to radio."

Small Tome looked up and smiled sympathetically. He wasn't sure that there was really much point, but if that was what I wanted to do then he was not going to be the person to stand in my way.

"No wari, Will. You go radio."

"Right, off I go."

The municipal radio was kept at the provincial office, which was tucked just behind the bank. Walking up the white

steps, along the veranda, and through the door marked RECEP-
TION, I found myself in front of an immense woman, who was
sitting behind an enormous typewriter hammering away at the
keys with an alarming ferocity. With a final *ping!* and a mighty
swipe that sent the carriage whizzing back over to the left like a
train hitting a brick wall, she looked up. "Morning!" she shrilled.

"Yes, hello, morning. I wondered if I could use the radio. I
am trying to contact the *Maoaoa*." The name of the ship was
almost impossible to pronounce. Every time I tried I gave the
impression of struggling with ill-fitting dentures.

The woman stood up and came busily from behind her
desk in her bright yellow-and-orange-patterned dress. Pushing
past me, she opened a wooden cupboard. Inside the door hung
a small mirror and, alongside a stub of wilting lipstick and a garden rake of a comb, stood a new radio. She switched it on,
adjusted a knob causing a torture chamber squeal, and twisted
the central dial a couple of notches. All of a sudden we found
ourselves in the middle of a maritime stag party. Voices shouting
and laughing, intermingled with snatches of rowdy singing and
music, crackled across the airwaves. Grabbing the handset, one
hand on her hip, she barked some harsh instructions in Pijin.

As if by magic, silence suddenly fell over the South
Pacific. The woman recovered her composure, patted her hair
in the mirror, and called for the ship in the sweetest of tones.

"*Maoaoa, Maoaoa, Maoaoa,* here Provincial Office. Come
in plis."

Silence.

I practiced mouthing her pronunciation of the ship's name
behind her back until, swinging from one haunch to the other,
she caught sight of me in the mirror and frowned. I hastily
rearranged my lips into a neutral smile.

"*Maoaoa, Maoaoa, Maoaoa,* come in."

Silence.

Frustrated by the lack of response, she lost her temper and

bellowed a stream of invective across the airwaves. I shuddered as she announced, with a grabbing and wrenching hand action, what she proposed to do to the unfortunate skipper should he fail to respond.

Terrified silence.

She threw the handset back into the cupboard and slammed it closed.

"Nobody on ship."

I dodged as she strode back to her desk and, without a word, carried on with her pounding at the typewriter. Muttering garbled thanks, I fled.

Back at the wharf, Small Tome and the two boys had nodded off. Fine lookouts, I thought grumpily as I settled down under the tree to keep watch for the ship. The radioing episode had, it seemed, been more emotionally draining than I had realized, because after a short while my eyelids began to droop.

Some time later I opened my eyes, woken by the birds above me, now chattering with nervous incessance. Out in the bay I recognized the green, wooden cargo ship—the *Mowwow*, the *Mowerwower*, or however it was pronounced—that I had seen loading on the wharf in Honiara. It looked fantastic against the blue of the sea.

"Tome, Luki, Hapi! Look, it's here, wake up. The ship. It's arriving," I said, suddenly coming giddily round with that terrible, disorienting, encompassing sickness that comes with the realization that you should not have been asleep at all. I used to suffer from it a lot driving my car and sitting in examination halls.

"Huh?" The trio sat up in perfect unison.

By now, I was on the end of the jetty. They jumped up too, and the four of us watched the ship chug through the calm waters. Our own boat, in which we'd laid a plastic tarpaulin to protect the sacks from leaks, was ready.

Something, though, was not quite right. To reach the jetty

and avoid the shallow reef, the ship needed to turn in quickly after it had come between Kundu and the other Kundu, tucking itself inside the white stick that had been planted in the reef as a channel marker. Yet it seemed to be plowing straight to the next point and on round the island. We waited, uncertain, willing it to come toward us. It did not, and it was not going to.

We tumbled into the canoe. Such was my haste that I slipped on the plastic sheet and found myself flat out in the bottom of the canoe as Luki feverishly tried to start the engine. Such was his enthusiasm and enviable strength that the starting rope snapped, and he too found himself lying on his back. The *Maoaoa* was disappearing into the distance.

"Come on, Tome." The normally irrepressible Small Tome was looking rather bleary. "Let's see if we can get this engine going."

Annoyingly, the piece of rope that Luki was still holding was just too short to be of any use. Small Tome staggered off into the bushes, to return, after a short while, with a piece of bush liana.

"Do you think it'll work?" It looked too spindly to be of much use.

"No wariwari," said Small Tome, yawning as he removed the cover from the engine and wrapped the vine round the groove on the top of the motor. The ship had all but disappeared round the corner. He put a couple of twists round his hand and pulled. The vine snapped, but not before the engine coughed and fired. He pushed the gear lever into reverse, and we slipped away from the jetty. Swinging the long canoe round, we set off in pursuit of the *Maoaoa*. Although traveling much more slowly than we were, the coastal trader was now a hazy mark, a possible mirage, far off along the coast.

As we negotiated the marker stick, the wind picked up, and soon waves were breaking against the hull of our boat, bursting into spray. Within minutes we were soaked, but we were slowly gaining on the ship. I could now make out the color of its hull again and see the black blotch of dirty diesel that rose from the rusted funnel. We could see figures leaning against the rail as they stood high up on the flat deck.

Then, of course, our engine misfired, and the boat suddenly slowed before lurching forward. I turned around in alarm. It missed another stroke. Small Tome leaned down and squeezed the rubber bulb of the fuel pump. He looked up and grinned as we surged again. "Look, not too much petrol, I think!" he said, picking up the orange can and waving it cheerily. The others laughed.

But now, fortunately, the *Maoaoa* was only a couple of hundred yards away, and with Small Tome draining every last drop we were finally slopping in her wash. As we came alongside, Luki reached out and grabbed on to the edge of a porthole. A row of absorbed, black faces peered down over the side. "What are these idiots up to?" read their collective expression.

Not that I cared much. We were nearly out of petrol and soaked to the skin. The canoe, by this stage, was rocking dangerously as it banged against the side of the larger vessel, and I was beginning to feel queasy.

A man wearing a black cap, an anchor stitched in gold at its center, joined the crew, leaning down to look at us. He shouted something.

From his expression, I was relieved that the wind scooped up his words and ran away with them. Standing up, or rather at a sort of three-quarter squat, I hung on to the side of the ship. Small Tome, who was sitting by the engine, which, relieved by our safe arrival, had sputtered its last, tapped me on the knee.

"Go up on top," he shouted.

"How?" I shouted back under my armpit.

Just at that moment, by way of an answer, a rope ladder unraveled itself down the side of the boat. Grabbing on to it, I made my way up onto the deck. Pairs of hands helped me over the wooden rail. Looking down, I got a thumbs-up from Small Tome, who scrambled up the ladder behind me with the petrol container.

"What now yu lookim?" asked the bewildered skipper.

"I just wondered whether you had my chicken feed? Iu gotim kae-kae blong kokorako blong mifala?"

"What kind name blong yu?" He pointed at me with his chin.

"Will, Will Randall from Mendali."

One of the crew was dispatched into the bowels of the boat to have a look. A few minutes later a sack popped out onto the deck, followed promptly by the rest, which were handed from man to man to the gunwale where, by accident, I happened to be standing. Handed the first sack, I thought for a moment that I might disappear with it back into the hold. I struggled it to the rail and hung on as it dangled over the side of the boat. It pulled me onto my tiptoes, but Luki, below, held his arms up.

"Drop him now!"

He wiggled his fingers expectantly, and I let go. He caught it lightly and dropped it down at his feet. Soon all the bags had been loaded. Looking around for Small Tome, who had disappeared, I spotted him at the back of the wheelhouse with what was clearly now a full can of petrol. He shook hands with a man who, dressed in ragged overalls, was smeared in oil that shone lightly against his face.

"Well done, Tome. Where did you get that from?"

"Man here." He pointed over his shoulder to the stern. "Him wantok blong mi!"

Unerringly, everyone seemed to recognize their own in this tiny country.

We clambered back onto the ladder. Small Tome first and then I made the short but precarious trip down. With one foot on the last rung, I turned to step out into the boat, but as I did so my foot slipped and, losing my grip, I fell forward. Accompanied by a great "Ooh!" from the audience I ended up spread-eagled on the sacks of feed. In the process I barked my shin badly on the wooden side of our canoe and, as I gripped my leg, I realized there was now a cut in it about three inches long. The blood ran freely. I did not cry nor did I throw up, but I would very much have liked to have done both.

"Thank you tumas. Let's go, Tome!" I said, waving through a swimming head and gritted teeth.

Back home there was a great deal of clumsy excitement as the sacks were stored in the vestry. I limped to the benches outside my house, nursing a new bash, followed by Young John, the boy who, with his older brother Young George, had been chosen to look after the chickens during their short passage through our hands.

"So when kokorako come?"

He brought out my "First Aid for the Traveler" kit and placed it on the table in front of me. Discarding the information sheet (which suggested that if I were to go clubbing, I should avoid taking Ecstasy), I rummaged for a bandage between the clean needles.

He asked excitedly again. "When kokorako come? How many come?"

"Two hundred on Saturday."

Some sticking plaster and a selection of exotic condoms seemed to be the only barriers between me and gangrene.

"Two hundredfala!" Young John's eyes shone, particularly when I told them that I would buy them flashlights with which to patrol at night.

"Wetem battri?"

"With batteries," I promised.

≈

Mission Accomplished

Y ou fala make kokolako?" Harold, the eponymous owner of the Chinese store in Munda, asked in his own idiosyncratic Pijin as Fatty and I walked the gray rolls of fine-mesh chicken wire out of the door.

"Mi like fo' payim one hund'ed, no!" He paused, looking up into the air quizzically, and then dramatically raising two fingers of one hand. "Two hund'ed!"

He nodded enthusiastically, smiling broadly, and said something to his wife in Chinese. Her eyebrows, which for convenience had been removed and new ones tattooed in their place, frowned slightly as she replied. "Ah, gud, gud, gud, three hund'ed." Both of them looked quite delighted.

Not sure that we were ready to start trading in chicken futures at this early stage, I replied in the most businesslike, noncommittal fashion I could manage and promised to get back to them. Once outside, Henry, who had popped a roll of wire under each arm, was beside himself with excitement.

"Him like payim staka!" he exclaimed. "Staka."

Hang on, I thought as I dragged my roll behind me, that was all good and well, but we didn't actually have any "in stock" at the moment.

In any case, I was beset again by self-doubt. My dear old aunt had sent me a letter in which she wished me well in my ventures and wanted to know how I was getting on with the books. I needed to write and tell her what a venomous dislike I had developed for the smug, self-satisfied, and extremely successful Robinson Crusoe. He would not have had any problem setting up a chicken farm. Oh, no! And he would have had not just a couple of hundred but several thousand that he would have reared on his own with great success and then used them brilliantly to fly to safety. Grimble, of course, was still blundering around the bush, playing cricket, and addressing everyone, regardless of age or sex, as "old man" or "old boy." Stevenson hadn't done much but loll under one of the "giraffes of vegetation," whine about the heat, and worry about Mrs. Stevenson ending up in the cook pot. Just recently he had become most concerned when "Mrs. Stevenson had gone alone to the seaside of the island after shells." He had been "very sure the proceeding was unsafe." He did, however, concede that she "was prepared for any eccentricity." From her photograph, she certainly looked it.

Anyway, at the end of her letter my aunt had added a P.S.: "Of course we'd chickens during the war, dear. They had a very nasty habit of dying."

My confidence in our project slipped again.

By the time we returned, my bashed leg hurt properly. I had scrubbed it as much as I could bear with antiseptic and had cobbled together a makeshift dressing with the sticky part of the plasters and some cotton wool. It had been fairly disastrous.

Now, as I rested my leg, I was aware of an odor vaguely reminiscent of one that I had smelled when, on a cross-country run, my foot had become lodged inside the body cavity of a decaying rabbit. I lifted the offensive limb onto the bench and peeled off my dressing. The wound—and I can only apologize for this description—was pink, swollen, and bubbling with pastel green pus. As I squeezed tentatively, a great gush splattered onto the wooden seat. I thought it smelled terrible, but this, it seemed, was a matter of opinion. Flies seemed to find it delightful and paddled about in it enthusiastically.

Old Eliza, Ellen's mother, on her way back from her garden, found me in gymnast pose holding on to my poor shin to stop it stinging, throbbing, and aching all at the same time. "Ooh, no good. This one need bush medicine," she declared.

She scratched her wrinkled head and took a serious drag on her foot-long cigarette. Scooping up her bananas and beans, she went slowly back to her house. When she returned, she was carrying a pestle and mortar and some large green leaves. Sitting quietly, watched by curious if not sympathetic children, she mashed the leaves into a thick brown paste not dissimilar, in texture at least, to a cowpat. This she applied with her fingers and tied it all in place with a strip of a faded Hawaiian shirt.

(I would like to tell you that this traditional cure worked wonders and that my wound healed overnight. Sadly, all that happened in that passage of time was that it swelled up something rotten and red lines went inching up my leg. Geoff gave me a dose of antibiotics so powerful it would have had a broken-down nag up and running.)

With only the most cursory of glances at my injury, Imp came over to ask, rather sheepishly, if I could organize the building of the chicken house as his wife had told him that he had to go fishing.

So I hobbled off with Tassels and attendant children down the path that led to the gardens to find a suitable site. Checking my notebook, I remembered that Warren had suggested a location that was cool, airy, and near a water supply. We chose a plot in the shade of a grove of coconuts. It was only a short distance from the village, a small promontory in the elbow of a deep stream that babbled out of the side of the hill a few yards higher up. The area was cleared in a short hour.

The single most useful piece of equipment, in fact the only tool that each islander owned, was a bush knife, a flat-bladed machete about three feet long. Its uses were multifarious, and training started straight from the cradle. Small children, both boys and girls, no taller than the knives themselves, would drag them around, taking practice swipes at anything in their paths. By the time they were ten or twelve, they would be expected, as they were now, to fell a tree with an eight-inch-thick trunk in no more than three or four strokes. The accuracy and precision of these strokes were breathtaking; time after time they unerringly struck the same spot. This said, bush knife usage was not incident free, and missing tips of fingers and toes and a few vivid scars bore witness to the occasional mistake.

Bush knives were not used just for felling and clearing but also for weeding gardens and digging out roots, for splitting coconuts, for shaping paddles and walking sticks and, not least, for mincing the ubiquitous sticks of tar black tobacco.

"Now we just need to measure out the dimensions, and then we can mark the corners with posts."

In vain, I tried to free the knife that I had borrowed from Barnabas, Stanley's older brother, from the tree in which it was now firmly stuck. Smiling at him, I patted the wooden handle so that he would know where it was and started to pace out the floor. Using a ball of string that had made its way into my rucksack and a couple of half-remembered formulae, one of which, in hindsight, was probably more suitable for calculating the surface of a sphere, we tried to get the four corners of the house to square. But they would not. We arranged every form of parallelogram but never a rectangle and, now that a sizable audience was spectating, I began to feel the heat even more than usual.

After shifting the markers again and squatting down and lining up and closing one eye and opening the other and holding out a thumb and sticking out a tongue, all of a sudden everything, with a huge relief, fell into place.

Henry and two other gargantuan men acted as human pile drivers to place the uprights, and onto these they fitted the roof rafters. The women sat in gaggles, laughing and chatting as they sewed the sections of leaf roofing, which when completed were passed up on top to be tied in place. The children unrolled the chicken wire around the bases of the posts and held it up as Small Tome hammered it into place with some U nails bought by the kilo at Harold's. Slowly the panels were put in place on the roof and tied securely. Someone appeared with a door, which was hung on wooden hooks.

It was an impressive, sturdy construction, and standing back, arms folded, I felt pleased by the achievement.

Sadly, though, there was no time for self-congratulation. Everything had to be readied for the arrival of the new incumbents. After the long wait, time was rapidly running out. This, however, was something that I was used to.

Thick, olive green bamboo pipes from a nearby clump were split in half along their lengths and filled with water. Coconut shells, steadied like so many half rugby balls on top of small mounds of sand that Innocent had brought in trickling handfuls from the beach, were filled with feed, and the floor was swept. We were ready. Well, fairly ready.

Launching the canoe at sunrise, we set off for the airport. Everybody had wanted to greet the new arrivals, but places were limited. Luta, as chief, selected Young John and Young George, who were to act as future guardians, and me, as the individual who had caused all the trouble in the first place, to make up the members of the welcoming committee.

There was a point of entry across the reef on the Munda side that we often used as a shortcut. It was a short passage that ran along the lip of a lozenge-shaped island. The water here was so shallow that it was necessary to paddle or use a long pole to punt the canoe across the dead coral, which was now inhabited only by the sea slugs that were as attractive as soapy, moldy, rotting loofahs. (It is interesting that, once given their French title, *beche de mer,* they immediately commanded astonishingly high prices in the fish markets of the Eastern world.)

Luta knew the approach well, which was vitally important as, in rough weather, there was a risk of being dumped onto the rocks by onshore waves or hitting the ledge of the reef and pitch-poling, cartwheeling the whole boat on its length. This morning, however, there was no danger—the sea was glassy flat, and the tide was so low that the moment we crossed from the open sea onto the top of the reef we ran aground and came to a halt. Sliding forward in our seats, we hoped to inch the boat across the reef by the movement of our bodies. It had no effect. Everybody got out into the ankle-deep, bath-warm water. Removing my leather boots, I too stepped out, but my feet were not tough enough to walk on the sharp coral or to contemplate stepping inadvertently on one of the revolting slugs. I ooh-ouched along a few paces but, as I was obviously holding up proceedings, Luta suggested that I get back into the canoe. I rather shamefacedly agreed. Only once on the short crossing was it deemed necessary to pick up the canoe and its contents and carry it.

Eventually we were across and arrived without further incident at the airstrip. A few minutes later we heard the buzz of a plane. It landed from right to left, disappearing momentarily behind the trees before turning and taxiing back toward us.

Eventually the propellers stopped spinning and the pilot dropped out of his seat to open the door for the passengers. Then he went to the rear, twisted down the handle of the triangular luggage compartment door, and pulled it open. Of course it was very unlikely, practically impossible, that the chicks would be here.

We froze in horror.

With a good deal of panicky cheep-cheeping, dozens of small, yellow, momentarily rather enchanting balls of fluff were hopping around the hold. In the middle, in flagrante delicto, a number of small feathers floating around its mouth, was a black cat.

Georg, the eccentric German who lived alone with his transistor radios up at Iriri, had finally become fed up with the endless nocturnal caterwauling as he tried to tune in to *"Frühstückstunde"* on Radio Dortmund. So, in search of a bit of peace, he had sent his cat in a cardboard carrier to Honiara to have it castrated. On its way back, with peculiarly less on its mind than before but peckish after a lean stay at the vet's, the cat discovered to its joy that it had been placed on top of a huge carton of bite-sized Chicken Delights. It had scratched away enthusiastically and managed to escape. Knocking the lid off the box of treats, it had dipped in.

The first of the chicks fell out of the hold and dropped headfirst onto the tarmac. Slightly stunned, it stood up and started to waddle off. The cat decided to make good his escape and shot off in the direction of the bank, pursued by his owner. "Komm back, Schatzi! Bitte! Schatzi!"

We dived in. Fortunately, the box of chicks at the bottom had remained unscathed. I handed it to Luta while I and the two Young boys scrabbled around, scooping up the wriggling little bodies and putting them as gently as possible back into the other box. Every time the lid was lifted to put one back, five or six made a break in different directions, striding out on spindly yellow legs, their little heads jerking back and forth like cartoon characters. Eventually we managed to push them all in and press the lid on tightly. We rushed through the considerable crowd toward the beach and boat.

Fortunately the tide had risen sufficiently for us to be able to streak back across the reef. When we came into our bay, the whole village had collected on the side of the jetty. The two boys hurried the precious boxes to the house.

"Now." I addressed the assembled children in Pijin. Once a teacher always a teacher, I made sure that I had their undiverted attention before I went any further. "Now, I don't want all you children to run around the house. You will frighten all the kokorako. So over the next few days you can't go . . ."

My voice trailed off as the last pair of bare heels sped in the direction of the chicken house. Soon I was left alone in the middle of the village. With little choice, I sighed and followed them.

That evening, over the card table, the story of the morning was told and retold. Everyone wanted to hear every detail. Mothers, suckling children at their bare breasts, shook their heads and then threw them back in laughter as they heard how the cat had run away and how we'd had to pick up the little creatures one by one.

Later the two Young boys walked past, shining their new flashlights. They both had their bed mats rolled under their arms and sheets draped over their shoulders. I asked where they were going.

"Mifala go sleep long house blong kokorako. No good somefala come stealim."

No good at all, I agreed.

"I think the Commander would be happy tumas about this," said Luta, smiling, after everybody else had drifted bedward. "Now we can start to do some improvements in the village."

"I hope so, I hope so!" I was certainly happy. Despite lengthy complications we'd come far, and I thought that even if we'd not yet returned the village to its former glory, the Commander would have been happy with our achievement. I did know, however, that there was still a worryingly long way to go. With the words of my old aunt's letter running through my head, I went up the steps into my house.

CHAPTER 16

～

The Feast of St. Andrew

Happily installed in their new home, the chickens pros-
pered, and so now, after our varied exertions, it was time
for village life to return to normal. Time slowed back to a gentle
drift, and comfortable, settled, content with my new home, I
floated along, meandering distractedly through the days and
weeks. Attempting to govern or hasten the timing of events was,
as I had learned, a fruitless task, so I took off my watch and put
it at the back of my wooden cupboard. Soon the white mark that
the manacle had left on my wrist faded, and finally disappeared
into the deepening tan of my forearm.

Daily routine was marked by little more than the rising
and the setting of the sun, by light and dark, by morning and
evening, and was intruded upon only by the occasional appearance of hunger and thirst. Often, particularly after tending to
the needs of these two, I would only too agreeably comply with

my leaden eyelids' request that I should lie down for an hour or two. Trained as I had been to sprint out every morning from the starting blocks of ambition and achievement toward an ever more distant, often invisible, finishing line, I needed, perversely, no little self-discipline to break out of the habit of trying to get things done.

Many were the days when simply nothing happened, but this inactivity only heightened the pleasure of waiting for the few special events in the village calendar, high points of the year which, as they approached, were enthusiastically saved for, discussed, and planned. A few days after the arrival of the chicks, one such day came round and, as there now really was some cause for celebration, I had been much looking forward to it.

Somewhat incongruously, the most important day of the year at Mendali, after Christmas and Easter, was St. Andrew's Day. This was not, it transpired later, the result of any Scottish connection. I had half-expected to find myself dining on homemade haggis and sweet potatoes, the festivities coming to a close only once we'd finished kicking up our coconut kilts and dancing endless reels around our bush knives to the tune of bamboo bagpipes. Fortunately St. Andrew, the fisherman, was the patron saint of the village church, and in his honor a day of mainly religious celebration was to take place.

In the Solomon Islands, Christianity, rather than being flashed about as a minority fashion accessory, was treated by one and all with a gravitas that was all the more impressive in a world where nothing was taken too seriously. Christianity alone, with its call to prayer twice daily, three times on Sundays, provided any social structure to the day; its followers lived, as much as I could observe, fairly steadfastly by its teachings, or at least as well as anyone can while being permanently hounded by Temptation. Every islander was expected to be a signed-up member of at least one of the numerous churches available, and it was therefore useful, for once, that I had been baptized. The consequence of a reluctance to adopt one brand or another, at least for appearances' sake, would have been definite censure.

The flip side of the Solomon ecclesiastical coin was that people tended to be worryingly receptive to the various religious road shows that paddled around the islands. Every half-witted, crackpot, dishonest, unscrupulous, hypocritical, and, more often than not, American church was in evidence, generally represented by an individual who was a fine example of all these characteristics. He—and generally it was a he—scattered leaflets bountifully as he urged curious villagers to join up and cough up. "Yessiree, pay your way in this life and get a free ride in the next!"

A particularly dubious character stood almost daily in the marketplace at Munda. Black-browed and silver-haired, he would berate his audience for every conceivable vice, many, if not all, of which he shared. Certainly his penchant for young Solomon Island girls was widely reported. On one occasion, as he held forth, I crossed between the women seated on the ground among their piles of produce and politely declined one of his proffered sheets. Seeing that he might be missing out on the opportunity of saving an obvious sinner, he leaned over to me and, with his moist, colorless lips almost touching my ear, breathed in a Southern drawl, "Can't hurt you, can only help you."

I had shuddered and hurried on.

Father Joshua, by contrast, was a thoroughly likable Solomon Islander. He was the roving vicar of the Western Province but, with no transport of his own, he was forced to hitch lifts around the islands with a bottle of wine and a few wafers in his rucksack to bring communion to the outlying villages. A young man recently married and now provided with the requisite armfuls of gurgling babies, with his easy manner and his genuine interest in his congregations, he was a popular visitor to Mendali.

On the few occasions he stopped overnight in the village, he would stay in my house, or rather in his house. For the official title of my residence was Small Padre House, in this case the *small* referring to the size of the house, the padre being of perfectly average proportions. Father Joshua would insist on sleeping on the floor of the front room, lying beatifically on the mat that traveled with him. In the morning I would come guiltily out of my room to find him asleep, his head propped on a sack of rice, an impromptu pillow, his only covering, his communion robe, pulled neatly up to his chin.

On this St. Andrew's Day he had arrived by canoe to lead the service accompanied by the older, but only recently qualified, Deacon Hilary, a jolly, rotund man bursting with enthusiasm for his new vocation and beside his considerable self at the prospect of delivering his first sermon.

Everything was now ready for the big day, which had, apart from the continuing prosperity of the chickens, been the sole topic of conversation for weeks. Not only would we have "the Service" to enjoy but also, possibly more important, we'd have "the Feast."

Local politicians, currying favor with their prospective voters, had arrived in canoes loaded to the gunwales with a seemingly endless number of sacks of rice, flour, and election promises. Cardboard boxes of hard navy biscuits—which had been such an important dietary supplement to the sailors of yesteryear—protected by plastic from weevils, paper packets of tea, and several hundredweight of sugar had all been hoarded in readiness. For two nights previously the men had set off standing in their canoes, spears in hand, in pursuit of the fish course. Lazy parrot fish, attracted by the bright light of the kerosene lamps balanced on the prows, bumbled to the surface and were swiftly skewered before being dropped flapping and twitching into the bottoms of the boat.

I had been partially responsible for the main course,

although admittedly somewhat against my will. For only the morning before I had been doing some hit-and-miss weeding of my little patch of garden. Pinching out the impertinent shoots that had appeared overnight, I had been trying to check their spread, which, like thick fur creeping over the ground, would soon ruthlessly choke out the efforts of my infant seedlings to reach maturity.

I was alone in the jungle, my only audience a pair of chatty, middle-aged cockatoos who, sitting on a branch of a mahogany tree, oohed and tutted comment on my clumsy efforts. Staring back at them, I wondered whether they tasted anything like chicken.

High up and bored, a sea eagle planed in circles, like a boy on a bicycle in the park waiting for his friends. Yawning, it finally headed off over the false forest floor of treetops, its tawny wings beating in slow motion. Fat, wet splats of rain began to fall and, as they became steadier, I sheltered under the broad protection of a banana tree. On the other side of the valley, under the arch of a feeble rainbow, came two girls running through Old Edith's garden, each guiltily clutching a papaw to her chest with one hand. With the other they held, above their heads, huge palm leaves that hung down to cover their entire bodies. At this distance, they looked like a couple of crafty green beetles scurrying along, picking their way through the undergrowth.

As the clouds tumbled down the side of the mountain and pushed out across the sea, allowing the sun to glare down once more, I returned to my task. Steam trickled upward prehistorically, and it seemed a country where bizarre creatures might appear—great lizards risen on their hind legs, or rabid beasts, half man, half shark, growling in the forest around me. I laughed, and the two cockatoos sighed.

Without warning a tremendous commotion came some fifty yards above me. I straightened and looked up, but my view was blocked by a row of incandescent chili bushes. With a dreadful cracking and crashing, an enormous pig came bursting through the screen, bearing down on me and my garden, bristling with thick black hairs, full tusks under its snout, and its two thin front legs working double overtime below its corpulent bulk.

It would be pointless to claim that I was unconcerned by this spectacle, but there was no time to run, even if I had been able to move my legs. So, for want of a better option, I sat down firmly on my fledgling tomato plants.

Close on the pig's tail, wriggling through the shrubs, emerged two lanky village dogs, greedy, sweaty tongues lolling between bared teeth, and close behind them came the leaping figures of Hapi and Luki. As one of the dogs lunged, the terrible boar veered to its left and headed off in the direction of the stream, Hapi and Luki giving chase. I gave hottish pursuit and, following the course of the flattened vegetation, I eventually found the hunters and the hunted a few hundred yards on. Luki was now astride the pig's back waving a large surgical-style knife rather as a rodeo rider waves his hat. By now the dogs had the bucking animal pinned down by both tearing ears and, with an almost considered stroke of the knife, Luki sliced open its neck. Hapi beat the two hounds back from the fire hydrant of blood.

The boys were already tying the boar's legs together with vine chopped from the closest tree when, as if tired and very slightly irritated by the whole exercise, the beast gave up. Pushing a pole between the two pairs of trotters, the boys easily lifted it, slung upside down, onto their shoulders. Setting off triumphant, they waved back. "Nice one, Mr. Will!" they called.

Well, I supposed so. I wiped my mouth with my shirt, swallowing hard a couple of times.

A carefully timed program of St. Andrew's Day events had been drawn up and written out, but nobody had the faintest intention of abiding by it. "Activities" were supposed to include "kastom" dancing, singing groups, and dramas, but the only two certainties were "the Service" and "the Feast."

It was for "the Service" that I was waiting in the churchyard under the shady branches of one of the rain trees, so called for the wide, feathery leaves that offered some protection from the regular and often violent downpours. An iron cauldron was being readied under Ethel's expert supervision for the huge quantity of supersweet, pitch-black, bladder-defeating tea that would be drunk throughout the later celebrations.

Although it was still very early in the morning, the day already held the heat and humidity that, switching themselves idly with birch twigs, Scandinavians lock themselves away in small rooms to find. I had been beginning to regret my decision to wear long trousers and socks. But as I looked toward the village and saw the first of the congregation walking toward me down the path, I felt some relief that I had made an effort to dress for the occasion. Gone were the ragged shorts and betel-nut-stained T-shirts of the men; gone too were the tired curtains that were normally wrapped above or below the women's breasts, patterned and spattered by endless babes in arms. In their place were smart black or blue shorts, white shirts, and colorful floral dresses, straw hats, and shell necklaces. I smiled and whispered "Gud morne" as I slipped off my shoes and we went into the comparative cool of the church.

The font, filled with fresh water, had been drawn up to one side of the altar. Father Joshua, who was still outside in his white robe enjoying a last-minute betel nut and a huge cigarette, was clearly hoping to fulfill a number of his duties on this one visit from his vicarage on the other side of the lagoon.

On both sides of the aisle, the nave had been decorated with a profusion of flowers, and greenery had been woven around the rafters and tied to the ends of the pews to create a fittingly biblical avenue of palm trees the length of the nave.

Above the altar, suspended by two lengths of fishing line, hung a huge heart-shaped wreath woven from hibiscus and frangipani.

The church's bell, which had been salvaged from the Commander's launch before it had sunk in a storm, was now energetically rung. As the sound of the last sharp clang rolled away across the water, the service started.

Selwyn Fly, our choirmaster, sang the first line of the opening hymn solo into his gray beard, peering at his handwritten, water-stained words through his elderly spectacles. From where I stood behind him, I could see the piece of wire that held the frames to the right earpiece. He whipped them from his nose and lifted his head as the rest of the choir joined him in singing the softly ululating tune. Unaccompanied, they sang in parts, the men behind me and the women on my left across the way. This layered, complicated mix of sounds and words seemed to transform the church building into a complex but extraordinarily beautiful human accordion. As I gazed past the decorated pillars to the blues of the still sea and the island of Kukurana across the channel, the music increased in volume, and I was very nearly, suddenly and unexpectedly, reduced to floods of tears.

The procession made its way to the altar, led by the irrepressible Small Tome, dressed in one of his most lavish and intricate robes. As he advanced, he swung a brass incense burner filled with smoking ngali nut oil around and around as a medieval knight might have brandished a ball and chain on his way to battle, or a Japanese might demonstrate a martial art: a three-hundred-and-sixty-degree swing with every step. Then, as he brought his other foot level, the chain came to rest by his side, and then another step and another swing and onward. Slowly and seriously, he made his way toward the three shallow steps that led up to the altar.

Behind him, in attendance, came Brian, a young lad who

had the triply difficult job of holding a small bowl of oil steady, keeping step with Small Tome, and avoiding the dangerous metal object whizzing in front of him. He carried out his duties impeccably—as the solemnity of the occasion demanded.

Behind them now came the splendidly dressed Father Joshua, in surplice of red and gold, and beside him the wondrously corpulent Deacon Hilary, the cord of his robe tied in a tight knot around his remarkable girth. His round, cheerful face had already developed a sheen that was broken only by the droplets of sweat that ran down in little streams from his graying hair and met like lemmings on the end of his chin.

Next to come were twelve boys of nine or ten, smart in shirts and shorts that seemed to have escaped too much rough-and-tumble on the way to church. Every boy held a stick, at the top of which he had spiked a candle, and each one of these seemed to lean at its own idiosyncratic angle. Those whose candles leaned too far backward spent much of the time trying to avoid the hot wax that rained down in soft white spots onto their hands. Each boy also possessed a different sense of rhythm and level of concentration but, miraculously and with only the minimum of jostling, the group arrived at the altar without mishap. As the boys filed to either side and Small Tome accomplished a magnificent seven-hundred-and-twenty-degree whirl, the last notes of the hymn faded away.

The service was a traditional but simplified form of Anglican worship, to suit the islanders' way of life. The Lord's Prayer read, "Give us this day our daily food"—bread not featuring greatly in the local diet—and parables were rich in metaphors of fish and palm trees, low on asses and lambs. Father Joshua whisked us efficiently through the order of service.

Then Deacon Hilary, his finest hour upon him, gave an upbeat sermon in Pijin, which included, he told us, a *very* funny story about an iguana and a giant and hundreds of people who only narrowly avoided getting eaten—by either the iguana or the giant or possibly both. I was not entirely sure.

Sadly, Deacon Hilary's words fell on the sandy ground beneath our feet, as none of the children, at whom the cut and thrust of his discourse was aimed, understood any Pijin, and as a result the whole tale was about as illustrative as a slide show for the blind. Undeterred, Deacon Hilary laughed uproariously when he reached the end, slapped his juddering thigh several times, put his back out, and had to sit down unceremoniously on the first pew available, scattering little blond-haired girls onto the floor, their pretty, engraved faces alive with alarm.

The first verses of the Kyrie Eleison had been sung when the whole congregation froze at the sound of a loud rattle outside. The smallest children, who had now managed to divest themselves of their clothes and had begun to build sand castles in the aisle, scuttled back onto their pews. For in the doorway appeared, silhouetted by the dazzling morning sun, a group of crouching figures. Led by Hair and Tassels, all six men and boys were dressed in loincloths, braided headbands of dolphins' teeth and beads decorating their hair and foreheads. White lime streaked their bodies and faces and, bandolier style across their chests, they wore thick chains of shell jewelery, each shard shining like mother-of-pearl in the soft light. Around one ankle of each dancer was tied a cluster of dried nut shells, which created an impressive rattle as it was shaken and stamped on the floor, and in their hands they carried palm leaves to represent paddles. With swooping, bobbing movements, they canoed their way through the congregation, their amplified steps providing a rhythm to the singing that now struck up again. Finally, they lined the three sides of the altar and came to rest. They remained head-bowed and motionless as the last note of the amen drifted out of the window on the scented air.

Carrying on regardless—as you must when your church is

invaded by six warriors in an invisible war canoe—Father Joshua broke bread, poured wine, and served communion. Again my eyes prickled and I feared that I would have to use sand in my contact lenses as the excuse for my red-rimmed reappearance in the village.

Once we were all outside, the atmosphere relaxed, and children, unleashed from the strange restrictions of church, broke loose of parents and ran amok among the huts, pausing only occasionally to kick a cat or torment one of the multitude of scabrous dogs that loped around the fringes of the "motu" mound. Here, underneath a pile of banana leaves and stones that had been heated throughout the day by fires built on top of them, resided the pig. As the leaves were pulled away, I was greeted by the most peculiar sight. It appeared the animal that had been of perfectly normal porcine proportions that morning had, in the heat of the fire, melted and collapsed. It was now flat out on the floor with all four limbs splayed outward, rather as a tiger's skin might be laid out in a baronial hall. Congealing puddles of fat lay in pools on its back or dripped down its snout, leaving dark, oily marks on the dirt. It had not, it appeared, been skinned, and the bristles stood up in affront at such treatment. The eyeballs could not, fortunately, stare accusingly as they had popped. I was not surprised. Anyway, this was the treat that we'd all been waiting for—the cause of much salivating and stomach rubbing. I made a mental note to stick to the sweet potatoes—again.

Joining the men by the cauldron, I sipped an enamel mug of tea and watched the women busying themselves laying the table. Down on the floor went the palm leaves, and onto these were dropped whole sweet potatoes, leaf parcels of rice, whole "motued" fish, and slabs of tapioca pudding.

Meanwhile, the pig was carved and carried over from the oven by finger-licking ladies. In the gloom it was hard to see which of the pieces of pig to choose. The trick, I quickly learned, was to wait politely until everybody else had rummaged about and then help yourself from whatever remained. As the local diet normally included next to no fat, slabs of greasy skin, warts and all, to say nothing of the thick black hairs that stuck between your teeth, were considered a great treat to be chewed on at length with sighs of satisfaction. I could then surreptitiously select the tastiest and juiciest bits of meat. Blubber an inch thick was carved into squares and added alongside. I could see Fatty eyeing one hungrily and jostling for the right spot at the meal.

Deacon Hilary had now made a full recovery and said grace. Silence but for the sound of tearing fat settled over the proceedings. For five minutes. Then the leaves were rolled away, the scraps thrown to the dogs, and the fire at the end of the clearing stoked. We were ready for the "Activities."

The Mother's Union were first "onstage" with tales from the Bible—the choosing of David to be king and the rather gruesome death of John the Baptist. Ellen played an enthusiastic Salome, holding up a coconut with a smiley face drawn on it to represent the unfortunate man's head. They finished with a cautionary tale about, as far as I could gather, avoiding pregnancy unless married. This was given extra visual impact by the production of the same coconut, this time wearing swaddling clothes, from underneath Young Margaret's dress. From the looks of surprise and mystery, it appeared that this strange disclosure had been enough to dissuade some in the audience from pregnancy at any stage, under any circumstances.

Next were the dancers and singers, shifting gently over the ground as they sang in their local language, using undulating arm movements to signify the sea and come hither love. No applause came from the crowd, only the occasional appreciative murmur. Fingers pointed at the most shy of the performers, and smiling mouths whispered into ears, resulting in gentle giggles. Out of the gloom behind the table appeared Small Tome. He was holding one of the only two bottles of the deep red jam fruit wine that I had produced and some glasses. He filled two of these and signaled that I should push them in front of the two clergymen sitting on either side of me. I shook my head, not wanting to, but he insisted. So I slid one bottle in front of Father Joshua, who lifted and sniffed it suspiciously. He declined it by smiling and pushing it back in front of me. I handed it to Deacon Hilary, who picked it up and sniffed it.

His face lit up. "A hot one, I think!" he exclaimed enthusiastically as he took his first sip. Unfortunately he went on to take several more, and as the evening wore on he became more and more animated, talking loudly at inappropriate moments, slapping his neighbors on the back, and guffawing with laughter. His face gleamed in the firelight. Small Tome looked on approvingly, delighted with his handiwork.

Much later, with only the embers of the fire and the gigantic moon to light them, from far away in the bush came the sound of Tassels's Marching Band. Slowly the music got closer and closer, until boys and girls of all ages singing songs of Jesus and joy in the world marched into the clearing. Each was equipped with two thin sticks about a foot long and a small flat piece of wood, on which they beat out the rhythm. The four columns of children parted, and from the gloom behind them came Tassels himself, dressed in the tightest blue pinstripe bell-bottoms and a flouncy white shirt. As the children marched in intricate formations behind him, he drummed out his own tattoo with a pair of leather cowboy boots, their metal-tipped toes glinting in the darkness. Voodoo witch doctor, dancer, and acrobat all rolled into one, he danced as if all our lives depended on it. The crowd loved him. Whooping and shrieking with delight, they watched in awe as he pouted and leered at the bemused Father Joshua, who nevertheless voiced his enthusiasm. Bloated and dazed, Deacon Hilary managed only the occasional hiccup.

For over two hours, the marching band pounded out tunes until, with a breathless and sweeping bow from Tassels, they disappeared into the night.

As I stumbled exhausted down the track past the church, voices called from the dark *"Rodo diana"*—Good night.

"Rodo diana, William."

"Rodo diana, everyone," I thought contentedly as I clambered over Deacon Hilary, who was snoring like a two-stroke engine. Then I skirted round the serenely sleeping form of Father Joshua, who, with his hands folded on his chest, might have been an effigy on a tomb. Chutney and I slipped quietly into my room.

~⊃≈

CHAPTER 17

Murder Most Fowl

K illing 'em is pretty easy. You just grab the little bastards like this and twist and pull. Twist and pull, right?" He made a gruesome turning and snapping hand movement and a strange squelching noise out of the side of his mouth. I took a deep glug from the green bottle in front of me.

By chance, I had run into Warren in Munda, and in exchange for a couple of beers, which seemed to serve as expat shell money, he was giving me a last-minute refresher course in chicken slaughtering for beginners.

"Then what you gotta do is hang 'em, yep, hang 'em high. Get a clothesline or something."

Hang them? Surely it was a bit late for that.

"Not by the neck, you stupid bastard! By the legs. Then the blood runs down to the head and you don't get so much dark meat, do ya!"

I supposed not. This was not quite as straightforward as I had hoped. I ordered two more bottles of SolBrew.

"Then you gotta heat up lots of water."

Water?

"Yeah, water, that's what I said, isn't it?"

I agreed that it was.

"Right, anyway, then you dunk 'em in and that loosens the feathers and then you pluck 'em easy. Don't leave them too long or they'll start to cook."

Of course.

"Then you've got to draw them."

Pen and ink or charcoal? I decided that facetiousness was not going to impress my Australian friend, who now embarked on a long and pretty grisly description of how to gut and clean the birds to "industry standards." Perhaps, I thought, perhaps we should keep the chickens a little longer, just to make sure that they were really up to weight.

"You'll be right. It's a piece of piss, mate! I love it, it's the best bit when you get into it."

Best bit! It sounded like an extremely unpleasant night-mare, which until now, in my still fairly abstract concept of poultry farming, I had found easy to overlook. Now, in the clear light of the fast-advancing day, I was not at all certain that I was the best man for what was going to be, it seemed, a very messy job.

This first shipment had been experimental; we would all follow the whole procedure through, and once we were happy that we knew what we were doing, it was my intention to build more houses and to slaughter every couple of weeks—dreadful though the thought was. I was keen that the villagers should understand the whole process and took one or other of them to the bank when I sent funds to Mr. Wu or ordered more feed. Although I felt impossibly bossy and hypocritically know-all, I regularly inspected the houses and checked for cleanliness,

water, and food; everyone else good-naturedly set about learn-
ing the trade. It struck me, as I spoke to Warren that afternoon
at the lodge, that this had been a good choice of business
because it was financially and logistically simple to manage.
Mind, we'd not yet accomplished the last phase . . .

For now some six or seven weeks had slipped by, and the
little balls of fluff had disappeared, to be replaced by plump,
healthy white birds with red combs and bright, suspicious eyes.
Recently, I had taken to whistling nonchalantly as I walked past
their house, looking in every other direction as if I were hardly
aware of their existence. I trusted that they were unaware that I
was in fact about to be personally responsible for their cold-
blooded (or, if I left them in the scalding water too long, warm-
blooded) murder.

Although an enthusiastic carnivore, I had never really considered having to kill animals in order to be able to eat them.
Plastic supermarket wrapping had had a wonderful ability to
absolve me of any involvement or guilt. A smartly designed label
reduced the contents of any chilled package to the status of
"meat" rather than what it really was: a body part of a pig, cow,
or sheep, or in this case the whole corpse of a chicken. Marvelous, really.

Of course—I convinced myself—our chickens had not
had a bad life, just a rather brief one. More by luck than by good
judgment, we'd built the house to just the right proportions, and
even when fully grown they still roamed freely among the extra
foodstuffs that Young John and Young George delivered every
day to supplement their pellets. Households supplied their
kitchen waste, and the chickens feasted on old rice and sweet
potatoes, delighting in pecking away at bits of pudding and the
odd kernel of coconut.

The children loved to watch them go about their business.
Sitting cross-legged on the ground outside the wire, they would
stay for hours, mouths half open, fascinated by their own farm-

yard soap opera. Some claimed that they were able to recognize individuals and had named them after English footballers, whose fame had spread even to this remote spot, situated as it was on the unfashionable outskirts of the global village. There was certainly an aptness in this choice of names, I thought when I peeked into the coop and witnessed the inane strutting, the self-obsessed preening and vapid posturing of its inmates.

However, inevitably, the time had come for us to have to sell them, and I knew, in practical terms, that this really meant that we were going to have to do away with them—kill them.

One of the biggest problems, apart from the practicalities of dispatching chickens, was our lack of refrigeration. In the heat we would have to deliver them pretty quickly to purchasers. Orders would have to be taken in advance, because two hundred chickens all dressed and nowhere to go was an unimaginable disaster, requiring every man, woman, and child in the village to consume a brace at a sitting.

So, order book in hand, George Luta and Small Tome paddled around the islands in search of prospective clients. Harold, the eponymous owner of the town store, agreed to take one hundred, the guesthouse another fifty, and, surprisingly quickly, various friends and wantoks snapped up the remainder. Delighted, they returned home, sold out in less than a day.

On the final evening we planned the whole operation with military precision; admittedly that of a rather ill-equipped, disorganized, and, in my case at least, cowardly army, but we were, nevertheless, pleased with our preparations. At first light, we would motor, engine willing, to borrow Geoff's large insulated chest, fill it with ice, borrowed from the rest house—Ellen had a wantok who worked there—and then we would hurry back to the village.

Somebody, not as yet nominated, would kill the chickens, employing either the Warren method or one of a variety of different ones as proposed by members of the committee. To my great surprise, the normally mild-mannered Small Tome volunteered to go in single-handedly and decapitate the lot of them with his bush knife. Although this plan of attack had its supporters, I was relieved that Stanley managed to knock it on the head, as it were, by running around the table doing a remarkably realistic impression of a headless chicken. Everybody thought that this was tremendously funny, which I suppose it was.

Although unresolved on the finer points of this aspect of the campaign, we moved on to stage two: plucking and drawing. A rather unwilling group of women and children were assigned this task and presented with small knives, the machetes adjudged to be too cumbersome. Once the chest was filled with the first hundred birds, packaged in plastic bags bought from the Chinese store, it would be lugged aboard the canoe and rushed to the various customers. Then the whole procedure would be repeated. It was all pretty straightforward.

The pop-popping of the outboard as it headed out to Munda woke me, and I spent the morning sloping around my house, taking a feigned interest in a cash ledger book that I did not fully understand. However, when the canoe returned I felt duty bound to go out onto the jetty.

"Everything okay? Get the ice all right?" I asked when I saw the large blue container.

"Every something number one. No wariwari" came the reply.

"Good, good." Turning, I started to tiptoe back to the house.

"So now, Mr. Will make a workshop and show everyone how to kill and prepare chicken."

Stanley!

"Me, oh, no, I don't really know how."

"Yu whiteman, yu savvy," he said, taking my hand. He was smiling mischievously.

Why did anybody think I knew anything? I didn't have a clue. They were all quite wrong. It was all the fault of the other expats, who pretended that they knew everything.

As if walking toward my own execution, I led the good-natured crowd to an area a few yards from the chicken house, where my string had already been tied between two trees and the tea cauldron was steaming with hot water.

One of the boys disappeared into the house and reappeared holding one of the birds in his arms. It sat there perfectly calmly as I paced up and down, wishing that I were wearing a black hood.

"Well, what you do, you see," I attempted, pointing at the unfortunate creature. "What you do is . . ."

"Yu whiteman, yu showim mifala," said Stanley seriously, failing to realize how close he was to being throttled himself.

All of a sudden, as the crowd murmured its approval, the warm, distinctly alive chicken was in my arms.

"Hmm, okay, right, what you do is . . ." Avoiding the temptation to stroke it, I cautiously put my fingers around its throat. I was sure I could feel a pulse. Gazing around me as if I was engaged in nothing more nefarious than waiting for a bus, I squeezed gently for a few seconds and let go. Looking down, I could see that my victim was not, as I had hoped, miraculously departed this life but instead, quite unperturbed by my ministrations, still very much with us.

Oh well, here goes. I grabbed and throttled for all I was worth. After a great deal of flapping, some not inconsiderable squawking, and quite a degree of scratching, the bird broke free of my grasp and flopped onto the ground.

It was only then that I remembered Warren's advice.

"Hold the bastard by the feet, pull down on its neck hard, and then twist up. Piece of piss, mate."

Piece of piss. Piece of bloody piss!

I reached down and grabbed the slightly ruffled fowl as it attempted, under cover of the increasing mirth, to withdraw discreetly.

Right. I turned it upside down.

Pulling like there was no tomorrow, which as far as the chicken at least was concerned was the idea, I began to fear that my arms were not going to be long enough. It was stretching like a piece of rubber. Then, suddenly, I felt a slight pop and crack. Cautiously removing my hand from its neck, I held the bird up and, shaking it slightly, checked closely for signs of life. Dead, definitely defunct, I thought, with huge relief.

"Right, so that's pretty easy. No problem. You see? Then you just hang her up like this," I explained in the style of a presenter on a television cookery program, as I put a couple of loops of string around its claws and let it bob on the line.

"What you want to do now is leave her for about ten minutes. This allows the bloo—"

To my horror I was suddenly aware of flapping behind me. In vain, I tried to shield it with my body by standing on my tiptoes and spreading my arms wide. At last all was still again. I sat down in a sprinkling shower of my own sweat.

"Then you just pop it in the water, you see, just quickly. Don't want to cook it, ha, ha!"

Ten or so minutes later I found myself dipping the dead bird into the tea urn and withdrawing it hurriedly as if it were my own hand. To my great relief it was still dead.

"Then of course you can just pluck it." The feathers did come away amazingly easily. "And then you just take out everything inside. So, everybody happy?"

"But suppose yu showim mifala dis one?" Stanley grinned.

There is little point in going into the finer detail of the next stage of the operation. Suffice it to say that a few hours later, or so it seemed, I was ready to wash the gore from my hands, forearms, and, strangely, knees. I tottered off in the direction of the stream, leaving the object of my attentions looking as if it had been rolled with heavy machinery.

I scrubbed at the sticky residue. Out, out damned spot!

"So there we are. Everybody savvy now?" I asked on my return.

Stanley surveyed the carnage and was, I could tell, quietly impressed.

"I am just going to do some work with the books. Can you just finish the job off?" I exited before anyone could ask for more tips.

Later, from the table outside my house, where I hid behind the seven columns of my accounting book, I could see the villagers at work. Some staggered around in small circles, like drunkards trying to pull corks from bottles of wine, heaving for all they were worth. Others hung out the chickens on the long, bouncing string, a row of large white handkerchiefs. Figures farther down the production line untied them and dipped them in the black pot. I blocked my ears and hummed when one of the handkerchiefs squawked and flapped as it touched the hot water. The women, sitting on the strip of beach, their feet washed by the warm sea, plucked away as the melody of the song they sang and a few downy feathers floated over to me across the still water. By lunchtime the first batch was ready and the canoe disappeared again in the direction of Munda.

"Missis blong Harold, she wants to use scales. She says she won't buy any small one." Hair and Tassels, Delivery Manager, was most concerned on his return.

A few of the birds had looked a little underweight, I was willing to admit. I thought about using my first-aid needles to inject them with water, which I knew was good business practice in England, but suggested instead that our packers push some lumps of ice inside each bird—just to keep them fresh. Unfortunately, Mrs. Harold, she of the tattooed eyebrows, cottoned on in no time and demanded that the birds be all emptied out before she weighed them. It was some months before I dared show my face in her shop again. In any event, she agreed to take them all at a slight reduction.

Later that afternoon, a happy group stood over the insulated chest. Two hundred had been sold, and the profits were good. We'd paid the money into the community bank account, and Tassels was holding the receipt, ready to show it off in the village. Strangely, despite the efforts of the black cat, there were still two full bags floating in the melted ice.

Delicious they were, too. Ellen roasted them with a few sweet potatoes in an oil drum full of hot stones, and we ate them that evening. I smiled as I served out the food among as many of my friends as could squeeze onto the two wooden benches.

As Small Tome rattled though grace, I looked out at the calm bay and caught a glimpse of the last of the white feathers as they floated away into the darkening shadows of the trees. As I shaded my eyes, I thought I could make out across the clearing the silhouette of an upright figure framed against the last shards of golden pink sun.

"Commander, sir!" I saluted smartly and thought I noticed a glimmer of a smile before he turned his back with hands clasped behind him and strode off into the darkness.

CHAPTER 18

꙳

Making a Splash

Just when this story was in need of a villain, one stepped out of the shade of a sloping lean-to and walked toward me with a broad smile. He was dressed in smart Western clothes, which seemed strangely incongruous in the rural setting. A shiny blue shirt patterned with tinselly thread was tucked into checked trousers, of the type favored by overweight golfers. On his feet were cartoon socks and soft white loafers. He was wearing a pair of sunglasses, which he did not take off as he stuck out his hand. I took it, and he squeezed mine slipperily.

"I hear we share an interest in birds of the feathered kind." He sniggered. He spoke excellent, almost accentless English. "Allow me to introduce myself, Mr. William. My name is Bunni. I am the son of Old Ezekiel. It certainly is the greatest honor to meet you. We are most fortunate to have you among us. We are poor island villagers, and we can learn so much from you."

He appeared to revel in his richly sarcastic insincerity. Although momentarily amused by his name, I took a sudden, surprisingly strong dislike to the man. As he cracked his knuckles, I read the raised inscription on a thick ring of the fakest gold, which he wore with flashing pride on his middle finger: EAT SHIT.

"Come let us sit down and talk. We've so much to discuss."

He held my hand, as was often the way among men in the islands when they chose to suggest a certain complicity. We walked hand in hand to the bench under the shade of a large sumai tree, and I just managed to control a strange urge to swing my arm and add a skip to my step. He pushed a small boy out of the way and dusted the seat for me.

"Please." He paused and licked his lips. "Let me tell you something about myself."

In fact I knew rather more about Bunni (pronounced as in Wuni rather than as in Peter the Rabbit) than perhaps he realized, for his name was often mentioned in the area. Youngest child of eleven, he had been born in Mendali but had been sent by his proud father to a boarding school on New Georgia. Here, he had done well in his exams and on leaving had been offered employment in the newly founded National Bank of the Solomon Islands. After a few years of hard work he found himself manager of the branch at Gurava. Success indeed for the young man from the island backwater.

It was a pity therefore that, as a result of the stresses and strains caused by the responsibility of his job, he began to confuse the bank account numbers of his customers with that of his own. Earnings paid in by local villagers no longer went toward their savings for old age but instead went toward funding the increasingly expensive tastes of the young Bunni. Now he liked to arrive in the village reeking of prosperity and cheap aftershave, dispensing generosity—cheap plastic gifts bought in the Chinese bazaars of Honiara—to his wantoks. The older villagers were greatly impressed and congratulated Old Ezekiel on his son's success. The ancient man simply shrugged his shoulders, accepting it as a natural consequence of the boy's parentage.

Fortunately or unfortunately, depending on whose perspective you were to take, a junior office assistant thoughtlessly slammed the till drawer hard on Bunni's fingers by uncovering, inadvertently, the misdirection of the funds. Filled with youthful indignation, the clerk, rather than asking, as a maturer man might have done, for a slice of the profits, took his discovery to the regional manager, who, although by no means guaranteed a place in heaven himself, had no choice but to dispense with Bunni's services.

Too embarrassed, if not ashamed, to return to the village, Bunni limped away to Honiara. After a period of sleeping on various wantoks' storeroom floors, he began to learn a little about the still relatively newfangled concept of business. Soon he too was adept at buying something at one price and selling it at another, extortionately higher. Eventually he bought a house and started his own family, which were, he quickly discovered, two crippling expenses. As the problems in Guadalcanal exacerbated and opportunities became scarcer in town, his thoughts turned to his home village.

Returning one Christmastime, he was greeted with open arms by his friends and family, most of whom, as was the way with these trusting people, either had forgotten or never truly believed the tale of his dismissal from the bank. Little by little he convinced his relations of the benefits of his latest scheme. He needed them to dive the deep pools of the lagoon and collect the huge crayfish that teemed there, the huge crayfish that commanded such incredible prices in Honiara. New hotels had sprung up after Independence in 1978 to cater for the crusades of aid workers that arrived in hordes to satisfy their craving for seafood and their urge to condescend.

Once the crayfish were safely packed in ice, he explained, he would accompany them in person on the *Iuminao* and supervise their sale. As soon as sufficient funds had been collected— a few days at most—he would then, of course, send his family the pay for the work they'd carried out. He offered them a handsome wage.

With enthusiasm for Bunni's clever idea, many of the young boys and girls jumped into their canoes, ready to set out for this exhausting and often dangerous work. It had been a good year for crayfish, and within two days they had collected enough to fill several large insulated containers that stood on the jetty. Everything went according to plan, and Cousin Bunni set off to get the best prices available.

"Bunni—him savvy now," everyone agreed proudly as they waved him off.

Beset by an impressive variety of obstacles that blocked his return to Mendali, Bunni did not come back in a few days or even a few months. A year or so passed, and there was still no sign of him or, more to the point, of any of the wages.

In the interim I had arrived. When I first began to get to know the area a little and shop owners and local businessmen found out where I lived, I had been surprised that so many of them asked me whether I had seen Bunni or when he might return. They all seemed very keen to talk to him.

"So maybe you and me can do some business?"

Bunni was still holding my hand.

"Well . . . I am not sure that . . . the thing is . . . it might be . . ." I stumbled as I withdrew it.

"Maybe I buy some chickens, you buy some chicken?" Fortunately he had provided me with an escape.

"But the chickens are nothing to do with me. They belong

to the community, and all the profits will go toward projects in the village."

"Yes, but you and me . . . How about maybe you buy some chickens, I buy some chickens?"

For want of a better argument, I repeated what I had just said.

"Yes, of course, I understand." He sighed.

"Understand?"

"Always the same with whiteman. Mmm, yes, I think you come here to steal the money from the village," he murmured, nodding out at the sea and then looking around him as if he meant that no one else should overhear our argument. He released a long sigh.

"What! You, er . . . I, no, no no, ha, ha, no, what?"

"Yes, that is it. I see it now. You think you can come to steal from the people here. You think they are stupid perhaps? But it is not as easy as you think."

I supposed he should know.

Removing his sunglasses with a flourish and standing up like the heroic defender of the people that he saw himself to be, he spat hard on the ground. Only when he looked at me again did I realize that he had an unmistakable squint. At first I wondered whether he was doing it on purpose, the trick of a second-rate entertainer to frighten the children and make them laugh all at the same time. I certainly felt like running away, chuckling as I went.

"Yes, you are a con man. I know it now," he exclaimed triumphantly, with the revelatory tones of a detective in the last scene of a mystery story.

"No, no. Not at all. Perhaps you are right, perhaps we could do some business. What a good idea. Excellent, yes . . ." I finished brightly but without much conviction. Unsure how to handle him, I decided that there was little point in arguing any further and attempted instead to placate him.

"We will see." He glowered darkly before stomping off, if such a thing is possible in a pair of white leather shoes and Mickey Mouse socks.

I was shaken by this short altercation. It was the first time that I had experienced any ill feeling from a Solomon Islander. Seeking out my good friend Tassels, I asked him what he thought.

"No wari." His face cracked into its familiar, lined smile. Leaning his head back and bunching his hair in both hands to the top of his head, he laughed gently, but I could tell that he was less than his relaxed self.

Small Tome was a little more forthcoming. "He is very jealous man. He covets our chicken."

This came as something of a shock. I had never considered that our chickens might be covetable.

"He wants to grow chicken for him, but you and me start before. Now him jealous tumas."

"What do you think he might do?" I asked nervously.

Small Tome was at once uncharacteristically serious. Now, for one of the first times since we'd met, his bright, cheerful face grew grave. (The only other occasion had been when he had accidentally pulled up one of Ellen's runner bean plants and I had told him that she was after him.)

"Oh sorry, Mr. Will, but him one cranky man. Problem: him got staka education but him no got any common sense. Maybe him try for stop yume?"

Well, I supposed, we would just have to wait and see. At least Bunni was living not in the village but way down the coast with some of his wife's wantoks, so it was not going to be a daily issue.

As it turned out, I was not to see Bunni again for some time, and the unpleasant scene was quickly lost among the stream of beautiful days that floated by as unconcerned as the clouds over the peaks of Mount Reve on Randuvu. More chick-

ens came and went, and little by little the village began to prosper.

Repairs to the church were soon possible, and Imp, the
village carpenter, and his assistant, Gordon, set about the roof,
pulling off the old, rusting corrugated iron, removing and
replacing rotten rafters. Smart gutter pipe ran along the edge of
the new sheeting, and from it a pipe led to a new, larger, steel
rainwater tank. After a few storms, it brimmed with clear, fresh
water straight from the sky.

Tins of paint were sent from Honiara, and the villagers
repainted the inside of the church a bright blue and green, mir-
roring the colors of the natural world in which we lived. A visiting wantok painted pastoral scenes on the wall behind the altar.
Shepherds and their flocks grazed alongside the Virgin mother
and child and a full-length, rather gruesome picture of the cru-
cified figure of Christ.

On the roof the two workmen waved hammers in greeting,
their mouths full of nails as they balanced on rickety homemade
ladders. Stanley and Small Small Tome helped out, scampering
along the ridge, carrying equipment and refreshments for the
workers. Small Small Tome would call out hellos in his strange,
strangulated voice, and Stanley would urge me to be sure to
attend that evening's service as each morning I set off for my
garden.

For just as things improved steadily in the village, so was
there promising horticultural progress. Although I had suffered
an initial setback when the small garden I planted soon after my
arrival was washed away one night by an abnormally heavy deluge, I had enough enthusiasm to start again. Sporadic agricultural espionage had produced a number of helpful tips, and
now, like the villagers, I took to hooping banana leaf shelters
over the fragile seedlings, sheltering them not just from the
incinerating sun but also from the marble-size raindrops that
would otherwise squash them flat. I discovered, because Jane

had told me during my stay in the capital, that the soil was badly leached by the high rainfall, so I experimented with various natural fertilizers. Randall's Number 1 mix was a secret combination of seaweed, leaf compost, rotten wood, and fish bones, of which there was no shortage. This and some mature chicken muck I combined in a battered oil drum.

After a couple of weeks, I spread it liberally on the ground and dug it in with the new spade that I had bought myself as a birthday present. The plants thrived, but the smell, certainly for the first week, was unspeakable. Their faces wrinkling in disgust as they passed my plot, the women returning from tending their own gardens would peer curiously into mine. What on earth was the whiteman up to? But soon the garden bloomed, and I was able to bring a veritable ratatouille of firm, fresh garden produce to Ellen's kitchen that would have had even Crusoe tearing his unkempt hair out with envy.

Tomatoes, peppers, eggplants, and cabbages of every variety grew in abundance, and soon the villagers were able to take the excess vegetables to market, where they sold almost before they had got out of the canoe.

It was with a woven basket containing a selection of these vegetables that I set off in the middle of one afternoon to visit my friends the Kings. Originally from the hills north of Melbourne, they and their three refreshingly pleasant children lived and taught as volunteer teachers in a secondary school up the coast of New Georgia, far beyond Munda at Beulah. On a number of occasions I had much enjoyed their witty, relaxed company at the rest house, and the last time we'd met, they had invited me to spend the weekend with them at the school.

I had been in the Solomons long enough now for lengthy boat journeys to have lost their novelty. My main aim was to reach my destination without getting burned raw by the crematorium sun, soaked to the skin by the impish rain clouds, or, of course, drowned by my own not inconsiderable incompetence.

This said, I now felt confident enough to skipper my own boat without the need for a crew and could happily punt my way over the reef to Munda, an hour or so away, to visit the shops or bank or, pointlessly, the post office.

I loaded up my canoe with the necessary kit: life jacket, water bottles, a long pole, sun cream, and more than enough petrol to get me there and back. Henry Fatty popped the engine on the back of the boat, and as long as that did not break down all would be well. I was waved off at the jetty as usual by the children; Stanley, who reminded me sternly that I should attend church on my arrival; and Ellen, who, I think, suspected that I was really heading for the fleshpots of Munda.

I pulled the starter rope that Geoff had kindly repaired. Firing immediately, the engine quickly settled down to a smooth hum—a promising, if slightly unexpected, start—and I set off out into the channel.

A few rain clouds were blowing away from me, the gray mist below them drenching somebody far off in the distance. Up ahead all was fair, and the motion of the boat lessened the heat of the sun off the surface of the water. Now confident, I pushed my sunglasses up onto the bridge of my nose, but they soon slithered back down to the tip on a slide of cream.

I had not seen a soul since I had left the village and waved to Imp, who was fishing off the tip of Te Ana Lasi, and I settled back down to enjoy myself. Up ahead was what appeared to be a large oil slick, but as I neared I discovered it to be a mass of red, apple-size jellyfish. In the middle floated a giant turtle, enjoying a lazy late lunch. Raising its head as it heard the motor approach and looking mildly irritated by the interruption to its unexpected gastronomic treat, the shy creature dived below the surface. As I passed overhead, I could see it disappear like a broad brown plate.

A little later, the surface of the water broke and, throwing itself into the air, an eagle ray shot upward, its beak, which lent it its name, pointing straight at the sky. It performed a back flip and then crashed back into the water with a gigantic belly flop. The spray flecked my face, refreshingly cool. This was the life, I thought—this was the life, a beautiful, warm, uncomplicated, uncluttered life.

This was a life to be led at a pace you chose, not one that was thrust upon you. A life that was not luxurious but one that was remarkable in its ability to provide such magnificent sights as I had just witnessed. I was in love with this Solomon Time.

The farther across the channel and into the deeper water I traveled, the greater the swell became. No waves, just a lolloping roll that picked up the boat, tipping it slightly and then setting it softly down again. Its rhythm was pleasant, and I made myself comfortable in the stern of the boat, resting my bare feet over the side. Behind me, as I looked over the foaming wash, I watched the village disappear out of sight, the nearest islands that fringed the reef now a good five hundred yards away. There was no land ahead of me for a couple of miles, just open sea. On I motored, rising and falling, carried along by the huge power of the water, able only to take pleasure in the ride.

Suddenly there was a bump underneath the boat and the engine slowed. I looked over the side to see a coconut spinning back to the surface with a fizzing in the white water behind me. I throttled back, found neutral, and swung the engine up. As the exhaust cleared the water, the engine coughed its annoyance loudly. The propeller was snarled with green strands of weed.

Leaning over cautiously, I freed the propeller with my hand. It was clear. Nothing too serious, but I would need to be on the lookout for any more flotsam and jetsam. I lowered the engine back into the water and set off again. All seemed to be well, but I continued at a slower rate. Peering up over the front of the bow, I could see coconuts and box-shaped sumai pods. I carved a careful route through them, and the way was clear for a while. As the sun started its languorous slide toward the sea, the two islands of Kiri Kiri rose up on my port side. Between them lay the passage that would take me through to the lagoon and on to Beulah. Slowly, I adjusted the tiller until my bow lined up with the space between the two islands and the boat began to run along the side of the swell.

As I did so I caught sight of what first appeared to be the antlers of a mighty Canadian elk or moose rising up from the water. I half-expected to see its begoggled face surface as, hopelessly lost, it moose/elk-paddled its way in search of home. I slowed down. As I neared it, I realized that the antlers were in fact the branches of an entire tree floating half-submerged in the water. Holding on to the throttle, I made the obviously not quite fatal error of standing up.

As I did so, the crafty sea took the opportunity to sneak up behind and gently tip me headfirst over the side of the boat.

⤳

CHAPTER 19

Once More unto the Beach . . .

Through the perfect blue, percolated with necklaces of tiny iridescent bubbles, I could see two strange, white sea creatures swimming toward my face, their tentacles flailing upward. After a moment of panic I realized that they were my hands, clawing for the surface, and breathed a deep sigh of relief. This, of course, proved to be a mistake.

Luckily, at that moment my head broke into the air and I swung myself around in a circle, looking for the canoe.

Of course, modern outboard motors are equipped with what is known as a kill switch. A line attaches you to the engine, and should man and machine part company, a plastic key snaps out of its clip and everything stops. Unfortunately, this was not a modern engine. What was more, Tassels, for greater snoozing

224

and fishing potential, had customized the twist throttle handle so that it would stick where it had last been set. As I had hit the water I hoped that the engine, for a reason best known to itself, would stall. It did not.

My sunglasses were now balanced on my top lip, so, having nothing better to do, I wiped the salt from the lenses, put them back on, and looked around again. I had hoped to see the canoe bobbing in the water like a horse that after losing its rider grazes, patiently waiting for him to stagger to his feet. Instead I glimpsed the boat puttering on steadily and in a perfectly straight line for the narrow passage between the two islands of Kiri Kiri. With it went my vegetables, my drinking water, and, most important, my inflatable life jacket.

It was a moment to take stock.

Right.

So here I was treading water. Water that, I seemed to remember from a chart in Gerry's office, was approximately 1,780 feet in depth. It was clear, quite clear—deep breaths—that I had two and only two options. Option One, I could head for land—far distant land—or, Option Two, I could stay where I was, which, for the moment, I found relatively easy to do. In fact, so warm and buoyant was the water that it was possible to lie fully stretched out on my back and, as long as I did not let my deep breath go, float with only the minimum of hand and foot movements.

It was Option Two then. I would just stay here until I was rescued.

It made sense: the last time that I had swum any distance had been in a suburban London swimming pool. I had been eight at the time and had received a sew-on badge for swimming twenty, possibly twenty-five yards backstroke. As I remembered, it had been something of a struggle. No, I would just wait for someone to pass by and pick me up. Someone was bound to turn up.

As the swell lifted me, I looked around. Miles of open water, no big boats, no little boats, in fact, nothing in sight at all. As I swept back down the slide of water, I tried to remember the number of boats that had passed me in the day, but my efforts came to naught. Even the elk or moose seemed to have disappeared.

Of course another perfectly valid reason for not hanging around unnecessarily in the water was the fact that the sea was absolutely brimming with sharks, and sharks are funny things. Somehow they manage to instill fear in practically everyone, and I fitted easily into the practically everyone category. I tried not to look down.

One of the glories of the Solomons, and it is well documented, is that their seas contain one of the largest number of species of sharks in the world. Mako, tiger, hammerhead, white tip, black tip, bronze whalers, gray whalers, big ones and small ones, long ones, thin ones, short ones, flat ones, slow ones, and fast ones—they are all well represented and all have in common, apart from horrible little black buttony eyes and totally undiscriminating taste buds, huge excesses of razor-sharp teeth. Rubbing one foot against the other, I was heartened to discover that both still seemed to be present.

Of course, the statistical chance of being attacked by a shark is small. It did strike me at that moment, however, that all the statistics I had ever heard quoted were based on samples taken from a broad range of the population. This broad range presumably included people who were, at present, walking down city streets, sitting in offices and traffic jams, watching television, or in the bath, where clearly the chances of being eaten by a large fish were slim. It had to be admitted, therefore, despite my every effort to think of a scientific reason why it should not be so, that I was running rather more of a risk than the average person. I started to swim.

It is interesting that—to change the subject and think of other things—the front crawl, the stroke preferred by modern swimmers, had been invented in the Solomon Islands. White traders had spotted the islanders performing this peculiar but effective action and had adopted it as their own. Not that that was of any great use to me; I had never got further than the backstroke. Nevertheless, by now I reckoned I had already quadrupled my personal best. When I bored of gazing at the sky, I turned onto my stomach and adopted an entirely new style, half frog, half drowning puppy.

Initially I found the going relatively easy, and if I alternated my two different strokes I could rest various hitherto undiscovered groups of muscles. They were having the shock of their lives.

My shorts, bought at an army surplus supplier in Brisbane, made of a thick, heavy-duty cotton, and furnished as they were with numerous pockets for water bottles, cigarettes, Swiss Army knives, et cetera, had proved to be excellent on dry land. Sadly now wet, they had developed the drag coefficient of a couple of heavy bags of shopping. Fond of them as I was, I was going to have to let them go, along with a smart leather belt, one of the many that I had received as birthday presents over the years.

Grimble had, under circumstances that I forget, been asked to remove his trousers. He had refused: "Dead or alive, said a voice within me, an official without his pants is a preposterous object and I felt I could not face that particular horror."

I, however, was not an official, and anyway this was only what Crusoe described as just another moment in the "uneven state of human life." So I stopped, wrestled the buckle undone, and yanked the buttons apart. Putting my thumbs into the waistband, I pushed down. Anyone who has tried this maneuver will know that it is actually very difficult to perform if you are also attempting to keep your head above the water. After rather a lot of unseemly struggling, I had them around my ankles. With a flick of my feet they fell off and sank.

Too late did I realize my mistake. In the process of divesting myself of my shorts, I had also managed to remove my underpants. A pair of medium-size expedition model boxers was now also commencing their long descent—somewhat to the consternation of any passing sharks, I imagined. In an effort to retrieve them, I scrabbled around below me but to no avail. They must have sunk quickly, wrapped as they were in my leaden shorts. At least swimming was much less difficult now that I was dressed in only a T-shirt and a pair of sunglasses, naked entirely from the waist down. In fact, it was almost a pleasure.

More worryingly though, I knew that my arms were beginning to tire. If I lay on my back and just kicked with my feet, then I could rest them, but progress was painfully slow. The quicker I could get out of the water the better. I was still not a little preoccupied by underwater predators, and my newfound seminudity had done nothing to improve my confidence. At least the swell seemed to be lessening and, in the calmer water, I could clearly see the two hummocks of Kiri Kiri. One moment they looked almost within touching distance, the next they seemed about as attainable as Alpha Centauri. There was no sign of the canoe.

Suddenly, as I paddle-steamed along on my back, my head connected with something hard in the water. Letting slip a popular vulgarity at top volume, I splashed epileptically away from the object. But whatever it was did not seem to be following me. I waited, my heart prevented from bursting completely out of my mouth by the firm clenching of my teeth. Strange though it may seem, up until this point I had not felt anything more than a vague sense of unease, a sense that I was in trouble but that somehow, at some time, my feet would touch sand beach again.

Now I was truly terrified. Drowning or being eaten had been only a televisual concept until now—something that happened to other people and then only on the news. All of a sudden it became a very real possibility. Here I was in the middle of the sea, half dressed, with nothing more than a pair of sunglasses to protect me, and I had just been attacked by an unseen aggressor.

Marvelous.

What I would have given at that moment to be back in my classroom. Leaning against a radiator teaching Robert and the rest, a whole class of Roberts if need be. The bell would ring and everyone would disappear through the door, wishing me good-bye until tomorrow. I would wrap up against the cold and switch out the lights. With a frost shimmering in the air, I would cross the echoing courtyard and get into my car. After a stop at the local pub for a beer and good company, I would arrive back at the house for a bite to eat in front of the fire, watch a film, and make my weary way to bed. Home sweet home.

Instead, I was bobbing helplessly in the middle of the Pacific Ocean on the cusp of extinction, or at very least running the risk of a nasty nip. But I would not give up without a fight. Mmmm Britannia, Britannia mm mm mm. I turned grimly about, seeking out my attacker—and then I saw it . . .

It was a coconut, a green shoot sprouting from the top. Then another one, and another. Swimming to them, I collected them with outstretched arms. They were surprisingly buoyant. Using them as a float, I settled down and kicked on with my feet. Reaching the islands was now a distinct possibility, and I allowed myself a smile. The sun had, however, now touched the water's edge and would, I knew, drop quickly out of sight. There was always a period of the night that was particularly dark, an hour or so between the setting of the sun and the appearance of the moon to cast its neon shadows across the islands. Once the sun was down, I would not be able to see a fin in front of my face. I splashed on.

It made little difference which of the two small islands I headed toward, as they were, as far as I knew, both uninhabited. Beautiful, circular, fringed with white sands and tufted with palms, they were the perfect get-away-from-it-all destination.

It had already crossed my mind that nobody was likely to come looking for me. The villagers were not expecting me to come back for a couple of days and, if I did not arrive at Beulah, the Kings would presume that I had not managed to get any transport, the weather was too rough to leave home, or, as often happened here, I just could not be bothered. With no telephone or radio in the village, there was no way of checking. I was not unduly worried by this, for the channel between the two islands was a pretty busy thoroughfare and I was sure to be able to hitch a ride, either back home or on to the school, whichever came first.

I was now exhausted but had lasted much longer than I had anticipated. Only a few hundred yards to go before I hit a small spit of sand, lit orange by the last of the sun, and I would be safe and dry. It was then that I felt a sudden sting on the ankle, a sharp stab. A while later numbness set in, then pins and needles began to prickle their way up my leg. Just as I was considering the possible repercussions of this creeping paralysis, the symptoms seemed dulled. I looked around as best I could and detected a number of small bubbles on the surface—the jellyfish that I had seen earlier. Imaginary stings covered my body. Nervously, I pushed on.

Finally, I experienced the delicious sensation of sand grazing my elbows and knees. After a careful inspection for teeth marks, it appeared that, apart from a nasty pink swelling on my ankle and a further last-minute one on my left buttock, I was unscathed.

On the other hand, I was incredibly thirsty. The coconuts bobbled randomly in the surf where I had dropped them. I sat down in the warm water and rubbed my toe. My tongue was as dry as a yam.

It is here that I write a few words of grudging gratitude to the coconut, because although at times I found it a supercilious, even occasionally downright unhelpful form of vegetation, without it I would certainly have spent a considerably less pleasant sojourn on my desert island.

This extraordinary tree provides an impressive range of products and fulfills so many vital daily roles it is difficult to imagine how the people of the Solomons would survive without it. So intrinsically important is it that a lease of land in the islands has a maximum tenure of seventy-five years—the life of a coconut tree. When the fruit is ripe, it obligingly falls from the tree and is ready to be harvested. The nut is encased in a thick, fibrous husk that breaks its fall, rebuffs intruders, and happily makes it buoyant should it fall into the water. Once the husk is stripped away, the nut is chopped in half to reveal two white hemispheres of kernel. The flesh, grated from the inside with a sharp instrument similar to that which is used to curl butter in smarter restaurants, is used as a flavoring for rice or the wallpaper paste that is tapioca pudding.

Alternatively, the two halves of kernel are dried over fires and packed tightly into hessian sacks. These sacks are shipped to oil-processing plants, where the kernels are crushed for the oil that is exported to the rest of the world, where it is used in vegetable oils, soaps, and margarines. Its leaves are woven into strong baskets for carrying vegetables, clothes, and babies, and it is from a "table" of these same leaves that many a feast has been eaten. The tough bark is stripped off and used to make rope, while the trunk itself is used for building bridges, houses, and canoes. Most important, though, the nut provides milk to drink—if you can open it.

Umpteen times I had watched youngsters stripping off the husks of coconuts with effortless ease. The prescribed method was to take the coconut in both hands and stab it onto a sharp wooden spike planted firmly in the ground. I did not have one. I broke off a tree branch, pushed it as hard as I could into the ground, and stepped back. It fell over like a fainting guardsman. I tried harder, and this time it snapped.

I noticed that the stump had a jagged point to it. I picked up the largest, most appetizing nut I could find and bashed it on the stick. It bounced off. I tried again with more success. It stuck—solid. Eventually with a splitting noise the husk began to tear away as I twisted. So, turning the nut, I repeated the procedure. Some more tore off. After about half an hour, I had stripped most of the husk away.

Now all I had to do was smash open the hard kernel. I tried hurling it on the ground, but it thudded dully on the sandy soil. I bashed it on a tree a few times, but the reverberations hurt my soggy hands. I even tried to throw it at the tree, but my aim was poor and I missed it five times for every one time that the two connected. On one occasion it rolled into the shrubbery, and I had to look for it like the lost ball at a village cricket match.

Abandoning the tree method, I walked round the island trying to find a stone on which to crack my nut. Five minutes later I had all but circumnavigated the entire island. It was only when I was a few yards short of my starting point that I found the perfect stone—a stone designed for the cracking of coconuts. I smacked my refreshment down a couple of times, and it started to leak. Holding it above me, I let the liquid drip down into my mouth. Delicious.

With my shirt as a pillow, I made myself as comfortable as possible on the sand. The warm breeze blew over my naked body, but by now, fortunately, it was properly dark and I am spared the embarrassment of having to describe the scene further.

With my eyes closed, I reflected upon my new position in life and found myself, somewhat against my will, agreeing with the profoundly obvious conclusion that Crusoe had come to when first he was cast away:

> EVIL: I am cast upon a horrible desert island, void of all hope of recovery.
> GOOD: But I am alive . . .

Although I should have stayed awake longer worrying about my situation, fatigue took a hand, and I quickly fell asleep lulled by the night song of that wonderfully named bird—the spangled drongo.

CHAPTER 20

~~≈~~

No Smoke Without Fire

Nudism, I had always felt—being modest by nature—was an activity best left to middle-aged Germans braving it on the Baltic. This said, in the warm air of the Pacific, it had its attractions.

It was perhaps only now, in the predicament in which I found myself, that I fully realized the benefits of a climate that was often intensely hot but never cold. Nights spent sleeping in the cool breezes that blew in from the ocean were remarkably pleasant, and as the days passed I had developed a healthy tan—if such a thing still exists. Henry Fatty had noted with some interest my ever darkening hue and one day had laid our two arms down on a table to study them. "Yu close up blakman now," he had said approvingly.

Comparing his deep black, muscled forearm to the pale rolling pin of my own, I had considered that there might still be some way to go, and now, in my present state of dress, it was only too easy to see the demarcation lines where the suntan ended and the almost shocking whiteness began.

Although I had been overcome with propriety when I had first woken, as the day progressed I became less and less self-conscious. By the time that the sun had cleared the sea, I had come to quite enjoy my newfound nakedness. Sand was a bit of a problem, of course.

I was aware, nevertheless, that I was going to have to attend to my appearance before I made any attempt to be rescued. So, I ventured into the bush to look for some materials that I might fashion into a temporary outfit. This shouldn't be too difficult, I thought, as I approached the suburban-garden-size patch of jungle. After all, people had used natural materials for centuries. Nowadays of course we were lucky enough to be able to slip into cotton and nylon and rayon and so on, but in times gone by man had had to use whatever the natural world had to offer. So that was exactly what I would do.

After all, Adam and Eve had just plucked fig leaves to conceal their newly discovered shame. Although I was not entirely sure what a fig tree looked like, there was bound to be something similar. As long as I avoided the nalato bush, the leaves of which left painful blisters wherever they came into contact with the skin, all should be well. Stanley had given me graphic depictions of the agonies endured by Japanese and American soldiers when they had availed themselves of the nalato leaf as alternative lavatory paper.

Equally illustratively, Small Small Tome had described the penis sheaths, surprisingly long wooden tubes worn by "bushman," the inland tribes who lived in the jungle on several of the Pacific Islands. Unfortunately, I had not quite understood the mechanics required to keep such an item of apparel in place, let alone upright.

I decided that something that required less technique in

the wearing would be more appropriate for my purposes and hunted around for suitable items. Although I was not looking for anything particularly showy, just something comfortable and casual, eco-tailoring proved to be much more difficult than I had imagined.

My first attempt was a disaster. Having affixed various greenery about my person, I stepped out onto the beach, but two experimental hula hoop wiggles of my hips later the whole arrangement fell into a heap around my ankles. It was clear that I was going to require something sturdier if I was to be able to hitch my way out of my present misfortune.

My next creation was a very authentic grass skirt that, if a little daring, at least seemed willing to stay put. I successfully made it down to the water's edge. I tried a few jumping jacks. Still fine.

As a final test, I took a short jog along the narrow strip of sand through the shells and leaves to a fallen tree some forty yards away. Things were fine for the first five, a little loose after ten, and before I had reached the twenty-yard mark I was tripped up by my waistband. Back at the drawing board, I finally produced a version that, if rather more constrictive, at least was solidly built. I ran gingerly to the tree and back. Ideal, if a little itchy.

It was a beautiful morning to be stranded on a desert island. Dragonflies with bodies as long as sparkling pencils hovered over the shrubs, their two sets of wings blurring as they searched out a bit of prey here and there. Below them foot-long geckos skittered across the sand in a bursting rush to get nowhere in particular. Shoals of near-oval, silver fish plip-plopped in and out of the water in such perfectly equidistant semicircles that they blurred into a solid mass, giving the impression of a hooped sea serpent undulating through the shallows. I sat down on the ground to watch them and wait for my imminent rescue.

Some considerable time later, and some even more considerable time after that, I was still waiting. Pacing up and down, up and down, I amused myself by writing witty messages in the sand and pondering the number of ways that there were to spell "wos 'ere." Eventually I grappled my way into another coconut, which slaked my thirst and put something into my rumbling stomach.

By now the sun had crept up to just the right angle to strike its fiercest, so I moved into the shade of the trees and fashioned a hat from two banana leaves. I would like to describe it accurately, but it was of no particular style. What do you call a man with two banana leaves on his head?

No boats passed. Nothing. Why not?

This was normally a busy thoroughfare, used by people living on outlying islands to ferry goods to and from the market at Munda. Confused, I consulted my watch, which I discovered was in my cupboard at home.

Sunday!

It was Sunday and it was church day and it was Day of Rest day and it was stay at home with the family day and do nothing very much day (not that this made it particularly exceptional). It was certainly not hop into your canoe and paddle around to see if any white man had been stupid enough to strand himself on any of the more remote islands day.

Or perhaps, for a reason unknown to me, nobody came by this way anymore? Perhaps someone had cast a spell on this passage and nobody dared brave the evil spirits that dwelled here now?

Spells?

Now, of course, I was just being ridiculous, sensational.

Evil spells, spirits, dear, oh dear. Ha, ha!

Well, in that case, why was the island of Tetepare deserted? A large island southwest of Randuvu, some twenty miles long, was now totally uninhabited. Why had nearly all the islanders there died of a plague and the rest taken to their canoes and fled? Because someone had cast a spell, of course. Imp had been quite sure of it.

The islanders, although firm in their Christian beliefs, still had a strong sense of the supernatural, and were forever telling tales of mythical beasts and spirits that lived in the jungle. Grimble had had to deal with a bunch called the Taani-kanimomoi— the whistlers of the dead—who would appear and smash your head open. It must have been pretty difficult to announce their appearance in a hurry.

He had been given a special incantation to recite if the Taani-kanimomoi were thought to be about. I remembered that it required an offering of food as an accompaniment, so I solemnly raised a shard of half-gnawed coconut in both hands in front of me. Right. Okay.

> This is the lifting up of the portion of the Ancestors.
> Here is thy food, Auriaria: I have committed no incest.
> Here is thy food, Tituaabine: I have not harmed thy
>   creature [the giant ray].
> I am excellent-e-e! I touch the Sun, I clasp the moon.
> Turn back the spirits of the death-magic: turn them
>   back, for I, Grimble [here I substituted Randall], beg
>   you.
> I am not lost. Blessings and Peace are mine. Blessings
>   and Peace.

This all seemed like pretty good gobbledygook, and I had no idea what incest had to do with it. I hardly knew how to pronounce the names of those I was calling upon for salvation, let alone who they were. What was more, the very last thing I felt was excellent, certainly not excellent-e-e.

Still, there had been no harm in giving it a go. There must be something in all this superstition. I knew that nobody in

Mendali—man, woman, boy, or girl—would consider venturing away from the village and into the bush after the sun had disappeared below the waves, for fear of the devils that came at night to lurk behind every tree or bush. Surprisingly, they were perfectly happy to go out on the sea or even in it in the pitch dark.

Anyway, someone was bound to turn up soon.

To take my mind off the prospect of a long, enforced sojourn, I set off in search of anything edible that did not come packaged in a husk three inches thick.

Inland, I came across a vine that grew prolifically over the stump of a long dead tree. On it were dozens of small, purple fruits. Although the skins were tough and wrinkled, the fruit seemed soft inside. I tore the skin, and out oozed a yellowish jelly packed with small seeds. I sniffed it cautiously, as if it were the bottom of a shoe. It smelled just like a glass of tropical fruit drink, but, not knowing at the time that it was a passion fruit and not wishing to add to my woes, I discarded it and moved on.

Close by, I came across a papaw tree, and in its top branches a few feet up above me hung its pendulous teardrop fruit, green tinged with orange. Papaw was highly overrated, tasting a little like nothing at all, but at least I knew it to be safe to eat. What, however, I did not know was that the papaw tree is not built to resist the close attentions of tall castaways. I inched my way up the fibrous trunk, imitating, with a little less grace, the method employed by the village children. I was a good two feet from the ground when with a crackling the whole tree snapped in half, leaving me on all fours over the log and my costume in tatters. At least the fruit was plentiful, and I ate two there and then, before taking two more back with me to the shore.

Wandering along the sand spit, I gazed down the channel and around the lagoon. Whichever way I looked, there was no sign of anybody.

Although I was aware that I had been marooned, half

drowned and pretty much naked, on a desert island, nothing seemed in any way extraordinary. If I had read this tale in England I would have been incredulous—just another unlikely piece of journalism in the Sunday papers, an entertaining story over a late breakfast. It was certainly not something that could happen to someone like me.

Now though, adapted to this different world, I considered my plight to be just one of life's little vicissitudes. In degree it was no more extraordinary than missing the last bus home or finding that the shop has run out of your favorite kind of dish soap—something to be taken in stride, with a shrug and a quiet sigh.

Hence I found myself considering quite soberly how I could best catch one of the many fish that flashed and spun in the water below me. I had heard tell that, in the east of the Solomons, fishermen would strip the bark from a certain tree and, folding it into a small parcel, dive deep to lodge it under a stone or a coral outcrop. A few minutes later, fish would surface belly up, stunned by a mild poison infused into the water. It was an easy job then to scoop them into the bottom of the canoe with a large landing net. Sadly, I did not know which kind of tree and, short of skinning a little off each of them or asking someone, I had no way of finding out.

Deciding to take a more orthodox approach, I started the hunt for some fishing tackle. I had a painful reminder of where I might find a hook. Walking back from the bush to the village one day after an afternoon admiring my vegetables and my horticultural prowess, I had lost my footing on a steep bank. Reaching out to slow my slide, I had grasped at the nearest greenery, and as it had slipped through my hands I had had the impression of being treated by an inept acupuncturist. After I had picked myself up, I had discovered that my palms were covered in small blood spots caused by curved, barbed hooks that grew along the edges of the leaves. This was the loya cane and very nasty, Luta had told me later as he cheerfully dug out the hard black tips from my soft flesh with the point of my penknife.

Finding a clump of this vicious plant, I broke off a few hooks and placed them carefully on a log. Line proved considerably more difficult to come by, but eventually I discovered some bark that seemed to tear off in fairly thin strips. As the water was shallow, I did not need any great length. After a couple of attempts, I ended up with a piece about six feet long, which I tied clumsily to one of the small wooden hooks; then I took a test cast. It floated. Tying a small piece of coral into the line, I tried again. This time it sank, and the hook hung relatively vertical among the fish that darted around it. They took little or no notice. Bait was what I needed. I retrieved the line.

After a rather peculiar dance, which incorporated rolling eye movements and slaps to various parts of my anatomy, I managed to swat a fly on my leg. Squidging its remains onto my hook, I tried again. This time the fish showed considerably more animation, nipping in to take little pecks. Out of the blue, a goldfish, of the size that you might win at a carnival or a fair, darted in. Scattering the other, smaller fry, it swallowed the fly, hook and all. I tugged excitedly, ready to do battle. The hook came off the line and my lunch swam off, coughing and shaking its head as if it had just swallowed a fish bone.

I gave up and went back to the shade of the trees. By this stage, it had dawned on me that, even if I did manage to land anything, I had no means of cooking it. In the village, I had eaten raw kingfish soaked in lime juice and coconut milk and sprinkled with coriander, but raw goldfish just did not have the same appeal.

So I set myself the task of lighting a fire. It was to be a challenge, man using the resources at his disposal to triumph against all odds.

I failed dismally.

Once in the bush on Randuvu I had seen it done. Old

Zephaniah, who was the brother of Old Ezekiel and, I think, grandfather to Small Small Tome, had been in a predicament. His ever-present cigarette had gone out. It was just beginning to rain, and one of the great drops that came splattering down landed on the bright red tip, which, with a resigned *pfff,* turned black. He cursed and asked round for matches. None of us had any. With a shrug he disappeared into the trees, returning after a few minutes with two short pieces of wood. Sitting cross-legged on the forest floor, he proceeded to do something that I did not realize was still possible. Putting the end of one stick on the ground and holding it at a shallow angle, he placed the end of the other on top of it. Slowly but purposefully he began to rub this one up and down. At first there seemed to be no change, but then slowly a groove started to appear, and the shavings that were worn away collected as fine dust at the bottom of the indentation. Firmly and patiently, Zephaniah rubbed and then, bending his craggy face over the two pieces of wood, the movement never ceasing, he gently began to blow. Almost as if he had achieved some holy act, some miracle, I watched as the first wisp of smoke started to twist up. He blew again, and the tiny heart of dust began to glow.

The others gathered round, joining him, communing with this moment. Placing small offerings, twigs and leaves, on the infant fire, they watched it grow until with an electric crackle the flames burst into life and the smoke rushed up through the thick, green growth above us and away into the sky. He then relit his cigarette and walked on.

I found two identical sticks, utterly indistinguishable from the pair that Old Zephaniah had used, and rubbed them together for about an hour. Absolutely nothing happened. Not even a groove. I threw the sticks into the sea in exasperation and lay back resignedly. As I did so, my makeshift skirt outfit finally gave up and gave way.

I was now rather glum. Beautiful though the island was, being stranded on it was extremely dull. When he was finally rescued, Robinson Crusoe discovered that he had been on his island "eight-and-twenty years, two months and nineteen days." I could only imagine he was easily amused. I had been here for only one day and was already bored witless. I was also under the distinct impression that this enforced solitary confinement would not do great things for the balance of my mind. I carved a notch in the trunk of a tree with the edge of an abandoned shell and tried to picture what sort of state Crusoe's trees must have been in by the time he left.

I lay down in the pale shade, closed my eyes, and listened to the rolling crash of waves as they broke endlessly. Day in, day out this sound would be like the hum of city traffic, worse in fact because it would not be interrupted by the hooting of horns, smashing of headlights, or screaming of enraged invective.

Then I heard it—a motor. No, no, it was an aural mirage, the first sign of impending madness. But, almost against my will, I listened again. No, it was true. Definitely an outboard engine.

I clambered to my feet and ran along the sand. Its bow nodding like a tired racehorse, a canoe was galloping across the wavelets that ran up the channel. I leaped up and down, waving both arms in the style of a kidnapped cheerleader, until the man at the tiller raised one hand in response and I saw the canoe readjust its line.

Salvation!

I punched the air and swung my hips from side to side in celebration. Only then did I remember that I was as naked as a jaybird. There was no time to wonder what a jaybird was or why it was permanently unclothed as I scuttled behind a bush. I grabbed my T-shirt from its peg in the trees, tucked it between my legs, and tied short sleeve to hem around my waist. It looked, I realized as I waded into the water toward my rescuer's boat, alarmingly as if I was wearing a pair of old-fashioned diapers.

Oh, well, what price freedom?

❧

Dokta Will

No harm done, I thought as Mendali came into sight. I was in one piece and so, fortunately, were the canoe and motor, which Benjamin, my phlegmatic rescuer, had spotted stuck, undamaged, in a hedge of mangroves a few hundred yards from his village. As the boat and outboard were important forms of transport between the islands, the relief poured off me when he told me of his discovery. He lent me a pair of voluminous blue shorts, which absentmindedly I almost put on over my T-shirt. He then helped me to relaunch my canoe and, once he was confident that I was under way, carried on fishing.

Back in the village, there was a disappointing lack of excitement at my return. Although I tried to leak the news that my trip had not gone as smoothly as intended, nobody appeared too interested in my lucky escape. Only Innocent, who wanted to tug the inflating cord on my life jacket, and Old Obadiah, who asked if he could have my undelivered vegetables, which of course he could, expressed any interest in me or my shipwreck. Everyone was trying to get to the bottom of a far more serious set of circumstances.

Despite their initial enthusiasm for sharing their charges' sleeping quarters, the two Young boys had discovered after the first couple of weeks, by which time the birds were a bit older and bolder, that a night in the chicken house was not quite the featherbed that they had initially imagined it would be. Having their faces regularly trampled by dozens of pairs of clawed feet, they quickly discovered, was not conducive to a good night's rest. Add to this the choking smell of ammonia and the incessant clucking chatter, and it was easy to appreciate why the boys had eventually picked up their mat beds and walked—straight back home.

They were, however, both conscientious in their efforts, forever walking back and forth to the house, swinging their flashlights and talking nonstop about the progress of the birds. At the very moment that I was waking up to face my first day of splendid isolation, Young John and Young George were arriving at the chicken house with buckets of feed and water. As they approached they discovered that the door to the house swung wide open. Immediately one brother blamed the other and vice versa.

Fortunately few of the fat, lazy chickens were curious enough to leave the comparative cool of the house with its readily available refreshments, so it was a reasonably easy task to shoo back inside those that had waddled out for an investigative morning stroll. Both boys swore at length that the door had been closed the night before.

The following morning the door was open again. We parted the squabbling Youngsters and assured them that they were not to blame, but it became clear, as we held hurried crisis talks over the card table, that this was not a coincidence. Perhaps, though, it was no more sinister than a curious child? Certainly all the chickens still seemed to be present and correct.

Nevertheless, we decided to take no further risks, and Small Tome, who was going to Munda that morning to sell some vegetables, brought back a small brass padlock and three keys. I gave one each to the two boys, which they hung round their necks on strings, and I kept the third one on a nail in my hut. The following night passed without incident, as did the next, and we began to think that whoever had been responsible had been foiled by the new security arrangements. Life, with a long sigh of relief, returned to normal.

Sadly, malaria was part of normal life in the Solomons.

In the middle of one wet night, I was woken by the sound of the rain playing timpani on the roof of the church. For the first time since I had arrived, I felt intensely cold—not just a case of the shivers but a cold that seemed to come from inside me and that caused goose pimples to pop up on my arms and chest. Then, as I knew would inevitably happen, I became fiery hot, as if my body had been pulled out of a freezer and shoved into a hot oven. I sat up awash with sweat, and Chutney mewed her sympathy from the enamel-topped table.

Shortly after my arrival in the Solomons, I had read, with no little interest, all about the symptoms of malaria on a "tick the boxes" sheet of paper that Geoff kept in his office to cheer up concerned clients. The main highlights to look out for included fever and chills or flulike symptoms—check, as Americans say—muscular aches—which were likely to give me less cause for concern—and jaundice ("yellowing of the skin and whites of the eyes"). In the gloom I held up my hands in front of my face, but I had no mirror.

The sufferer, I was informed, was likely to feel tired. I did, exhausted in fact, but was not sure whether this was a true symptom or just the result of being woken at some unearthly hour in the middle of the night by some thoughtless bloody rain cloud. Possible pains in the lower abdominal area accompanied by diarrhea had been the last telltale sign of approaching death.

Well—I smiled with relief—all seemed clear on that front. Then my lower abdominal area suddenly gurgled and twitched its disagreement.

The hospital at Munda was a cheerful, lively place, the pale blue buildings laid out round a white-hot sand parade ground, the purpose of which remained unclear. Small Tome had accompanied me lest I was too weak to make it on my own, and as we approached I pictured wheelchair parades, the sick and their smiling nurses in their bustling light green uniforms saluting Dr. James, who stood on a low podium, his stethoscope hanging proudly around his neck. The young, enthusiastic doctor from New Zealand had recently qualified and now found himself, after a sudden case of voluntary generosity, solely responsible for a hospital that provided the only health care in a fifty-mile radius.

"Reception" was the open veranda of the largest building and comprised two nurses seated at a camping table, on which lay a pile of registration cards and some glass slides.

Small Tome was most solicitous as we walked up the steps. "Oooh, malaria him rubbish something. One time me got malaria me close up die," he muttered reassuringly.

Actually, I felt a little better than I had the night before, although my joints had started to ache and my limbs were heavier than normal. I did also have quite a strong desire to be sick, but this may well have had more to do with the lurching, lolloping boat crossing we'd just made, Small Tome pushing our old motor to its limits to get me to medical assistance with the utmost urgency.

When my time came, I took the place of a young mother and her screaming, breathtakingly snotty baby at the flimsy table. I smiled at the nice nurse, and she smiled back. She took my details and asked me to stand on some scales, which she pushed out from under the table with her toe. Looking down, I read my weight to be nine pounds. I shot the nurse a concerned look.

Tutting, the friendly nurse pushed me off and, muttering an oath as she did so, jumped with both her smart black lace-up shoes onto the offending piece of equipment. Then she pulled me back on and the dial swung easily. I was going to have to cut down on the sweet potatoes. Oh, well.

"What kind problem now yu got?" she asked as she took my pulse.

I explained all my symptoms and pointed out how closely they bore comparison to Geoff's sheet. When I had finished Nurse summarized: "Hot, cold, sick-sick, belly run li'l bit." Rather more than a little bit actually, but it was only tempting fate to discuss it further.

"Finger blong yu."

"Hmmm?"

"Come finger!" Her kindly tone seemed to have evaporated.

Shyly, I produced my right index finger and, before I knew what had happened, the wicked witch of a nurse had pinned it down on the table and stabbed it with a small knife blade that she had been secreting about her person. Although it did not hurt much, I was greatly taken aback and hurriedly removed my hand.

The nurse, who was by now in free fall in my estimation, reached out again to seize my finger like a school crayon and rub it, none too delicately but with obvious enjoyment, on one of the glass slides. Handing it to me, she relinquished my wounded digit and pointed at an open window on the far side of the parade ground.

"Go lookim man with eyeglass."

I scowled at her and did as I was told. At the window was a bearded man seated at a table in front of a microscope.

Malaria, as most people know, is a parasite that travels from victim to victim by mosquito. What is less well known, however, is that there exist a number of different types of malarial parasite, which range from the relatively benign give-you-a-bit-of-a-headache-but-nothing-to-worry-about, go-home-and-sleep-it-off variety to the convulsions-and-almost-immediate-death, cerebral variety—the dreaded *falciparum* strain. The man through the window with the beard and the microscope was going to tell me which one he could see career-ing around on the slide. As I handed it over, I could imagine them: yellow circles with winking eyes and big, flapping mouths gobbling up all my corpuscles or whatever it was they did. It was not a great moment.

"S'pose yu like for come back behaen?"

Behind—later? How much later? They might have fin-ished wiping the plate by then. Beardo shrugged as he chucked the slide on the bench. Small Tome and I went over despon-dently to sit in the shade of the men's ward. A man with a mys-terious, patchy skin complaint that made him look like a short-necked, two-legged giraffe, offered us some pieces of his banana. Tome accepted, but I refused. I thought I might be contagious.

We waited for what could have been a lifetime, my symp-toms increasing all the while. Soon I was able to tick every box on the fact file sheet and could have written a short paragraph in the "Any Other Notes" section.

Eventually Beardy sissed at us and, head swimming, I staggered over to the window. He nonchalantly handed me a small, folded slip of paper. I stared at him intently for signs of great sorrow but, unmoved by my plight, he turned and took a slide from an old man behind me. I walked away like Long John

Silver holding the Black Spot—mind you, what were a few dirty smudges compared to raging *falci-thingummy*?

With feverish fingers, I smoothed out the piece of paper in the palm of one hand and then slowly opened one eye. "Negative."

It was just like opening exam results—in fact, in my personal experience, considerably better. The relief was enormous, and I released a loud whoop of delight. Small Tome was pleased for me, if a little surprised as I grabbed him by both hands and danced around in a little circle. The Giraffe Man clapped his hands with enthusiasm.

"So how are you?" Dr. James asked as he walked out of the ward.

"Fine, absolutely fine," I said, gleefully brandishing the piece of paper under his nose.

"Well, how are you feeling now?"

I stopped and had a feel. I had never been better.

Dr. James laughed. "Been out in the midday sun a bit long, I reckon. Make sure you drink plenty of water and try and stay in the shade as much as possible," he advised. "By the way, how's your medical kit look out on Randuvu?"

I thought of my prophylactics and syringes. Not very impressive, I admitted.

"What do you know about first aid? You could do a bit out on your island. Save you all having to come over here all the time. Here, follow me."

In a storeroom full of shelves but not a great deal else, Dr. James filled a small cardboard box with a selection of his scanty stocks: a number of bandages, clean white dressings in plastic envelopes, rolls of pink sticking plaster, and some fluffy, makeup-removal cotton. In one corner he slid a dark brown bottle of antiseptic ointment and told me that it would kill anything. Although I did not think this sounded very Hippocratic, I thanked him very much.

He disappeared into his office for a few minutes and returned to discover Small Tome and me rummaging through our new medical supplies.

"Here you go. You can have a read through this." He handed us a slim paperback with a large red cross on the front cover. "I've turned down the corners of the pages that'll interest you lot. Anything else you'll have to come in for."

I opened the book at one of the pages he had picked out. On a double spread was an extremely graphic picture of a young woman who it appeared had been the victim of a marauding chain-saw lunatic. Blood poured from at least five different locations, while a man knelt beside her ineffectually attempting to stanch the torrents with bits of cotton and sticking plaster. The page was entitled "Car Accident." I looked up frowning, and Dr. James grinned. "Cross out the 'Car' and write in 'Shark' or 'Outboard Motor,'" he suggested helpfully. "Read it up and keep it handy. You never know."

I thanked him rather doubtfully and promised that I would do as he suggested.

"Nice wan. Yu doktaman now." Small Tome shook me warmly by the hand. "Now mifala call yu Dokta Will!"

As we made our way back to the boat, I assured him that I was no medic. Having said that, I had shrugged off my malaria pretty successfully.

It was very kind of Dr. James to have given us all the supplies, but unfortunately it did seem that, now I was in possession of my booklet, the villagers considered that I had had bestowed upon me some sudden special knowledge. It was as if I had become qualified without having had to learn anything, almost as if I had gained a degree from an American university. It also seemed that the gift had sparked off a worrying spate of gruesome injuries. Once the news of my new title had spread, an army of walking wounded paraded outside my door.

Book in one hand and disinfectant in the other, I just had

to get on with it. Surgery hours were organized between the end of evening service and suppertime, and there were always at least half a dozen, usually small, takers. Until then the limit of my medical intervention had been to borrow someone's handkerchief and hand it to one of my pupils so that he could stanch a bleeding nose after a dustup at a rugby match. But now I found satisfaction in coping and dealing with the butcher shop appearance and awful smell of some of the injuries, cuts, and infections. There was a certain pleasure to be gained in applying a dressing neatly or removing one to discover that the wound had healed and that there would be no scar.

The pain threshold of the islanders was extraordinary, the stoicism with which physical injury was suffered remarkable. Perhaps this was because there was normally very little to take the pain away, no drugs or tablets and also remarkably little sympathy.

Innocent, in a flat-out charge to tackle one of my legs, had misjudged his launch and connected with the edge of the wooden bench outside Ellen's kitchen. In the process he had neatly pushed six bottom teeth through his lower lip, which lent him a curiously determined air. Once everything had been rearranged, there was still a long, wide gash on his chin that glinted whitely each time he smiled, which, actually, was not that often. Happily, though, the application of a goatee beard of bandages carefully stuck in place every morning resulted in hardly a blemish. The experience also seemed to have considerably lessened his enthusiasm for springing surprise attacks.

Tassels had succeeded, in his haste to find shelter from a surprise storm, in connecting with the corner of the metal roof of the vestry, thereby creating a flap three inches square in his scalp. In order to tackle the wound, it had been necessary to cut some of his legendary locks away from the top of his head. By the time we'd finished there was a hole in his hair that could quite easily have held a pot of geraniums and he was nearly in tears of dismay. I could think of no way of affixing the dressing, so instead I placed it on top of the wound, which still smoldered from the antiseptic, and wrapped a triangular bandage over the whole like a head scarf, tying it in a bow under his chin. I spent much of the next few days convincing him to keep it in place and the remainder of the time worrying that the rest of the village might expire from prolonged laughter.

One evening, as I was working my way toward the end of the surgery queue, one of Gerry's hire boats arrived at the jetty. Big Thomas, Henry Fatty's five-, six-, or seven-year-old, who had fallen out of a papaw tree during a scrumping raid on Ruth's garden, was just limping off with a new bandage around the deep hole that one of the branches had punctured in his not inconsiderable thigh. Next in line was Milly, a pretty little girl with blond hair and blue eyes in striking contrast to her dark engraved skin, who had, in a hectic game of wallop-another-small-child-as-hard-as-you-can-and-run-away, fallen and cut her shin deeply below the knee. Now it was her turn to sit up on the card table. She smiled at me weakly as I applied some of the hissing antiseptic.

We watched as three white men got out of the boat and approached Stanley, who was fishing from the jetty. They spoke to him briefly but, as he was keeping half an eye out for Chutney, whom he had rumbled a few weeks before, he just pointed with his chin to where I was standing by Milly. The three of them looked over. From their dress and the sounds that drifted ahead of them, I guessed that they were American. I was right.

"Hi there. You're Will, right?"

I agreed that I was.

"Mind if we look around?"

"Sorry, you are?"

"Oh, yeah. I'm Dwayne, Dwayne Tyler." The tallest of the three introduced himself. A thickset head possessed of two clay gray, unkind eyes jutted out chin first below a wide-brimmed hat. A big, buckled belt tilted below a belly born of beer and beefsteak.

"This here's Pat Dougherty," he said with a nod of his head.

A gaunt man with black, lank hair and two days' growth bristling on the graying skin of his face stuck out a thin, white hand. "Good to meet you, Will."

The third man stepped forward. He was slightly shorter than the other two, and his face beamed innocence if not intelligence.

"Howdy, the name's Clinton. I'm certainly pleased to meet you, Will."

"Clinton's our cattle expert."

"Cattle expert?"

"Sure." Dwayne looked me directly in the eye. "We've got a proposal for you, Will."

I lifted Milly off the table where she was sitting, her eyes boggling at not one but four different white people. Most of the children had become used to seeing me in the village, but it struck me then that perhaps they had not realized there were more like me. She hobbled off, no doubt to tell her friends of her extraordinary discovery.

"Yeah, we reckon you'll be interested in this one. It's a winner."

Go on.

"Well . . . my colleagues and I, yeah, we're planning to breed cattle in the islands, and we are pleased to tell you that we are looking at your land as a possible station."

"Err, hold on."

He was already using the too-good-to-be-true language of the professional salesman.

"I think you must be making a mistake. This isn't my land. It belongs to the villagers here."

"Yeah, we know that, but you could talk to the chief and tell him what a good idea y'reckon it is."

"Well," I said, trying to be diplomatic. "I think you might have to give me a bit more information, you know. Maybe some facts and figures?"

"Well, of course, pal. We don't have anything with us right at the moment, it's all back at the guesthouse. . . . Tell you what, we're going to be around a few days. How about you come over to Munda and have a bit of a feed, a few beers? We could talk it through."

I could not see any harm in that, and I had already planned to meet the Kings on Saturday morning to catch up on news after my aborted visit. "How about Friday evening?" I suggested.

They agreed. Dwayne asked again if they could walk about the village and bush, but I knew the women, at least, might be frightened. At any rate Luta, who as chief was really the person to give permission, was out in the bush collecting materials for a new house he wanted to build. I explained this and suggested that if they wanted to come back again then I would ask him and let them know on Friday.

"So why the Solomons?" I asked as we walked back to the canoe.

Clinton turned to me lazily and spoke slowly in a sleepy drawl. "Don't you just love the islands? Aren't the people just great?"

I did and they were, but that did not mean I wanted a herd of cows to share my discovery. Still, I was intrigued, and Friday would, I was sure, prove to be interesting.

That night our nocturnal visitor returned. This time the methods employed were somewhat cruder. When the lads turned up in the morning, the door had been forced off its hinges and removed. Again strangely, although greater numbers of chickens had poked their beaks out of the house, none seemed to be missing. Fortunately, Young George had the good sense to pour a thin trail of feed from some nearby bushes into the house. Pecking eagerly, the birds quickly bobbed their way back inside. Coconut leaves temporarily boarded up the hole, and later the door, still with its padlock and latch, was found stuck in the dark brown mud of the riverbed.

There seemed to be only one solution: night watchmen. Everyone was enthusiastic, and soon a team had been chosen and a roster of guards, two at a time, organized. When one shift had finished it would go and wake the next and so forth through till dawn. That night I saw the first two sentries setting off, flashlights in hand and stout sticks hoisted on their shoulders.

The following morning, I saw the same two returning.

"Bad luck. You had to do two shifts, did you?"

They looked rather sheepish. Actually no, in fact they had nodded off and only woken when the sun came up. As they had been sleeping in the doorway, all had been well, but after prayer, at which Stanley was, by now, practically ticking off my attendance, we held a short meeting. The workings of my old green and brass alarm clock were explained, and it was agreed that henceforth it would be kept in the broiler house. When it went off the guards would know it was time for the next shift to be woken.

I heard it ring periodically through the night as the guards reassured themselves that they really did know how it operated.

≈

CHAPTER 22

A Place in the Market

"How are you, my friend? Good to get away from the village, huh?"

There was a complicity in the question that I did not like, but I managed a suitably noncommittal answer.

I had arrived early for my Friday evening appointment at the guesthouse. The three cattlemen were already at the bar. They had, I suspected, been there some time. Dwayne swung round and leaned back on both elbows. "What are you drinking?"

As I could not remember the last time I had tasted one, and as I was clearly not paying, I asked for a glass of red wine. It was phenomenally expensive.

"Good idea, friend. I'll join you. Two bottles of y'all's finest red."

Titus, the impassive barman, produced two dusty bottles of the only one.

"Here you go, Will. Looks like crap, but it's all you can get out here, ain't it?"

Until now only Dwayne had spoken. Clinton beamed around the room vacantly, bouncing up and down on the balls of his cowboy boots. Pat Dougherty peered up at me, inquisitive as Mr. Rat.

"So, do you reckon they'll go for it?" He winked and twitched his nose.

Dwayne shot him a stare that suggested he keep his mouth shut and let him do the talking. Pat read the message loud and clear. Eyeing me beadily, he slunk back behind his warming beer.

Dwayne took over. "Why don't we sit outside? It looks like it's going to be a great sunset."

Indeed it was. We moved to one of the wooden tables by the sea. I sat on one bench; Dwayne and Pat took the one facing me. Clinton stood behind them with his arms folded, as if waiting to audition for the role of the stupid, tough guy in a cheap Western. I am pretty sure he would have got the part—he was a natural.

Calm now, the sea was lit the darkest blue and orange, the sun sitting huge on the horizon. A figure off to our right, silhouetted against the fire flickering across the water, dived from the jetty. The quiet splash sent gold, concentric rings spreading outward, and a while later the dripping head of a girl surfaced, flicking bright drops from her curly hair.

A pair of frigate birds, their sharply angled wings set in a plane, cast the last shadows of the day as they glided over us, coming in to roost.

"So let me tell you a little bit about our outfit." Dwayne startled me back to the conversation. "We call ourselves Island Gold . . ."

"Geddit, geddit? Island Gold?" Pat snickered.

Clinton obviously did not. He seemed about to say something but closed his mouth when Dwayne shot them both another glare.

"We're trying to introduce cattle ranches to a number of locations in the islands. Works in Vanuatu. No reason why it can't work here. We've got sixty million Solomon Island bucks sitting in the bank, ready to go if the landowners agree."

Pat nodded proudly but said nothing.

"You are investing that much of your own money here. Why?"

"Love the islands, my friend. Always have done."

"Go on," I prompted.

Over the course of a long and liquid evening, their scam became clearer. They had successfully raised the huge amount of money from a range of Middle Eastern banks, and they planned to lend this money to local landowners. Then they proposed to sell them cattle from ranches that they owned in Texas. Simple, almost simple enough to have been thought up by Clinton.

"So what sort of interest rate would you be charging on the loans?" asked a man who had by now consumed two large glasses of red wine and was badly out of practice. I need not have worried; it seemed that the others had given themselves a considerable head start.

Dwayne was irrepressible. "Couldn't tell you right at the moment. Can't quite remember. I'll have to check my records," he said without a hint of irony. "But you don't have to worry, they'll buy it."

So how would the villagers manage these animals, I asked. Most, as far as I was aware, had never seen a cow, let alone looked after one.

"That's the beauty of it. We provide a manager—someone like yourself. Then, of course, we charge a management fee. Ten percent."

Pat could no longer contain himself, and Dwayne, with a wave of his wineglass, let him run. "Yeah, ten percent of the first year's turnover. Ten percent of sixty million bucks." He relished the last line and took a celebratory swig from his beer bottle with a smack of his thin, wet lips.

We filed into the comfortable dining room. Dwayne pushed me ahead and sat at the neatly laid table, decorated by an arrangement of pink and white hibiscus and woven pandanus leaf table mats.

"Four lobster and loads of hollandaise, honey," Dwayne shouted at Rachel, the shy waitress, who blushed unhappily on the other side of the room. "All right with you, Will?"

I nodded and looked down at my hands, embarrassed.

"So . . . after the first year what's going to happen?"

Dwayne grunted a half laugh. "I expect they'll be able to cope. These natives aren't quite as stupid as you think they are." He flashed a wide smile at his colleagues.

I was speechless.

"Anyway, who cares? We'll be back in the U.S. You don't reckon we'd stay in this dump for longer than it takes to get the dough, do you? Too goddamn hot, and you've got to drink this piss."

It was clear that the more they drank, the more indiscreet they would become.

So what did they plan to do with the trees that at present grew so densely over all the islands? Wouldn't they have to be cleared to create space for pasture?

"Well, they'll all have to be cut down, of course, but we get the logging rights over that, so it should turn a nice profit as well." Dwayne laughed as he ripped the tail off his lobster and cracked the shell with his teeth.

"What happens if the landowners don't agree?"

"Oh, they will, you don't want to worry about that." Pat giggled as he rubbed imaginary notes between greasy thumb and forefinger and wiped the side of his mouth with his wrist, cleaning his whiskers.

"Anyway, that's where you come in, buddy. You can talk 'em round."

"Well . . . I'm not convinced . . ."

"So you like these natives, do you? You probably get a bit sick of them, hey? Wouldn't be a bad place, if there weren't so many of 'em. Ha!"

They sniggered self-approvingly, glancing at each other and me to affirm our complicity. Alcohol had reduced the three men to outlandish caricatures of themselves. Sloshing wine into glasses, they became less and less coherent, but what amazed me was that they were willing to take me into their confidence so quickly.

"Bet the girls are good for a ride . . . bit of a bang, right?" Dwayne finished his wine in one huge swallow.

Clinton reached out to grab Rachel as she walked past. She sidestepped and sensibly disappeared into the kitchen. Turning back to face us, he muttered absentmindedly to himself. "Love the islands. Yah, great . . ."

Several beer cans arrived and were expertly flicked open. I refused the one proffered. I'd had enough.

"Let's talk money, buddy. We can trust you, right, you being a white guy and all—even if you are a fucking Brit. Ha, ha! You'll be able to talk them round, right? If you do there will be a great big, nice, fat slice of the cake in it for you, friend."

Dwayne swung a heavy arm round my shoulders and gazed unsteadily at the floor.

"I'll have to get back to you, err . . . maybe tomorrow. I've got to go." I slid out of his warm grip and made my excuses.

"We're counting on ya, don't let us down now." Dwayne smiled and Pat winked as I backed out of the bar, promising to get in touch when or if I had any news.

"S'ya later, pardner." Clinton managed to lift his can from his chest, where it was balanced.

Once outside I hotfooted it to Geoff and Marlene's house, where they had kindly offered me a bed for the night. Marlene was away, but Geoff was still up. I told him about my evening. He listened closely to what I had to say. He looked concerned but not surprised.

"They come and go all the time. All sorts of different scams. Once upon a time they used to bring mirrors and beads to blind the islanders, now it's video games and CD-ROM presentations. Sometimes they're after the fishing, sometimes the gold, but usually it's the timber. I'll bet they want to get their hands on the trees. The cattle will just be a front."

"Timber?"

"Yeah, if they carry on flogging it at this rate, there won't be any left in ten years' time. A few backhanders and they'll strip Randuvu in front of your eyes. You'll all be sitting on a great big bald rock!"

"But who is doing anything to stop them?"

"Nobody. Not the government, not the Brits, not the Commonwealth, not the UN—nobody."

Oh, right.

"Well, what should I do?"

"Ignore them, just keep going with your chickens and they'll go away eventually. Just don't let them sweet-talk anybody in the village. They'll try and buy their way in if they can."

I was most concerned that they would try to convince Luta and the others of the attractions of their scheme. I resolved to forewarn them when I got back to Mendali.

It was a pleasant relief to see the Kings the next morning. They looked worried when I told them about my calamitous attempt to see them but laughed when I told them about my T-shirt and diapers fiasco.

"We heard about that at school." Sam, the eldest of their three children, grinned. "One of my friends stood up and told us all about this white guy who had lost his pants. I didn't realize it was you. His dad was the guy that found you. Everybody knows that story at my school!"

Marvelous, how my fame had spread far and wide.

When lunchtime came around, we decided to eat at the rest house but, working strictly on Solomon Time, the restaurant was closed and there was nowhere else to go.

"I could do with some fish and chips." I sighed wistfully.

"Don't you mean chicken and chips?" Sam laughed.

"Yeah, deep fried chicken and chips," said his father, Don.

Still hungry, we'd moved to a grassy bank between the rest house rooms and the sea, while the rest of the Kings had wandered down toward the hospital to see if they could buy any fruit from the nurses.

"That's what you ought to do, you know!" Don sat up suddenly.

"Who, me?" I mumbled into the crook of my arm. "Ought to do what?"

"Set up a fast-food outlet."

"What, fast food in the Solomons!" I laughed as I rolled onto my back and stared up at the ice blue sky.

"Why not? I am sure there's loads of people who work in the town who would want to buy a snack at lunchtime. Chicken and sweet potato chips. Rent a building here, get a couple of fryers. What else? Bit of red sauce, salt and pepper. Few napkins and some old newspaper. Away you go!"

I liked Don. He always made everything sound so easy.

"Well, I might think about it."

"So what would you call it?" asked Sam with a grin. I pondered the question a minute.

Don chuckled. "Chicken Willy's! You've got to call it Chicken Willy's."

"Yes, yes, go on. That would be cool!" said Sam with youth-ful enthusiasm.

"Well." I laughed as I sat up and brushed twigs from my shirt. "If we ever do start up a restaurant, then we'll call it Chicken Willy's, I promise."

"Bet you don't!" Sam sounded disappointed.

"Bet we do!"

And, to my very great surprise, we did.

On my return to Mendali, Luta listened philosophically to what I had to tell him about Dwayne and his cronies.

"No good then, Mr. Will?"

"No good, sorry."

He smiled broadly as he pulled a blackened yellow fish out of the fire. He tore off a piece with his steely fingers and handed it to me. "Commander always said they would not be Australian if they were honest." He nodded thoughtfully.

Coincidentally, the following day, somewhat to my alarm, Bunni paddled into the village. Sliding out of his light boat, he waded through the shallow wash, holding his tasseled moc-casins in one hand, his sunglasses stuck firmly in his tightly curled hair. He smiled up at me as I stood outside my house. "Good morning to you. Everything well with you?"

"Good morning," I answered cautiously. "Yes, fine, thank you."

Having had no encounter with Bunni since our first meet-ing, I was distinctly on my guard.

"So, how are the chickens?" he asked nonchalantly as he stepped into his soft loafers.

"Great thanks, yes, great . . ."

"I hear that you have had a few problems with them." He smiled neutrally.

"No, no, nothing really. They are all fine, just fine."

I peered as hard as I could into his eyes, but the dark glasses, which he had now slipped on, successfully hid any guilt lurking behind them. I could not ask him outright if he was responsible, so I let it go. He was sure to deny it anyway.

"Doesn't sound as if you will be able to do much with them if Luta goes ahead with these Americans."

I detected a triumphant note in his voice.

"How do you know about them?"

"They are my friends. They like to do business with me. You will see, soon we will have plenty of cattles here, and then your chickens will not be important anymore and everyone will be pleased that I have helped the community."

He sauntered off toward the village and, although I felt worried and depressed, there was not much I could do about Bunni, so I turned my mind to other matters.

Ludicrously, I had been giving some thought to the conversation I had had with the Kings. A fast-food chicken restaurant!

A fast-food chicken restaurant. Why not? It might be worth a try, and as long as we started simply we did not really have much to lose. In fact, it might even be quite a good adjunct to the chicken business.

I suggested it one evening at the card table.

"You like for try him, then him all right, Mr. Will." Everyone laughed good-naturedly, and I underwent the distinct sensation of being quietly humored.

Well, nothing ventured, nothing gained. Rather than get involved in the complications of finding or building any premises, we would start with a small stall in the marketplace. Keep it simple.

I rang Nick in Honiara from the new telephone box at the post office and asked him if he could buy a couple of the small gas rings that I had seen the day we'd found Mr. Wu. He sent them down on the *Maoaoa*, with two bottles of gas, two bright steel woks, and a drum of cooking oil. Astonishingly, the little wooden ship arrived on the day forecast.

Back at Mendali, Imp constructed a makeshift collapsible stall with two small supporting side walls and a hatchway, and at the back a clever folding serving counter with drop-down legs. Measuring it carefully several times, he ensured it was suitable to be transported by canoe, and once it had passed his rigorous quality control, we painted it a bright red with some of the blood left over from Christ's picture in the church. Small Tome, who had the neatest handwriting, painted CHICKEN WILLY'S in a blue semicircle over the top of the hatchway and, when it had dried, we stood the stall up in the clearing and stepped back to admire it. Very smart it looked, too.

Ethel, our forthright kindergarten teacher, bustled her way behind the counter and mimed serving food to passing customers. Stanley walked past, his arms outstretched, palms up as if carrying a plate. A latter-day Oliver Twist, he stopped in front of the hatch and Mrs. Bumble served up great dollops of imaginary food with her imaginary spoon.

One evening the cardplayers, forgoing their normal entertainments, wrote out advertising notices in crayon on sheets of the only exercise book that had not been smoked. Small Small Tome, who distributed the flyers, did such a thorough job in Munda that hardly a tree or door, wall or notice board did not flutter with the small pieces of white lined paper. With such punchy slogans as "Chicken Willy's him nice tumas," "Come long Chicken Willy's—staka good food," or the rather unfortunate "You like for taste Chicken Willies," if we were not at the cutting edge of copywriting then at least we were sure of plenty of interest.

Arriving early in the morning among the other stallholders unloading canoes and piling up produce along the water's edge, we chose a central spot. We set up the stall and arranged a table behind. The two aluminum gas rings with the two woks balanced on top caused a great deal of interest. A group of men, arms folded or holding hands, argued the gas ring versus traditional wood fire debate while our ice chest, which had been filled with jointed chickens, was stored behind the stall. In another container flour mixed with a secret combination of herbs and spices was ready to provide that unique CW taste experience. Sweet potatoes cut into chips and covered with salt water sat in a large plastic bucket under the table.

As the sun broke over the leaf roof of the guesthouse, shoppers arrived, keen to get the best and freshest of the produce. Yellowing green betel nuts were laid out in regimented rows, an occasional piece of torn cardboard propped up against them, announcing the price for the bargain hunter. Pineapples crowned every display, leaving their lingering scent on the air to mix with the smell of sweat and tobacco smoke as the hubbub of the market began to rise. Old women, their faces as wrinkled as the coconuts they were selling and surrounded by every conceivable kind of greenery, ferns, cabbages, and indeterminate edible leaves of every pattern, rattled off exchanges with their neighbors and the customers who paused to inspect the goods.

Children played alongside, occasionally entreating a parent or grandparent to buy them one of the lollipops from the stall run by the young, thin entrepreneur at the end of the line. He sold a range of luxury goods: sweets, single cigarettes, and balloons, one of which occasionally he blew up, his gaunt cheeks puffing until they met the rims of his cheap sunglasses. Holding it aloft, he would suddenly let it go, and it would spin flatulently around in the air for a few seconds before landing wetly in the dust, to be seized upon and fought over by a ball of children. He would smile at their excitement before turning to demonstrate a deft card trick to a group of astonished old men who would implore him to perform it again.

I retreated behind a pile of yams, and from this spy point I waited to see what would happen. Ruth rolled the chicken pieces in flour and popped them into the hot oil, where they hissed and bubbled before settling into a golden foam. Ellen dropped the chips gently into the oil of the other wok. Curious, the other stallholders and shoppers looked on as the smell of frying chicken wafted across the marketplace. $5.00 NO MORE read the sign that hung by the hatch. A number of people walked by and peered through the opening to see what this strange new addition to the marketplace was going to offer. There seemed to be plenty of interest, but nobody appeared to be willing to put their hands in their pockets. Perhaps nobody was hungry?

It must have been a good hour after we'd arrived that Geoff's mechanic, the inimitable Nob, appeared out of the side gate of the guesthouse. He came straight over to the stall and spoke to Ethel. Immediately she beamed and busied herself piling chips into a cone of newspaper. Finally she carefully balanced a large piece of crisp brown chicken breast on the top and passed it across the counter. Handing over his five-dollar note, the mechanic took the food and went and sat down under a tree by the jetty.

Every eye was on him as he took his first bite of chicken. Like that of a poker player, his face betrayed nothing, no flicker of emotion allowed his audience to know how much or even if he was enjoying his meal. He took another bite and chewed it slowly. Three inquisitive children walked over and sat at his feet, gazing up at him. After ten minutes or so he swallowed his last mouthful. Folding the paper carefully, he put it down on the ground beside him and looked over to the women at the stall. Ellen, absentmindedly holding an uncooked drumstick by her ear, and Ethel, her head tilted to one side, chubby hands resting on her hips, were both rapt with attention.

"Nice one," he called. "Nice one tumas."

Their two faces immediately relaxed into smiles as they

busied themselves over their pans. A few minutes later a woman in a floral dress, wobbling slightly in a pair of white plastic high heels, appeared. Carefully removing a five-dollar bill from a matching handbag, she handed it over to Ellen.

"One chicken and chip from Chicken Willy's," she requested. Then, looking round the marketplace, she giggled self-consciously into her hand. Loud whistles and a few raucous shouts of encouragement came from the crowd as she tripped away smiling, swinging her hips and waving her food in one hand above her head.

It all proved to be a far greater success than I could have imagined. A steady stream of people came to Chicken Willy's. When the chicken ran out, they bought just chips until they too ran out. Ethel and Ellen were delighted. Clutching the wads of blue five-dollar notes in both hands, they shook their heads and laughed, laughed until the stall began to wobble and the hot oil sloshed dangerously in the frying pans.

*

Chicken Willy's— Nambawan Nice One

Vhen Tassels and I pushed open the rusty hinges of the double front doors, the sight was pretty uninspiring.

Tucked just around the corner from the bank, the building was really too big for our purposes. It had, in a former life, served as one of the ubiquitous general stores, but now it was simply a large, empty room with a dingy back office. But, despite its unprepossessing appearance, this was more than just a scruffy wooden building—this was to be, we knew, the flagship of a phenomenon that might yet sweep the world.

I had spent that morning, as I steered us through the smooth, azure lagoon, reflecting on the distance covered since my arrival. Now we did have a "business," a moneymaking project that would provide the islanders, even at our present scale, with a healthy income. Whether they chose to expand the chicken farm or to pursue the fast-food sideline, how they chose to spend any resultant profits, to invest in their futures, or to amuse themselves must be entirely up to them. Indeed, if the whole were to come to a grinding halt after my departure, then this too would be their autonomous decision. Perhaps the teacher in me wanted to push to achieve the best results, but the rest of me, which by now was much the greater part, just felt very pleased and privileged to have lived this Solomon Time.

"Suppose you me look inside this one?"

"Why not?" replied Tassels, and grinning together we went inside.

The original counter had collapsed, leaving only the odd twisted nail sticking out of the wall. Working behind the till must have been a precarious pastime, as several of the floorboards were missing and nearly all the glass strips that made up the louvers of the windows were broken, cracked, or absent. The paintwork outside was hardly in evidence and some patches of leaf roof had rotted through, but there did not seem to be any major structural problems to overcome.

At the back of the building we discovered a brass standpipe overgrown with thick green vine. Stripping it away, Tassels twisted the tap open and, with a wheeze and a cough, rusty muck spat out until the water flowed clear and strong, splashing on the cocoa brown dirt before it puddled and dried into the cracked mud.

A few days after we'd settled on a rental price of fifteen chickens a month with the owner, the work team arrived to start the refurbishment of the hut. Imp worked with tremendous enthusiasm, always asking for my opinion on how something looked or whether something should be higher, lower, left a bit, or right a bit. Very often he would have me hold whatever was being positioned and skip a few feet away to judge it for himself. Holding his pencil at an angle he thought suitable, he would narrow his eyes and hum quietly. If things were not quite right, he would furrow his tattooed brow and pull gently on the piece of mother-of-pearl that was inserted in his earlobe.

Occasionally, but only occasionally, he would consult his apprentice, Gordon, and together they would crouch on their haunches to draw diagrams with sticks in the dirt in front of the building. Planks fashioned with axes were brought from the island, as were all the materials necessary to build the work tops and restaurant furniture. Geoff lent us his tools, and we spent some of our savings on paper bags of different-size nails.

Although the work was basic, it was tough, solid, and in its own way quite attractive. The tables were constructed from the round trunks of trees sawn into three- or four-inch-thick tops, supported by three reasonably straight lengths of branch, and around these were arranged three-legged stools of the same design. The counter was broad and smooth; it had been cut in one piece out of the jungle and oiled with coconut oil until it gleamed. Its front was decorated with broad cuts of bamboo, and pinned to these were fish shapes carved in wood by the children of the kindergarten. In the center, crowing loudly, was the silhouette of a large chicken. On the serving side were two long tables, where the cooking would take place. Here Ellen, Ethel, and their team would cook the food to order for our clientele. Behind in the small back room, two food preparation teams would be busy working, one group peeling and slicing the sweet potatoes, the other plucking, drawing, and quartering the chickens. The birds would be brought over every day and kept in a wire coop behind the restaurant until their order number was up. Freshness was our promise.

The broken windows were replaced with wire fly nets, and a large padlock protected the door. Above this Small Tome, standing precariously on a homemade ladder, painted our company name. He painted slowly and methodically, the tip of his tongue pointing out of the side of his mouth. Occasionally he came down to earth and, standing at some distance, waving his paintbrush flamboyantly, considered his progress. He used the same reds and blues that had decorated the stall, but now he cunningly highlighted each letter with white so that the whole stood out and could be read clearly from as far away as the airstrip. He also painted the front weatherboards of the building in thick stripes and the banisters of the small veranda at the front alternately in the same colors. When finally he was finished, we assembled outside and looked up at his work—it was the house that young Hansel and Gretel had discovered in the forest, good enough to eat.

Steady streams of onlookers stopped to inquire what we were planning. Small Tome would look down over his shoulder from his ladder, smile at his questioner, and gesture vaguely at me with his paintbrush before turning back to his work. Some passersby walked off shaking their heads, but most seemed enthusiastic.

Once again Small Small Tome was elected to go about the business of posting notices, this time to spread the news of our Grand Opening. His simple but extraordinarily expressive mimes, of people eating and dancing and generally merrymaking, ensured that soon everyone in the small town was talking about this exciting event.

Even the three American cowboys, who were still hanging round the islands, asked if they might come. They seemed strangely friendly, considering that my silence had to all intents and purposes demonstrated that I was not willing to help them. They appeared bullish, overly confident, too pleased with the way things were going. One day during our preparations, I had noticed them, in close conference, in the big leaf house at the rest house. Dwayne had seen me and had made a face that was an extraordinary combination of greeting and venom. I had waved lightly but, as I moved hurriedly away, I had spotted Bunni, standing behind him, talking animatedly to Pat and Clinton. He had winked at me in the most troublesome way.

On the other hand, the Americans had made no further approach to me or, as far as I knew, to anybody else, so I presumed that they too were just succumbing to the ether of Solomon Time. Anyway, with only a week to go, everyone in the village was working flat out—by our standards at least—to get ready for the big evening. From the telephone in the post office, which happily was still working, I had once again press-ganged Nick in Honiara into helping out. Now I asked him to try to find some paper plates, cups, and napkins. He was more than happy to help and promised that he and Jane would fly down especially for the opening.

"By the way, Nick, I know this is a bit of a long shot, but do you think there is anywhere in Honiara that you can get T-shirts printed with special designs?"

He laughed for a long time. "What, you mean Chicken Willy's T-shirts?" he finally asked incredulously.

"Well, you know, I think it might add a touch of class."

"I'll see what I can do."

He rang back later that same morning. He was sorry, but the best he had been able to find were plain T-shirts and a special material that could be cut into any shape and then ironed on.

"Where do you expect me to find an iron?"

"Use your initiative. You are bound to be able to use something. What colors do you want?"

Off the top of my head, I asked for red T-shirts and blue lettering, which seemed to fit well enough with the colors of the restaurant—our corporate image.

"I'll send them down on the next plane."

As good as his word, the T-shirts appeared the following day. I took them over to the village and explained that, as we were all working together, we should all be wearing the same clothes. This concept was greeted with some consternation. What on earth for?

"Well, you see, that's what people do because, well . . ." I trailed off.

"Oh, you mean like a football team?" suggested Luta.

Yes, that was exactly what I meant. Now everybody understood.

Ellen organized the Mother's Union into action and, with the help of the scissors I used to cut dressings and sticking plasters, letters were carefully cut out. These were laid on the T-shirts and carefully arranged into a circle, the CHICKEN arching over the top and the WILLY'S like a smiling mouth at the bottom. In the middle of each shirt was placed the outline of a cock crowing, or at least of a bird that was reasonably closely related. The cutouts looked magnificent, but I was concerned that we would never be able to get them to stick. Undeterred, the women lit a huge fire and, wrapping gray lava stones in banana leaves to prevent them getting either too hot or too blackened, they heated them in the embers. Held in bamboo pincers, the stones were applied to the task. One by one the letters magically stuck. Eventually the shirts were all finished, and Ellen, now indisputably in charge, tried one on to murmurs of approval from her audience. Then, with great care, she folded it up, and it was put away with the others ready for the big day.

On the morning itself, the younger children helped Old Edith to bring over the decorations that they had prepared cross-legged on the steps of her house. These they festooned across the ceiling and along the walls of Chicken Willy's. Decorations of remarkable intricacy hung from the dusted beams in yellows, reds, and bright greens, folded and threaded together like multicolored Jacobean ruffs. As Young John stood on his brother's shoulders to hang one of the garlands, I suddenly saw that they had been made from hundreds of old sugar and tea packets, sweet and biscuit wrappers dug out of the bins behind the rest house. Tinfoil, recycled from the same source and carefully washed, was cut into star shapes and interspersed with circles of plastic bag. I noticed, as I admired them, that one of the paper chains looped along the walls was made from colored advertisements cut out of Chinese newspapers. When they were all in place, the room took on an air of real celebration—it was going to be a proper gala event.

We'd no idea how many people to expect but decided to open our doors at dusk. Kerosene lamps, brought over from the village, were being filled and hung over each table, and the Sunday school choir and the Mother's Union were to provide a musical entertainment. Dressed in their smartest clothes, the children with, for the main part, clean faces and combed hair, were practicing in the corner. Tassels conducted with a gusto worthy of one of the big concert halls of the world, and their voices drifted out through the open doors.

As I wrestled with a bamboo cage of chickens, the evening flight to Honiara came low overhead to land. It touched down lightly a couple of times on the tarmac before swinging one way and then the other as it approached the small terminal. As its engines slowed and it came to a halt, I was much surprised to see Bunni emerging from the waiting room with his entire family and a considerable quantity of belongings. What was he up to now, I wondered as I straightened to watch. I knew enough about him to realize that all his actions were to be viewed with the deepest suspicion. Still, I thought, as the last of his small children disappeared into the white plane, at least he was going away. That had to be good news.

A few minutes later I noticed out of the corner of my eye the three Americans talking animatedly, even angrily to Luta, as they followed him up the short slope from the rest house. He appeared to be not a little nonplussed. As they approached, Dwayne fixed me with a wild stare.

"Where is he, you bastard?"

This was not a friendly question.

"Go on," he shouted. "Where is he?"

"Yeah, and where's our goddamn money?" Pat joined in.

Even Clinton looked a little perturbed.

"Hang on!" I said, surprised. "Where is who and where is what money?"

"The money we gave that guy. He said he was going to talk you around, show a load of money up front."

Dwayne's eyes were popping, and some ugly swellings bulged in his neck. "Sixty thousand bucks," he gasped.

"What guy?"

"Bunni." Luta shook his head in mock astonishment. "I can't believe this one."

His eyes sparkled as he looked up at me.

"You gave Bunni money?" I was incredulous. "Sixty thousand dollars!"

My last sighting of Bunni suddenly made sense. I grinned.

"Well, where is he?" squealed Pat.

"Try that plane." I could not stop grinning as we watched the white machine taxi unsteadily up the runway and disappear behind the screen of trees.

The three Americans grabbed their hats from their heads and set off in baking-hot pursuit. They too vanished, and a short while later we watched the plane rise into view with a mosquito whine and head out across the sea. We never saw any of them again.

Gradually people collected outside the restaurant, an atmosphere of friendly curiosity building as Luta and I walked toward the crowd laughing quietly. Low in the sky, the sun breathed its last and rested behind the mountain peaks of Randuvu. Slowly the light of the kerosene lamps began to shine through the windows, and figures bustled to and fro inside.

Ellen, resplendent in her T-shirt, appeared in the doorway

with a welcoming smile. Stepping out over the threshold, she spread her arms dramatically. "Numbawan kokorako ready now," she announced to the startled crowd. "Now yufala like for come tryim?"

Uncertain, the more intrepid shuffled forward. As they walked up the shallow steps and began to form a queue, Tassels's singers started to perform rhythmically. Friends began to appear. Nick and Jane, who had arrived on an earlier flight, walked up from the sea with Geoff, Marlene, and Gerry. Stanley, who was wearing a T-shirt several sizes too big for him and, it appeared—as it hung down around his knees—nothing else, brought them plastic cups of bush lime juice.

"I don't believe it, mate," said a voice from behind me as I went over to greet them.

Into the dim light cast from the doors of the shop stepped Warren, diminutive and hirsute as ever.

"Never thought you fellers would do it—good on ya." He winked at Small Tome, who beamed back.

Harold had managed to find some ketchup from one of his suppliers in Honiara and had brought an almighty bottle along as a gift. Pools of the red unguent sat in coconut shells on each table, and Silas, the postmaster, was dipping his chips into it with great aplomb as he chatted animatedly with the lady from the bank. He had brought me letters from a couple of my former pupils as a surprise present. What they would have made of this scene I found difficult to imagine.

Stuffing the letters into my pocket, I looked around. The noise level had gradually increased as more and more people arrived to congratulate the villagers, exclaiming how good the chicken was. Dogs, waifs, and strays who normally spent their time rummaging through the rubbish, to scavenge a scrap here or a nibble there, could hardly believe their luck, as bone after bone thumped onto the ground. They lay contentedly under the tables, drumsticks gripped between their front paws, gnawing on the delicious gristle and sinew.

I peered round the back and found Ellen plucking for all she was worth. "Ouff, everyone hungry tumas," she panted as the white down floated around her head like snow.

Warren was telling anyone who would listen about how he would personally take over the sizable order that Chicken Willy's was surely going to require every week. He would be able to provide me with a cheap gas freezer. I should just wait and see, Warren would sort me out. I didn't have to worry. It would be a piece of piss, mate.

The Kings appeared in their family canoe, and Sam ran up the shore to shake my hand. "Don't believe you all did it, Will," he gasped excitedly before he dived into the restaurant with his younger brother and sister. Don and Alice, his wife, laughed and shook their heads before they too sampled the fare.

We all celebrated long into the night. After we'd closed up the shop and said good night to the last of the customers, we settled at the bar in the rest house, drank much too much beer, and told the tale of Chicken Willy's. Eventually Tassels, Small Tome, Ellen, Ethel, Luta, and I wobbled back down the wooden jetty, got into the canoe, and set off into the star-filled sea. The night was fine and warm as we crossed the lagoon, and the phosphorescence foamed green along our bows. On our starboard side I spotted the twin humps of Kiri Kiri—my island!

"Tassels, I want to stay there tonight!" I yelled above the sound of the engine. "Will you drop me and come and pick me up tomorrow?"

"Why not? S'pose you sure, no wariwari."

I knew I could count on him, surprised as he was by nothing. We coasted over the black and white surf of the sand spit, and I stepped out. Coconut husks floated at my feet.

"You sure you want to stay here tonight?" asked Luta, surprised.

"Sure."

"Okay. No wariwari. *Rodo diana.*"

Out of the dark came flying a small yellow package, which landed softly on the sand beside me—my life jacket. Picking it up, I turned to walk up the beach, tripped, and fell lightly to my knees. Good nights rang out across the water as the canoe disappeared.

"*Rodo diana,* Chicken Willy!"

The laughter died into the sound of the surf as I lay down on my back, pulled the life jacket out of its holder and, without a second thought, pulled the rip cord. I no longer needed it. With a violent whoosh the plastic inflated between my hands. Tucking it behind my head, I closed my eyes.

Rodo diana. Good night.

Epilogue

Last night I dreamed I went to Mendali again, back to the turquoise seas and the sky.

I returned to an island adrift in time, to a village whose inhabitants floated through the gentle, unformed pattern of their days. I could see Small Tome standing by the porch of his church, lit by the sparkling sunshine and resplendent in one of his most colorful robes. He smiled as he watched the children appear from the toy town schoolhouse and rush toward the warm waters of the lagoon.

Beyond them, out off the small point where the skeleton house stood, a figure sat still in a smooth dugout canoe. The wisp of breeze that blew in from the Pacific ruffled the man's great frizzy fuzz of hair and fluttered the colored ribbons that hung down his back.

From one of the small kitchens, a steady thread of smoke rose a little before slanting away over Ellen's head as she sat in the shade and split coconuts with a glinting bush knife. Stanley, his friend Small Small Tome crouching by his side and staring intently into washed ink water, threw a three-pronged hook far out from the jetty.

Behind them, along the path that ran beside the clearing and under the broad branches of a ngali nut tree, came two other boys carrying new buckets filled with water and feed. On their heels tottered a naked black boy, a picture of innocence—until he picked up a piece of coral and threw it at a ginger cat that was slinking its way along a hedge of hibiscus. The cat hissed, flashing away up three steps into a leaf house that looked out over the bay.

Time had inevitably ticked by, even if in Mendali its progression had been all but imperceptible. The dawn of the new millennium was celebrated on the strip of beach by the village. No champagne, no fireworks, no promises to try to create a better world or even to go on a diet. Instead we sat and ate fish cooked on the fire, drank from coconut shells, and sang songs, the words to which I now knew by heart. "We are one big happy family . . ."

More than once during my stay in the Solomons I had almost felt that we were, but there was now a part of me that wanted to see other family and friends, and also wanted to find out how I would now react to the place from whence I had come.

Grimble one evening, no doubt after a couple too many sundowners, had burbled on about "never wanting to go back to civilisation again . . . about all the false values of it . . . about all these simplicities being enough for anyone."

But somehow they were not. I wished they were, but they were not. Not for always.

Standing on the jetty, watching a furious, splashing canoe race cheered on by the rest of the village, I explained to Luta, Tassels, and Small Tome that I was thinking of heading home.

"No wariwari." Luta turned his disappointed tattooed face to smile at me. "Butta yu come back lookim mefala?"

I promised that I would, for Grimble had, on the other

hand, been perfectly right when he remarked just before his own departure that "the islands are like a drug; they entice and they lull you. They will lure. You will be hooked. You will always want to go back."

They had, I was, and I do.

About the Author

Will Randall was born in 1966 and educated in London. He taught languages in the West Country for ten years before going to live in the South Pacific. *Solomon Time* is the story of his experiences there. He continues to travel, teach, and write. Visit the author's website at www.willrandall.co.uk.